Ascott R Hope

The Heroes of young America

Ascott R Hope

The Heroes of young America

ISBN/EAN: 9783743320017

Manufactured in Europe, USA, Canada, Australia, Japa

Cover: Foto ©ninafisch / pixelio.de

Manufactured and distributed by brebook publishing software (www.brebook.com)

Ascott R Hope

The Heroes of young America

PREFACE.

In the following pages it has been attempted to give some account of the English colonisation of the coast of North America and the foundation of that great country now known as the United States. On this side of the Atlantic, at least, the lives of the early adventurers who commenced and carried out that work are not so well known as they should be, though the record of their efforts is rich in incident, often of a thrilling kind, even surpassing that of the fictitious tales through which chiefly our young people get their impressions of America. What manner of men were those pioneers of civilisation, and what difficulties they had to encounter, I have tried to show in a narrative that, while not uninstructive, pretends to no grave and profound character. The ordinary rules of historical perspective have not been observed; my aim has rather been to put forward the picturesque features of the story in the hope of enticing young readers to a closer study of a subject as much neglected as it abounds in interest and information. Nor need I be afraid to appeal to that bountiful patron of light literature, the "general reader" of the period, for his notions of American history are often as vague as were my heroes' notions of American geography.

I have drawn my materials, as much as possible, from narratives and tracts, written at or near the time to which they refer. Among the chief authorities may be mentioned the collections of voyages printed by Hakluyt and Purchas, Captain John Smith's publications on Virginia and New England, the journals and letters of members of the Plymouth colony, and the early historians of New England. Since some doubt has been thrown upon the credibility of John Smith as historian, it may be well to remark that the so called "General History of Virginia," from which so many quotations have been taken in the section of this work headed by his name, was not wholly written by him, and does not exclusively refer to Virginia, but is rather a miscellany of papers on the theory and practice of emigration, including a compilation of accounts by comrades and contemporaries of his, the authenticity and accuracy of which there is no reason to impeach, and which are our main sources of detailed information upon the doings of the Jamestown colony. So far as matters

CONTENTS.

THE AMERICAN ARGONAUTS—p. 1.

I. Discovery and Spanish Colonization of West Indies and Central America.
II. Weakness of the Natives—Cruelties of the Conquistadores—Influence of the Catholic Church—Fruits of the Spanish Conquest.
III. French Explorations in North America—The Huguenot Colony in Florida—A Double Massacre—The Oldest Town in the United States.

THE FIRST ENGLISH PLANTERS—p. 30.

I. England enters the Field of Colonization—Sir Walter Raleigh—Sir Humphrey Gilbert's Expedition to Newfoundland.
II. Voyage of Amadas and Barlow to Carolina—Their Reception by the Natives.
III. Raleigh sends out a Colony to Roanoke—Quarrels with the Indians—Discouragement and Return of the Colonists.
IV. Another Colony settles on Roanoke—The Governor returns to England for Aid—The Spanish Armada—The Lost Colony of Roanoke,

JOHN SMITH—p. 68.

I. Captain John Smith's Services—His Early Life and Adventures—Renewal of Efforts to Colonize America—Smith Sails with London Colony for Virginia.
II. Character and Dissensions of the Colonists—Settlement on the James River—Ill-will against Smith—Sufferings of the Settlers—Smith Captured by the Indians—His Life Spared

by Powhatan—Friendly Intercourse with the Indians—Smith's Influence in the Colony.

III. Virginia and its Natives—Arrival of New Emigrants—Discontent and Delusions—Smith's Explorations of Chesapeake Bay—Dealings with the Indians.

IV. Smith Appointed Governor—The Unreasonable Demands of the London Company—The Absurd Coronation of Powhatan—Newport's Search for the South Sea—Smith's Way of Ruling—His Difficulties and Complaints—Renewed Scarcity—Smith goes to Buy Corn among the Indians—His Party in Danger through the Enmity of Powhatan and Opechancanough—His Boldness among the Enemy—Treachery of some of the Colonists—Encounters with Indians—Firmly Establishes his Authority—Progress of the Colony.

V. A New Government Appointed—The Officials Shipwrecked—The Colony Threatened with Anarchy—Smith Disabled by an Accident and Returns to England—State of Jamestown at his Departure—His Loss soon Felt—The "Starving Time"—The Colony Relieved by Lord Delaware.

VI. Smith in England—His Zeal for Colonization—His Attempts and Writings on New England—Progress of Virginia after his Departure—His Meeting with Pocahontas at Brentford—The Massacre of Settlers in Virginia—The Colony Transferred to the Crown—Smith's Works and Character.

The Pilgrim Fathers—p. 163.

I. Rise of the Puritans—A Congregation of Separatists takes Refuge in Holland—They Resolve to Found a Colony in New England—Voyage of the Mayflower.

II. Arrival at Cape Cod—The Country Found Deserted—First Encounter with Indians—Plymouth Chosen for a Settlement.

III. The Building of Plymouth—Incidents and Adventures—Hardships and Losses of the Colony—Better Prospects—Friendly Visits from the Natives—A Popular Government Organized.

IV. Treaty with Indian Chiefs—Slow Progress of the Colony—Danger from Indians—The Colony settled at Weymouth brings the English into Disrepute—A Sick Chief Cured—In Gratitude he Reveals Plot of Indian Tribes—The Plymouth Colony Resolves on War—The Indians cowed by Miles Standish—Pecuniary Difficulties of the Colony—Its Success and Importance.

The Heroes of Young America.

THE ARGONAUTS.

I.

WHO can tell what a thrill ran through the patient heart of Columbus on that memorable moment when at last he saw a light twinkling before his little bark, and knew that the guiding star of his faith was rising upon the horizon of ordinary men! What must have been the wonder, the joy, the self reproach of his timid and mutinous sailors, as with the day the land dawned upon them from that dark world of waters on which for weeks they had been wandering in despair! Words cannot express the emotions of that sunrise. The dreams of poets, the guesses of philosophers, the dim legends of old adventurers had indeed come true, and the eyes of Europe were dazzled by the light of the New World.

Columbus was to die without knowing rightly what he had discovered; still less did he foresee all that would come of his discovery. It was a time when the mind of the civilized world was at spring-tide; and great waves of new energy, already struggling against the old limits of thought and action, were gathering ready to rush into the channel which it was his lot to open. The same mighty forces that were to burst forth in the Reformation had given their impulse to the maritime enterprise of the age. Ships no longer crept cautiously along familiar shores, but, trusting to the compass, spread their sails to all winds and took bolder and bolder flights into the untried ocean. There were great men among the sailors of these days, men who were studious and devout as well as brave, men who had "sailed indeed not as the mariner Palinurus, but as the expert and prudent prince Ulysses." Columbus was the first among these men, but what he did might have been done by more than one of them who were so well able to follow when he had once shown the way. The time had come, and the man could not long have been wanting, even if the Genoese navigator, a pauper, and in the eyes of the world a madman, had carried his daring schemes down with him to the grave.

So, reading his story, we draw a breath of relief when Columbus has his reward within his grasp. The nature of his undertaking was such that mere chance might from day to day have forestalled or prevented him. His was that high and strong purpose which seems able to conquer even fate; yet when we consider the difficulties with which he had to contend, we are tempted to pronounce it a throw of the dice whether he or another shall first see that land which he so stedfastly believes to lie beyond the great Atlantic. Still more does it appear at the bidding of chance that to Castile and Leon he gave this new world. It is pitiable to think how he had to hawk about his mighty project, and saw age coming upon him before he could find a patron. From Genoa to Venice it went a begging; Portugal, which already took the lead in African discovery, had the refusal of America; it was France's or England's for the asking; and the grudging of a few thousand crowns had almost lost to Spain the mines of Mexico and Peru. The man was at last successful, and the country may be called fortunate that with so small a stake won this great prize at the very time when it found itself able to turn it to account. But, in the case of nations as of men, it depends on themselves whether good fortune shall be built up into true prosperity, or prove but the surer means of weakness and decay.

It is difficult for us, who see what Spain is now, to realize the part which it played in Europe then. Yet at the beginning of the sixteenth century the position of this country was not unlike that held by our own at the beginning of the nineteenth. A long course of internal dissension and foreign encroachment, which had both called forth and employed its energies, was at last brought to an end by the conquest of the Moors and the union of Castile and Aragon under Ferdinand and Isabella. The state thus formed of various races had many sources of strength ready to the hand of a wise government. Strange as it may sound, the principles of constitutional liberty were nowhere more at home in those days. In literature and the arts Spain was in advance of most of her neighbours. She had a bold and industrious population, and strong natural defences. The national spirit was martial and chivalrous; before long, the Spanish infantry were to be dreaded on many a European battlefield; and their great captain Gonsalvo de Cordova was the Wellington of the age. It would have been strange if their large seaboard had not tempted such a people to maritime adventure. They were beginning to rival the Portuguese in their career of discovery, while the commercial enterprise of both these nations was threatening the prosperity of the Italian ports, hitherto the chief markets of the world. In the romances of the Peninsula, ships and sea fights first figured largely among the giants, dragons, and enchanted castles that had filled older stories of the kind. A people's character may best be learned from what they love to read, and the popularity of Amadis de Gaul tells as plain a tale as the popularity of Captain Marryat. It was Hispania that in these times aspired to rule the waves, and before long it was to be the Spanish dominions over which men might say that the sun never set.

So when Columbus returned with his wonderful news, the Spaniards were both able and willing to enter upon the work thus set before them. They hastened to claim and to take possession of the new lands whose extent and features were yet unknown. It was long supposed by these navigators that they had reached one side of India, as the Portuguese approached it from the other. The Pope, who was then held to have at his disposal all parts of the world belonging to no Christian prince, granted

America to Spain, leaving Africa to their rivals and neighbours. An imaginary line was drawn down the Atlantic: to the west of this the Spaniards were to be masters, to the east the Portuguese. Thus, pushing on their discoveries from either side, they would in time, as they thought, meet in the Spice Islands or the mysterious country of Prester John. This arrangement was not always observed by the Portuguese; still less heed did the French and English mariners give to it; but in the main the history of the settlement of America is for almost a century the history of Spanish enterprise.

The Spanish character was marked by a strong tinge of romance; and the people who delighted in the gorgeous descriptions and wild adventures of Don Quixote's library, were ready to receive the most exaggerated accounts of the marvels of the tropical world. These exuberant forests and glowing skies seemed a very fairydom in the eyes of Cervantes' countrymen. Its fruits and flowers were wonderful and beautiful as those which hung in the enchanted garden of Apollidon. Strange and terrible as griffins were the huge reptiles which recalled the monsters imported into European fiction through the influence of the East. Each vast lake and impenetrable thicket might well be the abode of some such mysterious sage as Urganda the Unknown. These stupendous volcanoes, these earthquakes and hurricanes, were like the work of malignant and powerful sorcerers.

Here was cloudland made firm earth. Bold men hastened to try the chances of that magic region.

Poor men gladly fled from their creditors to those fortunate islands, where naked savages wore strings of pearl and ornaments of solid gold were freely trucked for trumpery toys. Pious men were no less eager to visit the ignorant millions who at all risks must be persuaded to change their hideous idols for the cross and the image of Mary. Cruel and imperious men were soon attracted to lands where it might pass for a Christian duty to shed blood like water, and where a Castilian boor could set his foot on the necks of Incas and Caciques. The more these men saw of the reality, the more wild grew their dreams. One discoverer, landing in central America, believed himself to have come upon the earthly paradise. Another wandered through the swamps and pine-barrens of Florida, hoping to reach the fabulous Fountain of Youth in which all the stains of mortality might be washed away. Explorers of the jungles of Brazil expected to find them defended by a race of Amazons. Grave hidalgos, learned geographers feverishly sought the road to El Dorado, where the ground was strewn with riches, as uncared for as the stones on the sierras of Andalusia.' Thousands of deluded mortals left their bones in pathless woods or on barren rocks over which they had toiled to find the golden city of Manoa.

It was small wonder if their heads were turned. Such adventures as those of Cortes and Pizarro, with a handful of men overthrowing empires for which hundreds of thousands were ready to die, read even now like stories of romance; to what a pitch then must the dullest imagination have been raised among the adventurers whose eyes first saw the golden Temple of the Sun and the glittering palaces of Montezuma! They did find gold so often and so little regarded by the natives, that they might be excused for supposing that those mountains and rivers concealed endless treasures. Every ship that came home brought specimens of these riches, and renewed the ferment of restless and covetous minds. Romance and religion had their share in the work; but gold was the great loadstone that drew the ships of Spain to the west, and gold was the temptation through which so many Spaniards lost their souls in this land of Eden. The story of their conquest is a story of sins as well as of successes and delusions. The record of their toils and hardships is a light one beside that of their inhumanity; even savage cruelties were outdone by the piles of corpses and the streams of blood over which these Christians struggled so madly in their search for unhallowed wealth; and their quarrels were as notorious as their cruelties.

With such a fever upon them, the *conquistadores* coming after Columbus soon forgot the pious aspirations of that great and good man who, by means of the wealth to be gained from his discovery of what he took for the gold mines of Ophir, known of old to Solomon, had ardently desired to restore Jerusalem and make it a sacred name throughout all the world.

II.

If the Spanish adventurers were almost intoxicated by the marvels which they found on every side, how great must have been the wonder of the simple natives who saw such strangers come among them as unexpectedly as if they had fallen from the clouds! The moving villages in which these white bearded men had crossed the ocean, the strange clothes and shells of iron with which they were covered, the magical instruments of which they were masters, their mysterious arts, their proud bearing, could not but persuade the Indians that their visitors were of some godlike race. Soon their awe was strengthened by unearthly terrors and new shapes of death. Fear fell upon them at the very sound of the thunder and lightning which the Europeans could produce at will; they were ready to worship the culverin or arquebus, which must have appeared to them like the spirit of their own volcanos, and which had a power of sudden destruction, "enough," as Montaigne says, "to fright Cæsar himself, if surprised with so little experience." Even more terrible was the unknown force of cavalry; rider and steed were taken for one animal, and whole hosts would fly before the hoofs of such a centaur. A certain tribe was once found praying to the skeleton of a horse. The fierce bloodhounds too that the Spaniards led about with them, played almost as great a part in the conquest as the sharp weapons and shining mail against which the savage clubs and arrows were shattered so uselessly; one dog was held equal to two arquebusiers. Thus the dragons, fabled to guard the treasures of old romance, were here upon the side of the spoilers. Even the alligators which basked upon the river banks were pressed into the service of the Spaniards and made to swarm in the moats of their castles. The fierce Caribs, the more peaceful inhabitants of the islands, the civilized multitudes of Mexico, were alike helpless against such arms and such allies. Only those tribes, here and there, who used poisoned arrows, had any fair chance of resisting whatever claims might be made upon them by so mighty invaders. For the most part, the Spaniards encountered no enemies more to be feared than the mosquitos which made some coasts almost uninhabitable.

At first the white men were generally received with kindness, and might have all they desired given freely or sold on easy terms. It was only when the natives had some taste of their rapacity, that they ventured to oppose it by violence and cunning, as was natural. This was a case where gentleness, patience, and friendly measures would in time have gained for the superior race far more than brutal force was able to secure. Cruelty better becomes weakness than strength. Yet little did the Spaniards understand that

>   . . . it is excellent
> To have a giant's strength; but tyrannous
> To use it like a giant.

Few of us indeed can rise above the temptation of being harsh and imperious towards a much inferior people with whose deficiencies and despised habits we come daily in contact. In British India, where the law protects all men from violence and gross oppression, the better class of natives too often complain bitterly of the manner used towards them by our civil and military officers. These are for the most part men of intelligence, culture, and a degree of humanity which would have passed for mawkish sentiment in the sixteenth century. The *conquistadores* were not even favourable specimens of their age and country. We scarcely need to be told that among the early adventurers were many outlaws and ne'er-do-wells, the scum of prisons and gambling houses, needy braggadocios, godless soldiers of fortune for whom the spilling of human blood was a pastime as well as a profession, men, in short, who would have been brigands and cut-throats in Europe if they had not been conquerors in America. Imagine how such a man, of mean birth and narrow mind, would behave when he found himself in a position to curse and beat a drove of his fellow creatures through whose exertions he hoped for sudden wealth. Why had they taken the trouble to come so far over the sea, if they were not to enslave those helpless Indians at their will! Decent, well meaning men, even men of real religious principle, looked at the matter in this way, and by the same temptations were soon drawn into some degree of the same inhumanity; the sons of the true church had small care of the rights of heathen. So before many years had passed the bewildered, crushed, and despairing natives found themselves toiling for others on the fields that were once their own, wearing out their miserable lives in the mines from which these greedy masters extracted the means of ease and pleasure, and perishing by hundreds under burdens which the stronger Spaniards would not touch with their little finger while one woman or child was able to crawl under their lash. It is a fearful story of wrongs, tortures, and sufferings. If we forget what human nature is capable of when it gives way to its evil passions, and read the accounts of writers who saw with their own eyes what was then done in that fair and rich region of earth, we may ask ourselves with a shudder if these Spaniards were not indeed beings of another sphere, fiends rather than men! The very cannibals, we are told, were known to loathe the flesh of these monsters in human shape.

The Spanish government, it should be remembered, showed more regard for the welfare of the Indians. But it found itself unable to oversee or control the proceedings of those who were on the spot. Besides, it was poor, and had no means of rewarding the conquerors except by allowing them to have their will of the lands and liberty of the conquered. Humane and pious scruples as to this wholesale enslavement were fitfully and doubtfully entertained at the court; and from time to time regulations were made to check the frightful atrocities of which some news did not fail to reach home, though the pious Isabella and the enlightened ministers of Charles V. could not easily learn the full truth. The colonists were ordered to treat the

Indians kindly, as if a bloodhound let loose into
the woods could be expected to fawn upon its
exhausted prey. The masters who were making
haste to be rich were admonished not to overwork
their slaves. It was declared that only the Caribs,
accused of cannibalism, and such Indians as might
be taken in war, should be reduced to slavery.
Negroes were transported from Africa to work for
the white men; strange to say, even the humanity
of the age seldom scrupled about the lawfulness
of holding the sons of Canaan in bondage. Such
regulations, however, were constantly disobeyed or
evaded by the cupidity of the colonists. At the
best, they would regard no more than the letter of
their sovereign's injunctions. When they wanted
slaves, and no wars were going on in which slaves
might lawfully be made, they did not hesitate to
march upon some peaceful tribe, with whom they
began proceedings by reading the royal proclamation
setting forth that there was one God, one Pope, and
one King of Castile, and requiring all people to give
their assent thereto on pain of war. The puzzled
and alarmed natives were probably unable at once
to understand or to embrace these strange doctrines,
so abruptly presented to them; and this Riot Act,
so to speak, having been read, it was considered
lawful to commence firing, and the unfortunate
people were without further forms put to death on
the spot, or made prisoners for a bondage in which
death was only more slow, scarcely less sure, if indeed they did not choose to be consumed in the
flames of their home, taking this for a more mer-

ciful fate than the swords and chains of the Spaniards. Millions are said to have perished thus. Whole families committed suicide, to escape their miserable lives; whole tribes died under their cruel tasks; whole islands were depopulated. Human life was held so cheap that when a gang of slaves were going along, fastened together by a chain, and one fell exhausted on the ground, his head would be cut off as the speediest way of setting the chain free and letting the rest move on without loss of time. In half a century from the time when the first colony arrived in Hispaniola or St. Domingo, its natives, two millions in number, had almost entirely disappeared, their places being filled up by negroes, more hardened to labour and more humbled to bondage.

The same tale is to be told wherever the Spaniards spread themselves like a pestilence, now hanging up thirteen poor wretches in honour of Christ and His apostles (a pious jest!); here calling by the name of the Holy Cross a town the foundations of which were wet with human blood; there founding a church to the Blessed Mother of Mercy amidst human groans and cries that might have made a very image weep. To this day one village of Spanish America will bear the name of some meek and reverend saint, while its neighbour is still remembered as Matanza, the place of slaughter. The white men who professed such horror at the human sacrifices of Mexico yet shrank not from turning whole cities and nations into a hecatomb on the altar of their greed. Need we wonder that the ignorant savages had small desire to seek the heaven in which they were urged to meet such Christians, a heaven in which they might still have prayers whipped from them at the church doors, and be tortured and robbed to furnish offerings to the Saviour, whose name was such a mockery in their ears! It is said that the slaves of a certain Spaniard were about to kill themselves in a body, but preferred to live when their master threatened to hang himself, so that he might accompany them into the next world.

These cruel conquerors were often good Catholics, according to their notions of religion; and we are not to be too hasty, judging by another standard, in looking upon them as hypocrites when they boasted of their devotion to the church and their zeal for the conversion of the heathen. We may know that God can only be worshipped in spirit and in truth; in these days it was too commonly believed, even by good men, that salvation depended on a mechanical operation of the sacraments. It was not thought to the purpose to make these poor Indians more intelligent, more self restraining, more capable of apprehending the truth; the work of the missionary was rather to force them to renounce one slavish superstition for another. The main point was to have them marked with the sign of the cross as a charm which should conjure the devil out of their hearts. For this kind of conversion, force seemed naturally a better instrument than reason. If the benighted sinners were not instantly convinced, and hesitated to receive the baptism of water,

Indians worshipping "the white man's God."
Page 15.

they might be given the baptism of blood with as little compunction as if they were dogs. With the awful fate of unbelievers awaiting them beyond death, a few stripes and tears more or less on this side seemed to make little difference. Severity towards many might be effectual in saving some, after this fashion of salvation. So the Spaniards may have lulled their consciences when in the name of heaven they turned earth into a hell, and "baptized a hundred with the sword for one at the font."

We may doubt whether such notions of religious duty be more ludicrous or more lamentable; but they were not inconsistent with doctrines which blasphemously represented the Almighty as a being with the intellect of an inquisitor and the heart of a despot. Such doctrines were little likely to awaken seared consciences or to move covetous breasts to mercy. Every mass, every offering, every formal confession and more formal absolution, only hardened the proud and orthodox lords of the New World in their accursed selfishness. Had they no sense of humour, to understand the contrast between their preaching and their practice? Surely then they must have felt the bitter unconscious sarcasm of a tale which describes how a body of these active disciples, armed to the teeth, marched forth to "convert" an Indian village, and found the frightened natives dancing frantically round a basket filled with gold, thinking thus to propitiate the Spaniards in doing honour to their god! A grimmer tale tells how Spanish prisoners were put to death by having melted gold poured down their throats. If this tale be not true it is a just parable, for so little indeed did the god avail them to whom they so madly devoted themselves. Better a thousand times that the ocean, which swallowed up so much of it, had always concealed the gold which they wrung by tortures from kings, crushed out with the life of nations, and washed from the soil by the tears of their fellow creatures.

What was called the Christian religion had a fearful share in the guilt of these iniquities. But no church is without men who are better than their doctrines. If the doctrines of the Catholic Church of that day were false and baneful, the conduct of many of the Catholic clergy rose far above the spirit of their theology, and furnishes the brightest page in the history of the Spanish conquest. The name of Las Casas is one never to be remembered without honour. At first himself a slaveholder, he was led to a sense of the wrongs which he and his countrymen inflicted on their victims, and of his own free will became the first abolitionist. Henceforward he gave himself up to the hard task of claiming justice and mercy for the slaves. With his brothers of the order of St. Dominic he braved all opposition in this holy cause; they constantly denounced the wrath of God against the tyranny which was enacted around them; from the pulpit they asked indignantly whether it could be right that their fellow men, for whom Christ had died, should be branded like beasts with red hot irons, and gambled away at dice from one dissolute master to another. The anger of the grasping colonists did not silence them; they visited Spain again and again, to besiege the court with their claims of protection for the unhappy natives; by their writings they filled Europe with the tale of their countrymen's atrocities. They gave deeds as well as words; they went to preach among the heathen a far other gospel than that which had swords as its texts and chains as its commandments. They sought to have a country set apart, where they might expose their lives in this truly Christian mission, and where no layman might be allowed to come to undo their work by his hunger for gain and thirst for blood. Alas! the poor savages did not know their friends, but taking these visitors to be like the rest of their race, massacred them in revenge for a kidnapping foray. Too truly had the monks foreseen how their fellow believers would preach the truth! Undaunted, they did not yet draw back from their labour of love. There was a district in central America into which no armed force could penetrate, so fierce were the inhabitants and so strong were their retreats; it was called the Land of War. Here the brethren had free leave to carry the cross alone and at their own risk. A little band of them hastened to this post of danger; at their mild bidding the unsubdued warriors laid down their arms, and henceforth that rugged country was known as the Land of Peace. For very shame, the slayers and enslavers could not but listen at length to teachers who gave such proofs of their sincerity; and they listened the more readily, no doubt, when they began to find how their shortsighted rapacity was undermining their own interests. Humanity got a hearing too late to save whole nations from being exterminated; but whatever amelioration was wrought in the condition of the Indians, when once the first fury of the conquest had passed away, was owing to the earnestness of these churchmen, who had come to the New World to seek no riches for themselves beyond the reward of him to whom it is given to gain souls. Their work in extending and confirming the dominion of Spain was in the end far greater than the share of the men of war. All over South America they spread their bloodless conquests, and established themselves by the force of a devotion that no dangers nor difficulties could overcome.

We cannot but admire the spirit in which these men laboured, yet we must grieve that such labours have been so barren of wholesome fruit. The Indians, their idols once thrown down, received easily the more superstitious part of their conquerors' religion; the yoke of Rome fitted them only too well. The lessons of submission sank but too deep into their character. With the wild freedom of the woods they have lost all energy and motive for exertion. Driven to their daily task, and secure of their daily food, they have become a listless and indolent as well as a docile flock. The monks have enslaved both body and mind, and diligently destroying the stimulating force of self reliance and free thought, have degraded rather than elevated their catechumens. So now, where the bell of the mission tinkles over *cañon* and *monte*, it speaks of peace indeed, but of a peace more akin to death than life: the peace not of smiling fields and busy arts and growing towns, but such peace rather as reigns in some pathless forest of the tropics, where the light of heaven is hid by unbroken masses of foliage, and the ground is choked by rank weeds, trailing and twisting between every mouldered trunk, where no breath of wind comes to stir the stifling air, heavy with noxious vapours, and ear and eye grow dull among the oppressive luxuriance of vegetation, swarming secretly with base and harmful creatures—a slumberous, sweltering, corrupting peace, broken only by the roar of the thunder and the crash of the earthquake.

If such evils came of the conquest of the cross, what might be expected of the conquests of the sword! Of these conquerors it may truly be said that only when they had made a desolation could they call it peace. They sowed dragons' teeth in the fields which they watered with blood, and they were to reap as they had sown. The history of Spanish America is a melancholy record of slavery and anarchy, of tyranny and revolution, of greed and poverty. Nowhere is the earth richer, yet nowhere is man more miserable than in the lands of gold and silver, of pearls and diamonds. Unable to conquer himself, he is powerless against nature, which still in these regions gives her strength to vegetable rather than to animal life, and sees the human soul dwarfed and withered amid her most prodigal bounties. The blessings of religion and civilization seem here to have turned into a curse, cursing alike those who brought and those who received the fatal gifts. The Spaniards have been tainted by the degradation of their bondsmen, for the cry of the slave against his oppressor is never raised in vain, and the lash of the tyrant as surely debases him who holds it as the cringing form on which it falls. Nor did their mother country long prosper on the wealth which these colonists gathered with such guilty hands. Soon she was to afford a memorable example that not thus are the true riches of a nation to be counted. All the gold sent home to Spain was found but a source of weakness when priestcraft and kingcraft were sucking out her life. Surely, we exclaim, hearing of her greatness and beholding her fall, the Avenger of the innocent has made inquisition for the blood with which she thus polluted her conquests!

In many books you may read at length these tales, more marvellous than legends, of how the modern Argonauts went to seek a golden treasure in the west, how they carried the plagues of Christendom to desolate America, and how they sent back poisonous germs concealed among their spoil. Our story is of heroes of another kind, who learned in time to look for no windfalls of precious ore, but to address themselves manfully to honest and patient work, which, in the long run, is the only thing that pays the world and the workers.

III.

Within half a century from the discovery of America, the flood of Spanish invasion had spread over the West Indian islands and the coasts of central America, and was rapidly making its way upon the southern continent, while to the north the ancient empire of Mexico was submerged beneath the rising colony of New Spain. Vasco Nunez had crossed the isthmus and discovered the South Sea. His countrymen were beginning to have some notion of the geographical features of the New World, though as yet it was unascertained what seas and straits might not divide it into a vast group of islands. The Spaniards now held at least the outskirts of the countries occupied by their descendants at the present day, and were firmly fixed in advantageous positions from which they might extend their conquest in every direction.

But here their progress stayed; and the most prosperous and famous part of America, that part which is called America *par excellence,* was left to be peopled and subdued by another nation.

Several attempts, indeed, were made to explore to the north. Expeditions were sent towards California, in search of the gold which was to be discovered there three centuries later; others sought the blooming shores of Florida, where Ponce de Leon was the first to land in 1512. Of these expeditions the most celebrated is that of Ferdinand de Soto, which wandered for years in the interior of the country to the north of the Gulf of Mexico, and left the body of their leader buried in the great waters of the Mississippi.

But the toils and hardships of these explorers produced no gold; the Spaniards, fearless in romantic perils and wild delusions, shrank back from the colder regions where nature refused to be conquered save by steady labour, and the sword was useless without the plough and the axe. Spain showed no readiness to push her settlements into North America, though, like a dog in the manger, she still claimed all the continent for her own. A new claimant soon appeared in these vast lists, where a century might well pass before challenger and challenged could come face to face. In the north France was, from time to time, to spend pains in clearing the ground and planting settlements, the fruit of which would be reaped by another nation.

It is notable that so many of the leaders of discovery at this time were Italians, setting out under the auspices of foreign governments. Columbus, as we have seen, was born at Genoa. Cabot, who first came upon the mainland while employed by England, was a Venetian. From Florence came Amerigo Vespucci, who had the undeserved good luck of bestowing his name upon the new world, whereas he was only the first to visit the southern continent. There was clearly room for a good deal of difference in opinion as to which people had any special right from prior discovery; the only great nation of the day—if Italy might be called a nation—that does not seem to have put in any claim, was the one to different states of which these men belonged.

Another Florentine, Verrazzani, entered the field in behalf of the king of France, and in 1524 surveyed the coast of the United States, and brought back such a report that his royal master began to think these countries had not been created for the Spaniards alone. The name of New France was given to the northern part, whither the French had already been attracted by the fisheries of Newfoundland, an important industry wherever the fasts of the Catholic Church were observed. France and Spain were playing that game at which Francis I. lost all but honour to his rival Charles V. There was therefore every motive for colonising, and the famous Jacques Cartier was encouraged and assisted with means to explore Canada. He sailed up the St. Lawrence and gave its present name to the wooded eminence of Montreal. Cold and scurvy drove him away; but once more he returned to his self appointed task, and behind him came a viceroy attended by the sweepings of the jails, who were thought good enough for such a doubtful enterprise. Failure was again the result. No precious metals or stones having been found, the newly opened country had small chance of attention from the government at a time when France was distracted by long and bloody civil wars, carried on in the name of religion.

It was an ill season to found colonies, yet the very stress of the times led to an attempt which for us has a special interest. In the middle of the sixteenth century Frenchmen anticipated the design carried out by the English puritans two generations later. A writer, whom his friend Montaigne believed likely to prove the greatest mind of the age, the shortlived La Boëtie, sick of the Old World, passionately adjured his countrymen to fly across the ocean from the evils of tyranny and bigotry. The same idea had already been conceived by a more practical spirit. Coligny, the celebrated leader of the Huguenots, undertook to form a settlement which should be not only the nucleus of a French empire in America, but a haven of refuge for his persecuted co-religionists. The king seems to have made no objection, and under Coligny's auspices a party of Calvinists was sent to Brazil. The Portuguese had already established themselves there, and the French colony was destroyed not only by fierce opposition but by the treachery of their own leader; yet Coligny did not abandon his bold and wise design, but turned his eyes towards another part of the coast, where he hoped to find no rivalry. The sunny shores of Florida and Carolina seemed to invite the sons of France to a congenial climate. Three successive expeditions were sent out under John Ribault and Réné Laudonnière, the latter of whom has left a full account of the fortunes of his ill starred companions.

Their story is a typical one, too common in the records of early colonial enterprise. At first all went well. The Frenchmen were delighted with the country and its productions; the low or gently undulating soil, well watered and covered with open woods and rich savannahs, promised them an easy settlement. They fixed themselves upon the

St. John's river in the north of Florida, and named their fort after their sovereign, Charles IX. The Indians gave them a friendly welcome, brought provisions, and eagerly sought the alliance of the powerful strangers. But soon ill feeling arose, and quarrels in which the arms of the Europeans secured them an easy victory but could not aid them against the consequences of inexperience and improvidence. Though the enterprise had been undertaken in a religious spirit, it as usual had enlisted dissolute and greedy adventurers of a character to ruin any community. Our own navigator, John Hawkins, who visited and relieved them, found that it was their own fault if they could not do well in such a land, "but they being soldiers desired to live by the sweat of other men's brows." They made twenty hogsheads of wine out of the grapes of the country, and learned to forget their troubles in sucking through a cane the smoke of a certain dried herb set on fire in "an earthen cup," after the manner of the natives. Hard work was in their eyes the worst of evils, and when they could no longer beg or buy from their neighbours they found robbery a precarious means of livelihood. So injuries and reprisals, waste and want, mutinies and desertion had nearly succeeded in stifling the birth of the young colony, which for some time received no support, the hands of its patrons being too full of troubles at home. Yet when the third fleet at last arrived, just as the starved survivors were about to abandon the country, the Frenchmen easily recovered their elastic spirits. Once more they seemed

to have fair prospects before them; but suddenly
a fatal cloud appeared upon the horizon.

It was not to be expected that the proud Spaniards would submit to this invasion of their vaunted
rights by foreigners and heretics. In 1565 Philip
II., according to the strange practice of the time,
farmed out Florida, so to speak, to be conquered
by Pedro Melendez, one of the ruthless *conquistadores* of South America. The new comers from
France had scarcely landed and were congratulating themselves on false news of the discovery of
gold, when part of the Spanish fleet appeared off
the harbour, making professions of goodwill which
were at once taken for what they were worth.
Alarm and dissension broke out among the French.
Ribault, the new governor, embarked with the best
part of the efficient forces, intending to attack the
Spaniards by sea. Laudonnière was left behind in
the fort with a garrison of invalids, boys and lackeys,
to protect the women and children. This weak
company kept a bad watch, and suddenly in a storm
of rain the Spaniards were upon them, having
marched, guided by a traitor, through several
leagues of swamps, lagoons and forests, from the
spot to the south where they had landed. A feeble
resistance was attempted, but the scene was a massacre rather than a fight. A few escaped into the
woods, and slinking through the reeds fringing the
river made their way to two small ships which
still lay at its mouth. The rest were slaughtered,
men, women, and children. Then upon these
human shambles the pious Spaniards did not fail

to raise their cross and offer their devotions to Heaven.

What was Ribault's fleet doing in the meanwhile? Alas! a storm had dashed it upon the coast, and the shipwrecked Frenchmen hardly escaped from the fury of the waves to fall into the cruel hands of their fellow men. Weak and destitute, they surrendered to Melendez, who butchered them almost to a man; a few who professed to be Catholics were saved. Nine hundred persons in all are said to have been killed.

The Spaniards proclaimed Philip II. king of all North America, and exulting over their easy victory addressed themselves to building a town at the place where they had landed on the day consecrated to St. Augustine, whose name was therefore given to this, the oldest town in the United States. This was in the year 1565. They also built three forts on the settlement of their victims, and proceeded, as was their wont, to make themselves a burden and a hatred to the Indians, already too little pleased with the manners of their former guests.

But before two years had passed an avenger of all this blood was on his way across the ocean. De Gourgues, a Huguenot gentleman of Gascony, was roused by the news which the French government heard with indifference. Borrowing from his friends, and selling a great part of his own property, he contrived to become master of three ships and a hundred and fifty soldiers, with which force he put to sea, as if for an ordinary voyage of discovery. But when they came near the American coast he disclosed to his men what he had in mind, and they swore to carry out his stern purpose of revenging the death of their countrymen. They landed in the St. John's river and made a dash at the forts. The Spaniards in their turn, taken by surprise, were beaten, though they much outnumbered the assailants. Each of the three forts was taken and razed to the ground. Scant quarter was given to those who had shown so little mercy in their hour of triumph. The Indians gladly rose against their oppressors, and filling the woods drove the fugitives back upon the arms of the victors. Those who were made prisoners were hanged upon the very trees on which the bodies of the French had swung beneath this inscription: "*I do this not as unto Frenchmen, but as unto heretics.*" So now De Gourgues answered Melendez with bitter irony, burning the letters into a wooden board: "*I do this not as unto Spaniards nor mariners, but as unto traitors, robbers and murderers.*"

Such is the dark story of the first European settlement within the bounds of the American republic. De Gourgues, unable to do more with his little force, returned at once to France, where the government was so far from caring to follow up his bold stroke that he was obliged to conceal himself from the consequences of its displeasure. Florida was tacitly given up to the Spaniards, and the French names which had been bestowed upon features of the country, were wiped out in blood.

But Spain thought little of its new acquisition. A few hundred Spaniards settled at St. Augustine, letting themselves be befooled by the oft repeated tale of a marvellously rich city lying somewhere in the interior. An attempt at discovery was made towards the north, but nothing came of it. The conquerors of the West India islands and Mexico and Peru, left the Atlantic coast to be peopled by as daring and more sober minded adventurers. But Florida, being so near their other possessions, was retained, and, with a short interval of English occupation during the last century, vegetated as a Spanish colony till 1819, when it was bought by the United States for five millions of dollars.

THE FIRST ENGLISH PLANTERS.

I.

WHILE the Spaniards and French were thus employed upon the outskirts of these vast and unknown territories, there appeared upon the scene that power which in virtue of courage, perseverance and practical sense was to found an enduring commonwealth across the Atlantic. England, now at rest from civil and religious discord, was awaking to her destiny as the greatest naval and colonising nation of modern times, and began to ask herself why she should not seek her share of these famed riches of the New World. In English ships the Cabots had first reached the mainland of North America. An English sailor had first circumnavigated the globe. There was more than one of his comrades who hoped to be the first to hit upon that northwest passage which, as people then believed, led direct to India; and though all attempts in this direction failed, every year was signalised by some new discovery due to English enterprise. Such men as Drake, Hawkins, and Frobisher were making the flag of England known and feared all over the maritime world. In the South Seas the Spanish settlements and treasure ships had to be constantly on their guard against her daring sailors; at the fisheries of Newfoundland the French were rivalled by her merchants. What then was to hinder her from exploring and settling on land, as she conquered and traded by sea? Had the Pope forsooth assigned the New World to Spain? So did that Antichrist claim to deal with the crown and the liberties of England! The newly discovered soil belonged to none but its natives, who might be won by kindness and fair dealing better than by rapacious conquest, or at least might be enforced for their own good to receive the blessings of Christianity and civilization. The pretensions of the Spaniards were but a challenge to the national spirit and the protestantism of England, now united in recognition of a common enemy.

The cruelty of gold-hunting filibusters towards the poor Indians, still more the atrocities of the Inquisition's bloody missionaries, made men shudder who had not yet forgotten the fires of Smithfield, and roused in the national mind, where the leaven of puritanism was already working, that righteous indignation which is one of the religious sentiments most easily excited in human nature. It was not difficult to bring our reckless mariners to take it for a religious duty to plunder papists, and to imagine those praises most acceptable to Heaven which were sung—

> Upon a harp made of dead Spanish bones,
> The proudest instrument the world affords.

Sentiment and policy were at one in this hatred of the Spaniard, who in the Netherlands had just taught Englishmen what they had to expect if ever the Pope and Philip could secure their vaunted rights over the dominions of Elizabeth. It needed little foresight to perceive that a struggle for life and death was imminent between the great Protestant and the great Catholic power. The wise statesmen of the one saw that a blow should be struck at that engrossment of colonial enterprise from which the other drew its riches. Besides, the population of England was expanding beyond its resources; and want began to be felt at one end of the social scale, while at the other increased luxury prompted to new means of gain. The country was full of restless spirits, stirred by the romantic notions characteristic of the age, and unable to find at home fitting scope for their activity. So it is not surprising that in the reign of Elizabeth there arose a general zeal for "plantation," as the phrase then was, inspired by various motives and sanctioned by the highest, which was on the lips of many men if as yet in the hearts of but few. The men who fostered and directed this zeal always declared, like Lord Bacon, that their purpose was "as well for the better increase of the trade of merchandise of this kingdom, as by conversation and commerce to draw those savage and idolatrous people to the true knowledge of God." And if our first colonists did not always present an example of the best fruits of Christianity, as understood in these days, they at least did not bring its worst to the work of conversion. Such violence and oppression as they were guilty of seem mildness and humanity when contrasted with the cruelties of the Spaniards; while among English colonists as among Spanish conquerors there were here and there men of true humanity and pure enthusiasm for the salvation of these ignorant souls.

The spirit of the time found its representative in the famous Sir Walter Raleigh. No story is better known than that of how this scion of a private Devonshire family rose rapidly, through his talents and accomplishments, to fortune and influence. No doubt he owed much to the fickle favour of Elizabeth, but such a man was sure, sooner or later, to win his way into notice. As a scholar, a gentleman, and a statesman, he was distinguished even among the many distinguished men of that court. His personal advantages might have made him a mere court favourite; but he was successful as soldier, sailor, trader, and author, and tried his hand at philosophy and chemistry, not without credit from his contemporaries. Yet it is by his attempts at colonisation, the part of his work which altogether failed, that he is perhaps best known to us; for though his efforts brought nothing but disappointment to himself, they paved the way for more successful settlements of the English race in North America. He was at once a poet and a man of business; the clear eye of practical foresight was united in him with an eager love of adventure and a sanguine imagination which, to the hour of his death, never ceased to dream of boundless wealth to be had for the seeking it beyond the seas. He shared, to some degree, the credulity of his age, when men easily gave ear to the most romantic stories of these lands of the sun from which the Spaniards drew such riches. "I tell thee, gold is more plentiful there than copper is with us," says a character in an old play, speaking of Virginia; "and for as much red copper as I can bring, I'll have thrice the weight in gold. Why, man, all their dripping pans are pure gold, and all the chains with which they chain up the streets are massy gold; all the prisoners they take are fettered in gold; and for rubies and diamonds, they go forth on holidays and gather them by the seashore to hang on their children's coats and stick in their children's caps, as commonly as our children wear saffron gilt brooches and groats with holes in 'em." If the ignorant could be brought to believe in this, their betters were often found to believe not much less; and it would have been surprising if such a man as Elizabeth's Captain of the Guard had not turned his attention to America.

Walter Raleigh's apprenticeship to arms was in the ranks of the French Huguenots, whose leader Coligny had been the patron of the ill starred expedition to Florida. The young English volunteer could not fail to have heard and to have been filled with indignation at the story of the cruel massacre of Ribault and his companions. If this were not enough to teach him the spirit of popery, he was in France, perhaps in Paris, during the horrors of St. Bartholomew's day, 1572. Later we find him serving against the Spaniards in the Netherlands, then struggling for their freedom;

and he returned to England a resolute enemy of these enemies of his religion, already in all but name the enemies of his country. He was still a young man when his half-brother, Sir Humphrey Gilbert, one cast in much the same mould as himself, engaged him eagerly in a work that was to make them both famous, though not rich as they hoped. This was at a time when the country was excited by the report of Martin Frobisher, who, in searching for the north-west passage, believed that he had discovered precious metals upon the icy shores of Labrador.

The queen was easily brought to see the advantages that would result from American colonisation. But it was the nature of this great princess to have at once a very keen eye for profit and a very close hand for expenditure; the sovereigns of England had already learned that, luckily for its people, they could only raise money by the sacrifice of power. Instead of supporting these designs with the credit and resources of the government, she preferred to induce private persons to undertake them by liberally promising rewards which cost her nothing. Gilbert accordingly, in 1578, received letters patent authorising him to search and take possession of any remote lands not actually in the dominions of any Christian prince, (the rights of heathen princes not being taken into consideration,) which lands were to belong for ever to him and his heirs, subject to the crown of England, which was also to be entitled to a fifth part of all gold and silver ore found therein. His title was to be established by his actually taking possession within six years from the date of the patent; and he was authorised to administer justice among his followers, and to levy war against whoever should interfere with his rights thus conferred, within a space of two hundred leagues.

With such prospects before him, Gilbert spent a large part of his own fortune in making preparations for a task that was almost beyond private means. There were many difficulties in the way, and the volunteers whom he could bring to join in his adventure were hard to manage. At the last moment his fleet was reduced by mutiny and desertion from eleven to seven ships, with which he sailed from the coast of Devonshire, a county that in this reign led the way in maritime enterprise. History gives no clear account as to the aims and doings of this fleet. There is some reason to suppose that Gilbert and Raleigh meant to begin their work by making attacks on the vessels or possessions of Spain, so as to gain means for carrying on their operations on a larger scale. In plain English, they were no better than pirates, setting out with the connivance of the government, though in her letters patent Elizabeth strictly forbade any hostile acts towards the subjects of princes with whom she professed to be at peace. Such piracy, in the face of such professions, was one of the leading features of her reign; it was held allowable, even honourable, as a spoiling of the Egyptians, and the leading men of the nation did not scruple to lend a hand in it, while the queen might be relied on to receive all complaints with no more than an affectation of displeasure. It would scarcely in her shrewd eyes have been policy to discourage such enterprise, when England might any day be at open war with Spain, and the royal navy must be mainly composed of private ships and sailors trained in these irregular hostilities.

It is not even known where Gilbert's fleet went to. Some suppose that their destination was the fisheries of Newfoundland; others, that they made for the West India islands in search of rich booty, and that now Raleigh may have himself visited* those regions which he afterwards laboured to colonise. In whatever part of the world it visited, this expedition gained neither profit nor credit, for next year it returned in a sorry plight, having been completely defeated in action with the Spaniards.

But Raleigh was not discouraged in his daring schemes by the failure of this first attempt. After three years, during which he had his hands full of fighting the rebels and their foreign auxiliaries in Ireland, the plans of Gilbert and himself were again brought under the notice of the queen. Now that bands of Spanish adventurers had invaded her dominions, Elizabeth was able to give more open encouragement to such naval incursions, but she gave very little else; and the brothers, after their recent losses, were too poor to furnish more than five ships, with which Gilbert set out for the

---

* "These islands with the rest adjoining are so well known to yourself," says one of his captains, addressing Raleigh in 1584.—*Hakluyt*, iii., 301.

northern parts of America, with definite intentions of discovering and of planting a colony. The queen was beginning to have such a regard for Raleigh that she would not allow him to go, and to this prohibition he perhaps owed his long and active life. His half-brother perished, and lost the glory of being the founder of New England.

Sir Humphrey Gilbert on his second expedition took two hundred and sixty men, among them such artificers as would be most useful in a young colony, also refiners and persons skilled in minerals, and a learned foreigner who designed to write the history of their doings and discoveries, and had already prefaced his functions as "special correspondent" by a laudatory piece of Latin verse, after the literary fashion of the day. As usual in such voyages, they carried a stock of "petty haberdashery wares" to trade with the natives, and besides "for solace of our people and allurement of the savages, we were provided of music in good variety, not omitting the least toys, as morris dancers, hobby horse, and May-like conceits to delight the savage people whom we intended to win by all fair means possible." These were times when Robin Hood and Friar Tuck still flourished in our sports; now-a-days an Arctic Expedition has more probably a troupe of amateur negro minstrels to amuse Jack, who may be unconsciously clearing the way for another as great change in popular amusements.

At the very outset this first English colony was met by misfortune. A contagious disease broke out upon the largest of the ships, the one contributed by Raleigh, and it put back into Plymouth; all his life its owner was destined to urge his countrymen across the seas, but to reap no profit there himself. The others continued their course across the Atlantic; and, passing through fogs and icebergs, arrived in seven weeks off the rocky coasts of Newfoundland and the well known "banks," which during the fishing season were marked by a multitude of seafowl feeding on the offal and garbage thrown out by the fishermen. Two of the five ships had parted company on the way; and the crew of one of them, a set of rascals over whom their captain had little authority, had found an opportunity of doing a stroke of piracy on their own account. Now the rest fell in with these stragglers, and sailed into the harbour of St. John, where were thirty-six fishing vessels of various nations, among whom the English seem to have lorded it, already in the full persuasion that it was their heritage to rule the waves. As soon as Gilbert displayed his commission, he was welcomed in the most friendly manner, and every ship in the harbour was taxed to furnish him with supplies. On Sunday, the 4th of August, 1583, in the full heat of Newfoundland's short summer, Gilbert landed and was shown an exceptionally pleasant part of the country, abounding in wild roses and raspberries, which the people engaged in the fishing trade called the Garden. Delighted with the appearance of the place, next day he set up his tent, and summoning the merchants and shipmasters of all nations, took possession in the name of his queen, and had delivered to him a twig and a clod of earth in token thereof. No one was willing or able to protest against these claims, so the ceremony was completed by the erection of a wooden pillar bearing the arms of England engraved in lead; and Gilbert proceeded to grant leases of the land which had hitherto had no owner. No natives were to be seen in this the south part of the island, which was so densely covered with trees and long grass that the exploration of it proved impracticable, and it was proposed to set the woods on fire as the only way of coming to a judgment as to the features and resources of the interior.

Sir Humphrey was greatly pleased with his new acquisition, especially with some ore which a German refiner declared upon his life to be silver, and which the commander had sent on board secretly, lest the French and Portuguese should get wind of it and report accordingly to their own governments. And whereas he had before thought little of the northern district of his dominions that were to be, intending merely to visit them, and assign them to be planted by others, then to pass on and settle himself farther south, he now changed his mind and resolved to take the north for his own share. But as the commission which he had received from Elizabeth provided that the rights granted him should lapse if he failed to take possession within a limited time, he must first go southwards and secure the country there by landing upon it and going through the same forms of asserting his ownership.

Desertion and sickness were rapidly thinning his

forces, so he made haste to depart, giving up one ship to convey the invalids home. With the three others he beat about between Newfoundland and Cape Breton, much troubled by currents and shoals, till in rough misty weather the largest ship, the Delight, ran aground, and was lost with almost all her men, the chief part of the provisions, Gilbert's books and notes, and the ore which he took to be so precious. The others continued to beat up and down, hoping that the weather would clear. But it continued rough and grew colder, winter now coming on, for which the adventurers were ill prepared with scanty clothing. Provisions also began to run short; and thoroughly disheartened by the fate of their companions and the hardships which they now experienced, some of them besought their leader to return to England, to which he agreed the more willingly that he hoped next spring to set forth again better provided.

But this was to be the gallant sailor's last voyage. Against the advice of his officers he insisted on remaining on board the smaller of the two vessels now left to him, the Squirrel, a frail craft of no more than ten tons, the deck of which was thought to be much overloaded. Still they were pursued by bad weather; men who had spent all their lives upon the ocean had never seen such violent seas, which again and again threatened to swallow up the little Squirrel. Ominous portents struck fear into the superstitious minds of the mariners. A monster was seen, in the description of which we get some hint of the celebrated sea serpent. Fatal lights were observed glimmering on the mainyard, as before the loss of the Delight there had been reports of "strange voices which scared some from the helm." The commander of the expedition, his head full of sanguine expectations from his next voyage, set a good example of cheerfulness to his men, and steadily refused to abandon the dangerous post which he had chosen. He was last seen sitting abaft with a book in his hand, and hailing those on the larger ship with the cry, "We are as near heaven by sea as by land." At midnight the watch of this ship saw the lights of the Squirrel suddenly disappear; she and all on board had been swallowed by the Atlantic. The Golden Hind, the only remaining vessel, passed through more stormy weather, but at last arrived safe in Falmouth with her woeful news.

Still Raleigh did not lose heart; rather was he inspirited by the reports brought home by the survivors. He knew that the fierce waves which had overwhelmed his brother were of as varying moods as a woman's love. Basking now in the halcyon days of the queen's favour, he trusted that the ocean would be no less propitious to him. From his royal mistress he procured a patent similar to that of Sir Humphrey, constituting him lord proprietor of such heathen countries as he should within six years discover, settle, and annex to the British crown. He then lost no time in fitting out a small expedition which should secure his rights.

II.

On the 27th of April, 1584, two ships, under Captains Amadas and Barlow, sailed from England to discover and report to Raleigh upon the capabilities of his yet to be acquired dominions. According to the notions of the time, they thought it necessary to make a circuit by the Canaries and the West India islands, fearing that the gulf stream would otherwise have carried them out of their course. On the 2nd of July they found shoal water, and a strong sweet smell as if "of odoriferous flowers" assured them that they were not far from land. Two days later they came upon a part of America, the conformation of which is such as might have well troubled these adventurers, since it is still the dread of more experienced mariners. The name of Cape Fear speaks for itself, and the old sea saying runs:

> If the Bermudas let you pass,
> You must beware of Hatteras.

The whole coast of North Carolina is fenced off, as it were, from the main ocean by a strip of barren land, edged with shoals and sandbanks, and even now inhabited by only a few hundred fishermen and pilots. North of the dangerous point of Cape Hatteras this long bank stretches almost continuously, with but two or three practicable channels giving entrance to the sound within, from ten to fifty miles broad, dotted with islands, and making shallow inlets into the mainland, the eastern part of

which is a low plain covered with swamps, lagoons,
and pine forests.

To this place, most unsuitable for the establishment of a colony, ignorance had guided the adventurers, rather than to the rich land and good harbours
which lay unoccupied at the distance of one or two
days' sail. Taking it for the continent, they coasted
for a hundred and twenty miles before finding safe
harbourage, and when at last they came to what
they supposed to be a river, they joyfully entered,
gave thanks to God for their safe arrival, manned
their boats, and hastened to take possession of the
country with the usual ceremonies. After their
long voyage they were well disposed to be pleased
with any land, and the spot in which they now
found themselves, seen to its best advantage in
the calm summer weather, excited their most lively
admiration. They wondered at the rich vegetation
which covered the sandy soil; the goodly cedars,
pines, and cypress trees were twined with vines
hanging from their branches, which also grew so
close to the shore that the sea spray dashed over
the clusters of grapes. The woods were filled with
game, and when for the first time an arquebus shot
awakened their echoes, whole hosts of wild fowl
rose up with cries of alarm. We may imagine how
eager these mariners were to stretch their legs in
this southern paradise, how they chased each other
through the woods like schoolboys, plucking the
delicious grapes, shouting after the astonished deer
and hares which bounded from their path, and
revelling in the cool shades stirred by refreshing

breezes. But when they reached a low height they found to their astonishment that they were not yet on the mainland, but on an island some six miles broad, beyond and around which lay the waters of what seemed to be another ocean.

Instead of immediately pursuing their voyage, the crews were well content to repose for a time in this charming situation. They could not but be curious to know whether the country had any inhabitants, and what manner of men they might be; it was not, however, till the third day after their arrival that three Indians appeared in a canoe, paddling toward the ships. Two of them held aloof, but the other showed great courage, for he landed, kept walking up and down on the shore opposite the ships, and waited fearlessly for the boat in which the chief officers rowed toward him. They were naturally not much the wiser for a voluble address which he made them in his own language; but he was without difficulty induced to return with them to the ship, where they soon found means of making him understand their goodwill. They gave him a hat, a shirt, and some other things, and made him taste of their food and wine, which he seemed by no means to dislike. Having been shown over both vessels, he returned to his own boat, where his first care was to prove his gratitude towards his late hosts. He fell a-fishing close by, and in half an hour had filled the boat with fish, which he laid out in two heaps on the land, making signs that one was for each ship.

Though there is no hint of the kind in the

narrative, one cannot help thinking that this savage would scarcely have shown so much confidence if he had not already come into contact with white men. There was a story among these people that years before a crew of Europeans had been wrecked on the coast, but nothing was known for certain as to their ultimate fate.

The news of this friendly intercourse soon went out, and next day the English were visited by several canoes, and in them no less a person than Granganimeo, brother of the king of the district. The king himself, it was afterwards explained, was lying severely wounded in war at the chief town of the country, six miles off. But his brother was a worthy representative of the royal family. He came attended by a suite of forty or fifty men. On his brow he wore a broad plate of copper, which the English fancied might be gold, the mark of high rank in this rude state. When he arrived his followers spread a long mat upon the ground, on which he sat with grave dignity and beckoned the strangers to approach, while his men remained standing in respectful silence. To the English he showed himself most condescending, and by signs gave them to understand that he welcomed them as friends. He then deigned to accept with evident pleasure the presents they offered him; indeed, he showed a very unprincely spirit of greed, for when they went on to make gifts to his chief men he snatched them up and put them into his own basket, and let it be known that it was his privilege to get everything that might be going. Nor was he above trading.

Of all the wares which were submitted to him, nothing better pleased his Indian highness than a tin plate, which he willingly bought for twenty skins, and, boring a hole in the rim, hung it about his neck with much pride. For a copper kettle the English got fifty skins; and the pearl ornaments worn by the chief's wife and her women showed that they had brought their goods to a rich market. Like experienced traders, however, they showed no eagerness for these wares, intending, if possible, to learn where the pearls came from, and whether they could not be had for nothing. While Granganimeo was by, no one else was allowed to do business, so that political economy was here at pretty much the same stage as in England, where the sovereign still claimed the right of fettering trade by the infamous system of monopolies.

Intercourse and traffic being thus established to the satisfaction of both parties, they soon became excellent friends. The Indians, cruel and treacherous towards their neighbours, regarded with awe these bearded strangers and the great ships in which they had come across the unknown ocean. They were never tired of wondering at the whiteness of the European skins, which they were not content with seeing, but must touch with their dusky paws. They would tremble with terror at the discharge of a pistol, and coveted a rusty cutlass as a treasure. Under the influence of such feelings they showed their best side to the English, who, on the other hand, admired the ingenuity with which those simple children of nature had learned to hollow out canoes by the aid of fire, to build and fortify wooden villages, and to provide themselves with garments, ornaments, and household utensils. They spoke most highly of the hospitable manner in which Granganimeo sent them almost daily deer, rabbits, hares, and fish, and sometimes melons, walnuts, cucumbers, peas, and other vegetables; they extolled the punctuality with which the natives kept their promises, the courtesy and ceremony which they seemed to observe towards each other as well as towards the strangers.

The following extract from Captain Barlow's narrative gives us a pleasant picture of native hospitality, with some hint of their way of living.

"After they had been divers times aboard our ships, myself with seven more went twenty miles into the river that runneth toward the city of Skicoak, which river they call Occam; and the evening following we came to an island which they call Roanoke, distant from the harbour by which we entered seven leagues; and at the north end thereof was a village of nine houses, built of cedar, and fortified round about with sharp trees to keep out their enemies, and the entrance into it made like a turnpike, very artificially. When we came towards it, standing near unto the water's side, the wife of Granganimeo, the king's brother, came running out to meet us very cheerfully and friendly; her husband was not then in the village. Some of her people she commanded to draw our boat on shore for the beating of the billow; others she appointed to carry us on their backs to the dry ground, and

The English welcomed to Roanoke.

Page 48.

others to bring our oars into the house for fear of stealing. When we were come into the outer room, having five rooms in her house, she caused us to sit down by a great fire, and after took off our clothes and washed them and dried them again; some of the women plucked off our stockings and washed them, some washed our feet in warm water, and she herself took great pains to see all things ordered in the best manner she could, making great haste to dress some meat for us to eat.

"After we had thus dried ourselves, she brought us into the inner room, where she set on the board standing along the house some wheat like furmety, sodden venison and roasted, fish sodden, boiled and roasted, melons raw and sodden, roots of divers kinds, and divers fruits. Their drink is commonly water, but while the grape lasteth they drink wine, and for want of casks to keep it all the year after they drink water; but it is sodden with ginger in it and black cinnamon, and sometimes sassafras, and divers other wholesome and medicinable herbs and trees. We were entertained with all love and kindness, and with as much bounty (after their manner) as they could possibly devise. We found the people most gentle, loving, and faithful, void of all guile and treason, and such as live after the manner of the golden age. The people only care how to defend themselves from the cold in their short winter, and to feed themselves with such meat as the soil affordeth. Their meat is very well sodden, and they make broth very sweet and savoury. Their vessels are earthen pots, very large, white and sweet;

E

their dishes are wooden platters of sweet timber. Within the place where they feed was their lodging, and within that their idol which they worship, of whom they speak incredible things. While we were at meat there came in at the gates two or three men with their bows and arrows from hunting, whom when we espied we began to look one towards another, and offered to reach our weapons; but as soon as she espied our mistrust she was very much moved, and caused some of her men to run out and take away their bows and arrows and break them, and withal beat the poor fellows out of the gate again. When we departed in the evening and would not tarry all night, she was very sorry, and gave us into our boat our supper half dressed, pots and all, and brought us to our boat's side, in which we lay all night, removing a pretty distance from the shore. She, perceiving our jealousy, was much grieved, and sent divers men and thirty women to sit all night on the bank side by us, and sent into our boats five mats to cover us from the rain, using very many words to entreat us to rest in their houses. But because we were few men, and if we had miscarried the voyage had been in very great danger, we durst not adventure anything, although there was no cause of doubt, for a more kind and loving people there cannot be found in the world, so far as we have hitherto had trial."*

The lady of Roanoke had certainly little to learn in the way of politeness, when she had a mind to

---

* Amadas and Barlow's Narration, Hakluyt, vol. iii., p. 304.

exhibit it. But this indiscriminate praise shows how Raleigh's agents were disposed to see all things in the brightest hues. By their own accounts these most kind and loving people, whose manners suggested the golden age, had recently exemplified such a high standard of virtue by inviting a number of their enemies to a feast and barbarously massacring them as they were praying before their idol. "Their wars," we are told, "are very cruel and bloody, by reason whereof and of their civil dissensions which have happened of late years amongst them, the people are marvellously wasted, and in some places the country left desolate." Something like this is what the enchanting prospect of most golden ages resolves itself into when seen too close; and our adventurers are not the first who have formed their judgment of others mainly from the treatment which they themselves have received at their hands.

After thus spending a few weeks off the coast of Carolina, and gaining some knowledge of the hundred islands which lie along it, Amadas and Barlow departed and made a short passage to England. They had on board two of the natives, who, we hope, came of their own free will, though from the too common practice of early explorers we fear it may have been otherwise. They brought home the most favourable accounts of the resources and beauties of the country, the name of which, as they reported it, was Wingandacoa. Elizabeth, entering into the enthusiasm aroused by their glowing descriptions, ordered it to be henceforth called Virginia, in allusion to her affected title of the Virgin Queen; and this name was long applied generally to the central parts of the American seaboard.

III.

Raleigh was now rich. The queen had granted him a share of the forfeited lands of the Irish rebels, and, far more profitable, a monopoly of wines, in which no vintner could now deal without paying one pound to this lucky favourite. He had no difficulty in finding poor men who were willing to become rich, and who believed that they had little more to do in Virginia than to open their hands and let riches drop down into them. So next spring he was able to send out seven ships under the brave Sir Richard Grenville, with a colony of about a hundred men, who proposed not so much to make their home in the new country as to stay there for the short time that, as they expected, would be required for them to make their fortunes. It was long before people came to understand that neither fortunes nor colonies are to be made but by patience and hard work.

After doing a little piracy against the Spaniards on the way, as well as boldly visiting the Spanish settlement of Hispaniola, where they were received with suspicious courtesy, (being too strong for other treatment,) and entertained by the spectacle of a bull fight, Grenville's fleet arrived about midsummer at the island of Wocoken, on which Amadas and Barlow had disembarked. One of the first things done was to send word of their arrival to Wingina, the chief of that part of the country, and the English seem to have been again received in a most friendly manner. The natives were eager to get clothes from them, preferring coarse and cheap ones to those of finer material, so that the views of both parties to the bargain were easily satisfied. The new comers confessed that the accounts of the climate and productions of Virginia had not been exaggerated. Everything bid fair for a prosperous settlement.

But before many days the cloud arose which was to be the wreck of the colony. The muscular missionaries of Elizabeth professed always a great zeal for propagating the Christian religion, but they too commonly showed themselves ignorant of its true spirit. Now began that long series of injuries and revenges which caused so much blood to be shed between the white and red men. The poor savages may have often been cruel and deceitful; they knew no better. But it must be confessed that the English have often been sadly in the wrong, even when, with a show of reason, they gave the name of justice to severities prompted by proud and hasty resentment.

One of the Indians was said to have stolen a silver cup, and when it was not returned on Grenville's demand, nothing would serve the hot tempered knight but burning the whole town and the corn on which its inhabitants relied for their support. Before the end of August Sir Richard returned to England with the ships, leaving this legacy of hatred to trouble the colony which remained under the governorship of Ralph Lane.

This colony fixed themselves at Roanoke, one of the northern islands of the archipelago, which then had opposite it a channel opening through the outer bank into the ocean, now quite choked up. From this centre they explored in various directions, and set off in search of the pearls and rich ore with wonderful tales of which the Indians abused their credulity; they were also led to believe that the South Sea lay close at hand, over the swamps of Carolina, none of them yet dreaming of the extent of the continent on whose outskirts they found themselves. A party going on such a wild goose chase were nearly starved, being reduced to keep Lent, for it was that season of the year, by living on their two mastiff dogs boiled with sassafras leaves, as the Indians on either side fled before their approach, taking away everything eatable.

Thus they were not long in finding out that they could not afford to lose the friendship of the natives. Their friend Granganimeo was now dead, and his brother Wingina was by no means so well disposed towards the settlers. This chief had recently changed his name to Pemisapan; it was very common for the Indians to change their names, and when we remember the difficulty that the English must have had in catching the strange sounds of their language we cannot be sure that we always have these names correctly given. The awe inspired by the white men was passing way. The small and scattered tribes, knowing no other weapons than clubs and bows, had at first despaired of resistance to them. An eclipse of the sun and a comet were supposed to have heralded their coming; the fact that no women accompanied the party argued them of more than earthly birth; they were taken to be immortal; they were believed able to cause sickness by shooting, like invisible spirits, in the air with invisible bullets. But when the savages found that their marvellous visitors were liable to hunger and thirst as well as to the familiar passions of anger and covetousness, they began to lose faith in their supernatural character, and to see some possibility of getting rid of them. To this end they proposed to leave their own fields unsown, so that the English might be able to get nothing from them, while they themselves should retreat to the woods and live as best they could by hunting. This plan was not carried out, but Wingina *alias* Pemisapan is accused of having conceived a bolder one.

If the story were true which was disclosed to Lane by a native prisoner, this chief had made a conspiracy with the surrounding tribes, all accustomed to cunning and surprises as their main mode of warfare; and the plot had been so artfully laid that the strangers might well have fallen victims to it. Between April and July they were in the greatest need, the corn which they had planted not yet being ripe. During this season the Indians proposed by all kinds of excuses to keep them ill furnished with provisions, while they treacherously destroyed the weirs which they had previously made to supply the settlers with fish. This would cause them to disperse over the island in search of food, while various native tribes were to assemble secretly or on pretence of performing the customary funeral rites for Ensenore, the king's father, in whom the English had just lost another friend. Then in the dead of night overwhelming numbers were silently to surround the cabins that the colonists had constructed for themselves. The reeds with which these were thatched might be easily set on fire after the hot dry weather, and the occupants would be knocked on the head as they rushed forth to escape the flames which were to be the signal of a general massacre. The rest, scattered in small parties, might also be taken at advantage and slaughtered.

Lane believed this story, and resolved to be beforehand with the savages in their design of massacre. He seems to have been one of those men who confound violence with vigour, and prefer to trust to the chance of a heroic operation rather than to the more difficult measures of patient skill. So, sending before him a false message that another fleet had arrived from England and that he wished to buy provisions, he marched off to the native king and found him attended by seven or eight of the inferior chiefs. At the most inappropriate signal, "Christ our victory!" given by the governor, the English fell upon the whole court and killed them with their pistols and other weapons.

But this victory was of little avail to the colony. They would now have the Indians as open instead of secret enemies, and could get no more supplies from them without fighting. They had been scarcely a year in the country, and already the fair prospects with which they entered upon their undertaking were overcast. No gold and silver had been found as they expected, but plenty of hardships and privations on which they had not reckoned. It had been promised that fresh supplies from England would reach them before Easter; but Easter was passed, and no aid came. They took themselves for deserted by their countrymen, and lost all heart; it seemed their sad fate to pass their lives in this barbarous country, where it was all they could do to get food to keep themselves alive from day to day. But as they gave themselves up to such dejected moods, news came that a large fleet was approaching the coast.

Instantly the colonists were on the alert. Was this an expedition of the Spaniards, who might at any time be expected to interfere with English settlements in the dominions claimed by them? But to their great joy it proved to be the fleet of their countryman Sir Francis Drake, returning home from the West Indies, where he had been giving the Spaniards enough to do to look after their own possessions.

Drake behaved most generously to the unfortunate colonists. He offered to leave them not only ample supplies from his own stores, but a ship in which they might quit the country when they pleased. But a storm came to interfere with this arrangement. The ship destined for them was driven out to sea; the harbour was shown to be an unsafe one; the colonists were thoroughly sick of their undertaking, and in short they asked Drake to take them home with him, which he did, arriving in Portsmouth after a passage of five weeks.

No sooner were they gone than the ship sent out by Raleigh with stores, which was expected before Easter, came just too late, and after seeking them in vain returned to England. And a fortnight later came Sir Richard Grenville, with three more ships, and made the same bootless search. He left fifteen* men on the island of Roanoke, and they must have been bold men, to keep possession of it. Then he also returned home, not without visiting the Azores, and doing a good stroke of piracy to pay for the expense of his voyage. In the same sea a few years later, this "man very unquiet in his mind and greatly affected to war" was to die as fiercely as he had lived, ordering his ship to be blown up with its last barrel of powder rather than that it should fall into the hands of the Spaniards.

IV.

It is said that a colonial settler seldom begins to make money till he has lost all that he took out with him. Something like this was the case of our early colonies; they only prospered after hard experience. It is well that there were found such men as Raleigh and Gilbert to spend their lives and fortunes upon the waste places from which posterity has reaped such abundant fruits.

The settlement of Virginia was still to be begun

---

* Smith says fifty, in which he seems to be wrong.—*General Historie of Virginia.*

all over again. As yet the only result of so much expenditure had been the introduction into England of two plants used by the Indians, which are now common features of our daily life, tobacco and potatoes. Sir Walter Raleigh has the credit of being one of the first English smokers of a weed which was then supposed to have excellent medicinal effects. "Taking tobacco" in silver pipes soon became the fashion, and the fashion spread gradually among all ranks. There are many ludicrous stories of the astonishment with which simple rustics saw men breathing out smoke and flames, and naturally took them for conjurors or worse.

But though many of the returned emigrants sought to excuse their desertion of the country by spreading unfavourable reports about it, there were others, and notably Thomas Hariot, a talented mathematician, who were better able to estimate its riches only awaiting development, and who urged that with time, industry, and prudence a colony could not fail to be in the end successful. Hariot wrote a faithful account of the produce and characteristics of Virginia, which showed reasonable men that this failure had been the fault only of inexperience and bad judgment. It could not be denied that the settlers had found it healthy; in all their hardships no more than four had died, and these four had gone out in bad health. With so little risk there was the chance of so much profit; Raleigh offered at least five hundred acres to any man who would join in the adventure. This soil thus going almost a begging was in parts very fertile; two tall crops of

Indian corn were known to be raised in one summer; and those who had penetrated into the interior of the country reported it even more desirable. So next year the lord proprietor was able to send out a hundred and fifty persons under a governor named John White; and this time it seemed that they meant settling in earnest, for they were accompanied by women and children.

Raleigh intended these emigrants to have been landed on the more favoured shores of Chesapeake Bay, where the wedge of colonisation was at last successfully driven in. But the best part of the summer was wasted in crossing the Atlantic, and the commander of their ships, with whom they seem to have got upon bad terms, refused to take them farther than the island of Roanoke, to which they first repaired to seek the fifteen men left by Grenville. They only found the bones of one. The fort and houses built by Lane were overgrown with weeds and gourds, among which deer were peacefully feeding. All was silence and desolation. By means of Manteo, one of the savages brought away by the first party, who had ever since remained faithful to the English, they learned that all fifteen had been set upon and slain by the remnants of Wingina's tribe, in revenge for the death of their chiefs. The murder of one of the newly arrived party proved this hatred not yet extinct, and the first thing the settlers did was to proceed to revenge in their turn, but in their haste for blood they made an unfortunate mistake, which is thus narrated.

"In the morning, so early that it was yet dark, we landed near the dwelling place of our enemies, and very secretly conveyed ourselves through the woods to that side where we had their houses between us and the water; and having espied their fire and some sitting about it, we presently set on them. The miserable souls herewith amazed fled into a place of thick reeds growing fast by, where our men perceiving them shot one of them through the body with a bullet, and therewith we entered the reeds, among which we hoped to acquite their evil doing towards us. But we were deceived, for these savages were our friends, and were come from Croatoan to gather the corn and fruit of that place, because they understood our enemies were fled immediately after they had slain George Howe, and for haste had left all their corn, tobacco and pompions standing in such sort that all had been devoured of the birds and deer if it had not been gathered in time. But they had like to have paid dearly for it; for it was so dark that, they being naked, and their men and women appareled all so like others, we knew not but that they were all men; and if that one of them which was a Werowance's wife had not had a child at her back, she had been slain instead of a man; and as hap was, another savage knew Master Stafford, and ran to him, calling him by his name, whereby he was saved. Finding ourselves thus disappointed in our purpose, we gathered all the corn, peas, pompions and tobacco that we found ripe, leaving the rest unspoiled, and took Menatoan, his wife, with the young child and the other savages with us over the water to Roanoke. Although the mistaking of these savages somewhat grieved Manteo, yet he imputed their harm to their own folly, saying to them that if their Werowances had kept their promise in coming to the governor at the day appointed, they had not known that mischance."*

This was scarcely the way to secure the affections of the natives. Yet it was a constant complaint that the poor Indians were backward in accepting the lessons of Christianity, so well taught them by precept and example!

Manteo was now christened and gratified with the title of Lord of Roanoke. A few days later there was another christening of the first child born of English parents in America, a grand-daughter of the governor, who was named after the country, VIRGINIA Dare.

The tale of the governor, so far as it relates to his companions, soon comes to an end. They seem to have been well satisfied with their prospects, for when it was decided that some one should return to England to represent their need of further assistance, it was difficult to find any who would consent to go. Finally, which appears a strange step, the governor himself, at the general request, reluctantly agreed to be their messenger, and after they had given him a solemn assurance that his property should be respected in his absence, he took a passage home in the fleet little more than a month

---

* Hakluyt's Voyages, vol. iii., p. 345.

after his arrival, leaving the rest to establish themselves in the town which, when built, was to receive the name of Raleigh.

John White duly arrived at home before the end of the year, but he found his countrymen with their hands full of work that made it impossible for them to attend to wants of his far off colony. The Spanish Armada was now being equipped, and England was straining every nerve to defend its very existence as an independent power. Every ship and sailor was needed for the running fight in the Channel during the last week of July 1588, on the issues of which hung such momentous consequences for the New as well as the Old World. It may be that to the heroes of that great fight and to the propitious winds which, as they doubted not, Heaven had sent to their aid, we owe it that to-day London is not the chosen home of tyranny and priestcraft, that rugged Massachusetts is centuries in advance of rich Peru, and that the American republic is other than the bankrupt states of the Pampas.

The storm came and burst upon our shores, and at last the nation could breathe freely. But it was not till the spring of 1590 that John White was able to come with three ships to the aid of his colony, which might by this time have perished with his daughter and his infant grandchild. He might have been expected to make all haste, yet his ships hung about the West Indies for the best part of the summer, playing the privateer among the Spaniards, an irresistible temptation to English sailors of the period. The weather also was against them; and it was nearly five months before they anchored off the banks of Carolina, and saw a great smoke rising in the island of Roanoke, which put them in good hope that their friends were still there and might be joyfully listening to the guns with which they announced their long delayed coming.

The ships remained riding at anchor two miles off that dangerous coast with its shoals and irregular soundings. Next morning in a gale of wind two boats made for the inlet through which Roanoke was to be reached. One of them crossed the bar in safety with no worse mischance than a wetting; but the other, badly steered, was upset, and seven of the crew were drowned in spite of all that could be done to save them. This so disheartened the seamen that they were for abandoning the search for the colonists; and when at last they were induced to go on, so much time had been lost that it was night before they came to Roanoke and too dark to let them find the site of the plantation. A great fire was seen burning in the woods at the north end of the island, to which they rowed and sounded on a trumpet many tunes of familiar English songs, but without getting any answer to their cries and calls. When they landed at daybreak they found the fire to proceed from some burning grass and rotten wood, but none of their friends were to be seen, and no signs of habitation except the print of naked feet of the Indians upon the sand. Crossing the island to the fort, they found it empty. The palisades were still standing, but the houses had been pulled down. In the enclosure were lying shot, cannon, bars of iron and pigs of lead, overgrown with grass and weeds. Close by they came upon a place where several chests had been hidden and dug up, their contents being now destroyed and scattered about, no doubt by the rude hands of the natives. Part of this property the governor had the vexation of recognising as his own, left there in 1587; his books torn from the covers, the frames of some of his pictures and maps rotten and spoiled with rain, and his armour almost eaten through with rust.

But there was one cheering sign in this scene of desolation. On leaving for England, White had arranged with the colonists that if they found it desirable to leave Roanoke, they should carve upon some tree the name of the place to which they removed. A cross was to be added as a sign that they had been in distress. No cross was now to be seen, but on one of the largest posts at the entrance were cut the letters CROATOAN. To the island of Croatoan then they must have removed, and as this was the abode of Manteo there was reason to trust that they were among friends.

John White's narrative says little about his own feelings, but he must have been a strange father and a bad governor if he were not most anxious and impatient to rejoin his old comrades when now so near to their probable place of abode. It was indeed agreed to go next day to Croatoan. But the weather grew worse and worse; victuals were

F

running short; the sailors found a difficulty in getting water on board through the rough breakers; out of four anchors the largest ship lost three, and was nearly driven on shore. These dangers seemed to warn them no longer to remain on this inhospitable coast. It was agreed that they should go to the West Indies for supplies and should spend the winter among these islands, picking up what they could in the way of trade or piracy, then return next spring to visit their countrymen, who, as they hoped, were safely settled in Virginia.

So, making no further effort for the discovery of the colony, they sailed away. Again the weather changed their plans, and they thought it best to run upon the wind for England, since it was too violent to let them work another course. On the way they fell in with an English fleet waiting to attack the Spanish ships coming home from the isthmus of Darien, and the mariners who were so little concerned about White's colony were very ready to take a share in this business. The ships made for Europe, spreading themselves over the coasts of Spain and Portugal, like a cloud of sea vultures hovering where prey might be expected. To rob Spaniards was now the height of patriotism, and many was the good galleon whose treasures in these days came to Plymouth when they had been shipped for Cadiz or San Lucar.

What must have been the feelings of the little colony, if from some retreat among the islands they saw the ships sailing away! Never again were they to see the face of their countrymen. It may

be that they had already perished of want or by
massacre; perhaps they had made their way inland
and were lost in the vast continent. Several attempts were made to find them; and Raleigh, after
he had given up his design of colonising Virginia,
spent much of his own money on this object, but in
vain. It has been conjectured that, believing themselves abandoned, they were received into a tribe of
the natives, whose descendants have been thought
to show marks of European blood. But the fate of
little Virginia Dare and her companions is buried
in mystery. No certain trace of them was ever
found beyond the ruins of the fort where English
civilization had again failed to gain a footing on the
shores of America.

JOHN SMITH.

I.

THUS far, the attempts to colonise Virginia have been like a fire lighted among a heap of green sticks, where it flashes up, splutters, smoulders and dies out with a little thin smoke, leaving only a few charred marks, soon to be hidden by moss and mould. We now come to the story of a man through whose diligence and ability it seems to have mainly happened that the flame, again kindled, was able to take firmer hold, and after many doubtful struggles with adverse conditions at last made head against them, and gathering fresh strength as it grew, began from this nucleus to spread its wholesome power through rank forests and rotting swamps.

It is surprising that the life of John Smith should be so little known in proportion to his merits and achievements. A former generation was familiar with the old chap-book tale which dwelt with such gusto upon his fight with the terrible Turk, Bonny Mulgro, and his unexpected good fortune when already in the hands of Powhatan's executioners. But probably half of his young countrymen, who nowadays so greedily devour fictitious narratives of absurd and impossible adventures, have never even heard the name of this hero; and nine out of ten of them are unacquainted with the story of his wonderful career, abounding as it does in incidents more strange than fiction. So strange indeed are some parts of this record, that it is hard to believe they can be true; certainly no inventions could be more dramatic and exciting. In America, where he is a more familiar name, there appears a disposition to exalt his claims as a romancer at the expense of his credit as an historian. This sceptical age, which laughs at the tableau of Alfred and the cakes, which makes a popular myth of William Tell's great shot, and which even disbelieves that Wellington at Waterloo cried "Up guards and at them!" is now asked to give up its faith in the most celebrated and striking feature of Smith's career. Matter of fact writers are found to give us reasons for treating with suspicion his own account of his rescue by Pocahontas, hitherto received as one of the effective scenes of history. But there is so little twilight in American annals that we cannot desire to abate our respect for this touching episode, and are not willing to inquire too closely how much it owes to the kindled imagination of the gallant adventurer. The man having undoubtedly gone through so many moving incidents and done so much real work, it seems hard to grudge him a little play of fancy in purely personal affairs. And in matters relating to the colony with the foundation of which his fame is identified, we may in the main accept his own narrative, written and published during the lifetime of many who were best able and by no means unwilling to correct him.

Our hero was evidently of a romantic disposition. We can guess that at the free schools of Alford and Louth he had often to smart for neglecting grammar and grave history to pore over the black-letter volume containing the "ancient, honourable, famous and delightful history of Huon of Bourdeaux," or the good old rhyme of Sir Bevis of Southampton, as well as the new narratives of travel which were beginning to supplant these chivalrous stories in their power of inflaming the imagination of daring youth. He surely had his head a little turned by the former class of literature when he built himself a pavilion of boughs in the Lincolnshire woods, and lived there in solitude, amusing himself by hunting and tilting at a ring. And it must be confessed that some of the early adventures which he narrates are fashioned quite upon the conventional patterns of chivalrous romance. He goes to the East and fights the Turks; overthrows three redoubtable champions successively in single tourney; is taken prisoner and favoured by the Turkish princess, Tragabigzanda, according to the received precedents of Esclarmonde and Josyan; is equally ill treated by her brother the bashaw, whom of course he kills and in due time escapes back to Christendom. All this is just what we should expect in a fictitious tale by such a writer, so that we are sometimes inclined to ask if the worthy captain may not have confused his actual experiences with the dreams of his youth. Certainly his account of his early life savours much of that kind of romance which the author of Don Quixote was about to explode, and to the general neglect of which Smith himself contributed so much by opening out a new field of real adventures as exciting as the absurd ones of chivalric fiction.

The age of chivalry had long been passing into the realms of imagination, and though this youth's character had a vein of romantic sentiment, it was mainly in harmony with the spirit of practical enterprise which now began to influence active minds. In his tourney under the walls of Regall, when, "the ramparts all beset with fair dames and men in arms," the champions galloped into the lists to the sound of hautboys, the fighting is done with lances, battle-axes, and *pistols*. Gunpowder had put an end to the resistless prowess of Lancelot and Amadis. John Smith, in his hermitage, no longer reads the "Arbre des Batailles" with its long winded precepts and institutions of chivalry, but Machiavelli's "Art of War." Beset by the Indians he challenges their chief, perhaps with a reminiscence of the famous story of Roland and Oliver, to decide their quarrel upon an island by single combat with equal arms; but with an eye to business in the needy state of his colony he proposes that the adversary shall bring baskets of corn, against which he shall stake the value in copper, and "our game shall be, the conqueror take all."

Even in youth his head was as full of resources and stratagems as of adventurous fancies. At the siege of Olympagh he contrived a system of telegraphing by torches, such as he may have read of in the classics during his school days, and such as is now proposed to be adapted to the Morse alphabet; spelling out letters by alternately showing and hiding the lights, he communicated to the garrison how they might second the efforts of the relieving force. In the night attack which followed he suggested that some thousand pieces of lighted match might be stretched upon strings, so as to be taken by the enemy for so many musketeers, and thus to distract their attention. Again, we find him employed to "put in practice his fiery dragons," by filling earthen pots with gunpowder and covering them with an inflammable paste thickly stuck with bullets, which were then set on fire and thrown by slings over the walls of a besieged city, wherever a throng of people was supposed to be, whose lamentable cries soon testified to the terror and confusion spread by these bombs. Another contrivance of fastening wildfire on the points of lances in a night attack shows him to have had a special talent for what he calls "fireworks," which should have gained for him among the Turks much the same reputation as that contemporary soldier of fortune, Guy Fawkes, bears among Protestants. But he was a stout fighter as well as a schemer. Wherever he took service, he seems to have been found a useful recruit. As a soldier, a sailor, a slave, and a traveller, he kept his eyes about him, and learned to turn his hand to whatever might be doing. This was the very man to be the founder of a colony.

Of one craft he scarcely became a master in his wanderings, that of authorship. "I confess," he says, "my hand, though able to wield a weapon among the barbarous, yet well may tremble in handling a pen among so many *judicious*." The work published under his name as a "General History of Virginia" is a compilation, to the various parts of which he stood sometimes in the relation of author, sometimes of editor; and it is marked throughout by a want of clearness and proportion, which, along with the looseness of spelling and punctuation that were characteristic of the time, make it often difficult to get at the meaning. We find constantly, however, in his writings racy, downright phrases, full of rough strength, which give us the impression of a man who had decided opinions, and a way of speaking out his mind that could not have been very pleasant to those who disagreed with him. Strokes of humour are not wanting; and though he tells us that the "style of a soldier is not eloquent, but honest and justifiable," he occasionally rises into a strain of fine writing. For example, let us take a passage from the memoirs of his early life.

"The Sunne no sooner displayed his beames than the Tartar his colours; where at midday he stayed a while, to see the passage of tyrannicall and treacherous imposture, till the earth did blush with the bloud of honesty, that the sunne for shame did hide himselfe from so monstrous sight of a cowardly calamity. It was a most brave sight to see the banners and ensignes streaming in the aire, the glittering of Armour, the variety of colours, the motion of plumes, the forrests of lances, and the thicknesse of shorter weapons, till the silent expedition of the bloudy blast from the murdering Ordnance, whose roaring voice is not so soone heard, as felt by the aymed at object, which made among them a most lamentable slaughter."

These highflown figures are of course after the taste of the period in which the author of "Euphues" set the example of an extravagant and conceited style, that now raises a smile where once it called forth the warmest admiration. It is only what one would expect of Smith. He was eminently a man of his age, of the age which was passing away rather than of that which, in his latter days, was opening on England. In spirit he was akin to the worthies of Elizabeth's reign, who went their way to heaven with a clear eye upon earth, believed sturdily in beef and beer, and thought no shame to hate Spaniards, papists, and cowards. The moral feelings of such a man were of the instinctive rather than the self-conscious kind; prudence, diligence, and discipline filled a larger place in his regard than refined sentiments; his conscience was not over scrupulous when loyal service or profitable business was in question. Though he might have a keen eye for a fool or a hypocrite, he was content, on the whole, to take his orders from the prince and his faith from the bishop. Like Parson Adams, he would have made very little difference between an atheist and a dissenter, but formed his conduct on the Church of England Catechism, feeling no vocation but to do his duty, as he understood it, in that state of life into which it had pleased Heaven to call him. It followed that he had little sympathy with the earnestness of the new party who were already beginning to agitate reforms in religion and politics. Towards the end of his life we shall find him laughing in his sleeve at the Pilgrim Fathers, whom he took for a set of half crazy fanatics, and prophesied their failure, for want of comprehending the higher aims which were their strength. But so far as the right was plain to him, he would do it with all his might, and stands for a good representative of that school of muscular Christians who are such excellent and useful fellows in their way, except when they take to trumpeting their own merits and abusing their more richly gifted and more subtly tempted neighbours. He was at least the very man to lead a forlorn hope of colonization into the perilous wilderness; and we cannot but choose him for the central figure of this part of our story.

John Smith was born of a respectable family at Willoughby, in Lincolnshire, in 1579. The first thing we hear of him is just what we might expect, that at the age of thirteen he sold his satchel and books with the view of running away to sea. This intention was prevented by the death of his father, who seems to have left him some small property, which, however, was taken such good care of by his guardians that he could find no means of indulging his roving disposition, except by becoming apprentice to a merchant at Lynn. But the drudgery of a counting house was not what he had bargained for; and when he found that the merchant did not send him at once to sea, "he never saw his master in eight years after," as he puts it in his biography. At last he contrived to get to France in the train of a young nobleman. At Havre he "first began to learn the life of a soldier"; but peace being concluded in that kingdom, he served for three or four years in the Low Countries, and thence passed to Scotland, where he had some reason to hope for the favour of King James. That monarch, however, had little regard for men of Smith's stamp, and he himself had not "money nor means to make him a courtier"; so we soon find him back in Lincolnshire, living in the woods as a hermit, with a touch of the poacher, to the great wonder of the neighbourhood.

A noble Italian gentleman, in the service of the Earl of Lincoln, drew him from this retirement to reside at Tattershall for a time, and no doubt kindled his mind with such descriptions of foreign countries that he was soon "desirous to see more of the world, and try his fortune against the Turks." He travelled through the south of Europe, and met with many adventures; among others, being thrown overboard by a fanatical rabble of pilgrims, who hated him as a Protestant and an Englishman, and declared they could have no fine weather while this Jonah was their fellow passenger. They also accused the English of being all pirates; and, indeed, Smith seems now to have had a turn at something which looks very like piracy, from which he gained five hundred sequins and other booty. After a visit to Italy he repaired to Vienna, and offered himself to fight the Turks in Transylvania, where his services were so distinguished that he says Prince Sigismund of that country rewarded him with a coat of arms bearing three Turks' heads, his portrait in gold, and a pension of three hundred ducats. But the Christian army being routed at the battle of Rottenton, he was wounded, taken prisoner, and sold for a slave to a certain Bashaw Bogall, who sent him to Constantinople as a present for his mistress, Tragabigzanda, pretending that he was a Bohemian lord conquered by his own hand. Smith narrates that this lady treated him with great kindness, and sent him to her brother, Timor, the Bashaw of Nalbrits in Crim Tartary, that he might learn their language and customs, with the hope of obtaining her hand when "time made her master of herself." There seems, however, to have been a misunderstanding somewhere, for the bashaw behaved to his captive with the utmost rigour, placing him among his other slaves, where, as the last comer, he became "slave of slaves to them all."

After enduring this kind of life for a time, and making many curious observations on the customs of this little known country, the ancient Scythia, he was employed as a thresher, and one day the bashaw "took occasion so to beat, spurn, and revile him that, forgetting all reason, he beat out the Timor's brains with his threshing bat, for they have no flails; and, seeing his estate could be no worse than it was, clothed himself in his clothes, hid his body under the straw, filled his knapsack with corn, shut the door, mounted his horse, and ran into the desert at all adventure." He was fortunate enough to reach safely the boundaries of Russia, and passed on to Transylvania, where he was received with kindness by

his old brothers in arms, and with substantial marks
of favour by Prince Sigismund. He now travelled
through Germany, France, and Spain, till, "being
thus satisfied with Europe and Asia, understanding
of the wars in Barbary," like a true soldier of fortune he repaired to the north of Africa. These wars
being ended, he went on board a ship of war "to try
other conclusions at sea," and we have a lively description of a fight with the Spaniards in which he
took part. At last he returned to England, still a
young man, but as full of enterprise as of experience; and of course such a man could not long
escape the influence of the loadstone which was so
powerfully attracting the adventurous spirits of the
day. In 1606 he sailed for Virginia.

This part of the world had by no means been lost
sight of in England during the fifteen years that
had elapsed since the mysterious disappearance of
White's colony. Sir Walter Raleigh indeed, after
spending forty thousand pounds on the work which
he had so much at heart, had given it up and
assigned his rights to a company which, in these
troubled times, had not been able to carry on the
execution of his plans. Now Raleigh was in the
Tower, conceiving those wild fancies of a golden city
in South America that were to balance the new
king's cupidity against his hatred of the imprisoned
hero, and to bring a stormy sunset at the end of his
varied life. But his friends Hakluyt and Hariot
were by their publications spreading a knowledge of
the more sure if less dazzling gains to be drawn
from Virginia; and now that peace prevailed under

a mean spirited and narrow minded monarch, who was yet not without some perception of the welfare of his people, funds and opportunity were found for new attempts at colonisation. Several private voyages for trade and discovery had been made, but it was seen that a well sustained effort, on a larger scale than private means would allow, was necessary to plant a permanent settlement.

Fortunately the matter was taken up by men of wealth and influence, such as Sir Ferdinand Gorges and Sir John Popham, the Lord Chief Justice of England. Two companies of "merchant adventurers" were formed, at London and at Plymouth, in which shares were taken by persons of all ranks. To these companies King James granted a patent of colonisation for all the land lying between 34° and 45° of north latitude, that is, the greater part of the seaboard of the United States at the present day, having then the French settlements on the north and Florida, claimed by the Spaniards, on the south. The northern half of this vast territory was apportioned to the Plymouth company, that part of England having most to do with the fisheries of Newfoundland. The southern division of Virginia, by which name the whole tract was then known, was granted to the London adventurers; and it was provided that neither body might plant within a hundred miles of the other. Authority over both was in the hands of a council in England, appointed by the king, who also held supreme power over the local government of each colony. The king was to have a share of whatever precious metals they might find, not to speak of any honour that might accrue to him from their doings under his auspices ; the companies were to be at all the expense and trouble. In such an arrangement we see no hint of the freedom and hatred of privilege which now characterize the United States ; but the selfish and stingy monarch was doing more than he thought to foster republican institutions. America owes little to the wisdom and liberality of our sovereigns.

It was with the London colony that John Smith cast in his lot, and we will now follow its fortunes over the Atlantic.

II.

The expedition consisted of three ships, the largest one of 100 tons, carrying about a hundred men, of whom one half were "gentlemen." We can imagine the sort of gentlemen they were : for the most part useless younger sons, ruined spendthrifts, idle fellows too proud or too lazy to turn their hands to any honest work at home. The colonisers of these days made a mistake of which the folly is not yet fully perceived ; they supposed that "the New World could be planted with the dregs of the Old." Very few of the number were artisans such as an infant colony most required ; and even those few were too much of the class who "never did know what a day's work was," else they would not have had cause to leave home. Among the chief persons were Bartholomew Gosnold, who had been the leader of a previous unsuccessful expedition, Edward Wingfield, a merchant, John

Smith, and Christopher Newport, an experienced sailor, who was entrusted with the command of the little fleet. But the council who were to govern the colony were not commissioned from the first; their names were shut up in a little box, only to be opened after landing in Virginia. This was an unfortunate mistake, for the adventurers almost immediately began to fall out, and were only restrained from abandoning the enterprise through the influence of a pious minister named Robert Hunt, who accompanied them, and more than once seems to have been able to calm their dissensions. Men in these days, it must be remembered, were accustomed to be governed by a strong arm and well marked gradations of rank; and this company, containing so many bad characters, found itself in novel circumstances without any authorized commanders and, worse than all, without occupation throughout all the tediousness and discomforts of a long sea voyage.

Six weeks they were delayed in the Downs by bad weather; nearly three months were taken up in sailing by way of the West Indies to the American coast, which they at last began to despair of reaching, and some were even proposing to turn back, when a lucky storm prevented them and drove them in sight of land. It is plain that John Smith during this time had been speaking out the honest hatred of selfishness and incompetence which marked him all along, and had thus made himself enemies. He was accused of being a mutineer and put under restraint; worse had almost befallen him. "Such factions here we

had as commonly attend such voyages, that a pair
of gallows was made ; but Captain Smith, for whom
they were intended, could not be persuaded to make
use of them." When, as soon as they landed, the
box was opened, and he was found to be named as
one of the seven who were to compose the council,
he was nevertheless not allowed to take his place
among them; and for some time still he remained
under the suspicion of conspiring to "usurp the
government, murder the council, and make himself
king," which probably means that he had a clear
idea of what ought to be done in their position, and
had no patience with the incapacity of those who
were unable or unwilling to do it.

On the 26th of April, 1607, the voyagers saw
with joy a line of white sandy downs and dark
pine woods, passed between the two points to which
they then gave the names of Cape Henry and Cape
Charles, in honour of the king's sons, anchored in
Chesapeake Bay, the "mother of waters," and were
delighted with the fair prospect of hills, rivers,
valleys, inlets, and islands by which they now
found themselves surrounded. "Heaven and earth
never agreed better to frame a place for man's
habitation," was their opinion after this long and
trying voyage, and they hastened to land among
"fair meadows and goodly tall trees."

It was, however, more than a fortnight before
they chose a beautiful situation for their settlement.
On the 13th of May they decided upon a small
peninsula, at high tides a complete island, on the
left bank and about fifty miles from the mouth of

the Powhatan or James River, at this spot about three miles broad and so deep near the shore that ships could be moored to trees while riding in six fathoms of water. This they christened Jamestown, and at once took possession and went to work. Wingfield was elected president.

Now for a time the emigrants plunged zealously into their various occupations. Some cleared land on which to pitch their tents; some laid out gardens; some wove nets; some made boards and barrel staves, to freight the ships with on their return to England. An old sail was stretched from branch to branch, and underneath this awning they sat daily upon fallen trunks while their minister read prayers and sermons from behind a bar of wood nailed between two trees by way of pulpit; as yet they had no time to make a better church. A small expedition went up the river to examine it, and visited Powhatan, the king of the country, who had sent them a pacific message and presents. Hitherto the natives had been on the whole friendly, or at least indifferent; but when this party returned, they learned that an attack had been made on the settlement while the men were working without their arms, and might all have been slain, if a shot from the ships crashing among the trees had not terrified the ignorant savages.

This was a warning to look to their defences, which the president was blamed for having neglected. The fort, hitherto merely a half moon of green branches, was now strengthened with palisades; the cannon that they had brought from

England were mounted; the settlers were armed and exercised, and learned to be cautious in straggling through the woods, where every tree might conceal an Indian, creeping among the shrubs like a wild beast and out of reach almost as soon as his arrow whizzed through the air.

It would have been well for the adventurers if their foes had only been without the camp. Busy as they were, they yet found time for dissensions. When they had been a month at Jamestown, Captain Newport returned to England with the ships, and some of the chief men proposed to send back Smith as a prisoner. He, however, took this occasion of insisting that the accusations against him should be brought to a head, and so well defended himself and proved the malice of his enemies before a jury, that he was not only triumphantly acquitted, but Wingfield, the president, was adjudged to pay him heavy damages for slander, which Smith generously gave up to the common stock. After this, through the exertions of Mr. Hunt, a temporary reconciliation was brought about; they all received the communion together, and Smith was admitted as a member of the council. Henceforth he began to take a leading part in the affairs of the little colony, which before long found itself in sore need of a clear head and a bold spirit such as his.

The potentates of the council were presently by the ears again, squabbling over kettles, whittles, chickens, rations of peas and pork, and so forth. The commonest articles of food became luxuries which the authorities were angrily accused of engrossing to their own use. Unfortunately the situation of Jamestown was swampy, and sickness soon began to prevail among the unseasoned settlers. Now that Newport had left them they were reduced to a scanty allowance of spoiled grain, and for a time could not go in search of better provisions, for what with these evils, and the heat and toil, at midsummer few of them were able to stand. Many a settler since then has passed through the misery of "chills and fever," and will sympathise with these first emigrants in the troubles uuder which even Mark Tapley found it difficult to be jolly. One of them* has left us a woeful tale of their sufferings.

"For the most part they died of mere famine. There were never Englishmen left in a foreign country in such misery as we were in this new discovered Virginia. We watched every three nights lying on the bare cold ground, what weather soever came, warded all next day, which brought our men to be most feeble wretches. Our food was but a small can of barley, sod in water, to five men a day; our drink cold water taken out of the river, which was at a flood very salt, at a low tide full of slime and filth, which was the destruction of many of our men. Thus we lived for the space of five months in this miserable distress, not having five able men to man our bulwarks upon any occasion. If it had not pleased God to have put a terror in the savages' hearts, we had all perished by those

---

* Percy, in Purchas: vol. iv.

wild and cruel pagans, being in that weak estate as we were, our men night and day groaning in every corner of the fort, most pitiful to hear; if there were any conscience in men it would make their hearts bleed to hear the pitiful murmurings and outcries of our sick men, without relief every night and day for the space of six weeks, some departing out of the world, many times three or four in a night, in the morning their bodies trailed out of the cabins like dogs to be buried."

In this distress they turned against the president, who, though a tract is extant in which he strongly protests his innocence, was accused of dishonestly using the public stores and of scheming to desert his companions in misfortune. It is difficult to ascertain the truth at the present day; at all events it seemed plain to the despairing community that this should be the scapegoat. Wingfield was deposed, and in his place was elected Ratcliffe, a weak and inactive man, who had the name of commander while Smith seems to have done the real work. As soon as the latter had shaken off his sickness he began to stir up the rest to mow, to thatch, to build, "himself always bearing the greatest task for his own share, so that in short time he provided most of them lodgings, neglecting any for himself." He sailed up and down the river, and scoured its banks in search of supplies. As soon as he turned his back, "all things were at random." Once some of the colonists stole the pinnace, a small vessel of twenty tons which had been left behind by Captain Newport, and attempted to fly for England. Smith arriving unexpectedly fired upon them from the fort, killed one of their leaders, and forced them to return.

There was indeed some reason to be fainthearted. Half of the little band died during the summer, among them Bartholomew Gosnold, one of the originators of the expedition. The rest came near being starved. For a time they lived on sturgeon and shell fish; later, corn, venison and other supplies were procured from the Indians, mainly through Smith's exertions; and in autumn the rivers became covered with wild fowl, and the rich soil yielded them fruit and vegetables in abundance. These supplies and the approach of winter checked for the time all thoughts of desertion, and Smith now applied himself to explore the country of which they had taken possession. And now came the celebrated adventure that had such effect on the fortunes of the colony.

He had ascended the river Chickahominy, running into the James river from the left, some way above the settlement. When his barge could go no farther, he left her with orders to the crew not to go on shore, which they disobeyed, and being attacked by the Indians, narrowly escaped with the loss of one of their number, who is said to have been burned to death after frightful tortures. Meanwhile Smith, accompanied by two Englishmen and two Indians, made his way in a canoe to the head of the stream; there he left three men while he himself went to shoot in the marshes, guided by one of the Indians, and unaware that

three hundred warriors were in search of him under
Opechancanough, one of the native kings or werowances, who ever showed himself a bitter enemy of
the strangers. This party, directed by a fire which
the two Englishmen had lit beside the canoe, came
upon them sleeping and killed them both with
arrows. Their Indian companion no doubt led his
countryman upon the track of Smith, who soon
found himself attacked by overwhelming numbers.

But he was not to be easily overcome. With his
garter he tied his unwilling guide to his arm, and
used him as a shield, behind which he plied his
piece so well that the Indians durst not come to
close quarters with him, while he himself was only
slightly wounded by the arrows. Then he began to
retreat towards the boat, but keeping a better eye
on his enemies than on his feet, he soon slipped up to
the middle into a muddy creek, from which he was
unable to extricate himself. Even then, he says, the
Indians were afraid to come near him, till half frozen
he at last surrendered, throwing away his arms.

The Indians drew him out and took him to the
fire; where, beside the dead bodies of his companions, they chafed his benumbed limbs. He had
now to look forward to torture and death; but our
adventurer's course of life had been such that he
never failed to have his wits about him. He had
already picked up something of the language of
these people; and he asked to see their chief.
On being introduced to Opechancanough, he presented him with a round ivory compass, covered
with glass, which called forth the wonder of the

Smith in the hands of the Indians.

Page 89.

savages. He next proceeded to give them a short scientific lecture, astronomical and geographical, which probably they did not understand, but which all the better answered his purpose of impressing them with his character as a mysterious medicine man. "Notwithstanding, within an hour after they tied him to a tree, and as many as could stand about him prepared to shoot him; but the king holding up the compass in his hand, they all laid down their bows and arrows, and in a triumphant manner led him to Orapaks, where he was after their manner kindly feasted and well used."

He was conducted with great precautions, three strong Indians holding him fast by each arm, and six walking on each side with their arrows ready fixed in their bows. When they thus arrived at this native town, which consisted only of thirty or forty wigwams made of mats, the women and children came out to stare at him, and the warriors proceeded to exhibit their accomplishments in a fashion which they thought calculated to strike the foreigner with awe and admiration. After performing some military exercises they rushed into a ring, in the midst of which stood the chief with Smith and his guards, and began to dance round him, screeching and yelling in a style that corresponded with their fantastic appearance. Their faces were painted with a mixture of oil and red dye; they were armed with clubs and bows; their clothes were the skins of beasts; and on their heads they carried a strange gear composed of such ornaments as the dried skin of a bird with outspread wings, set out with shells, feathers, pieces of copper, or the rattles of snakes. Having danced themselves out of breath, they shut up their captive in one of the houses, where he was guarded by no less than thirty or forty of these formidable braves, and where presently they brought him enough bread and venison for twenty men. Next morning he was again supplied on the same liberal scale, and he noticed that none of them would eat with him, which made him think that they were fattening him to eat him, so that "his stomach at that time was not very good." He also suffered much from cold, the weather being bitter frost and snow; but an Indian whom he had known before, and to whom he had given some beads and other trifles, showed gratitude enough to restore him his gown.

Six weeks he remained a captive. There seemed to be no immediate intention of putting him to death, and with his usual knack of making the best of circumstances he kept his eyes about him, and while watching for an opportunity of escape, made careful observations of the customs and resources of these unknown people. Savage-like they fancied that he must be possessed of supernatural power; so when he had been two or three days a prisoner, they brought him to a dying man, whose father was hardly prevented from killing him when he was unable to cure the patient. Smith offered to do it if they would allow him to go to Jamestown for a medicine which he had there; but this was a point of credulity to which he could not bring his captors. They informed him that they meant to attack the fort and offered him liberal rewards if he would assist them. At last he persuaded them to send a messenger with a leaf of paper torn out of a notebook he happened to have about him, on which he wrote to his companions, informing them of his plight, warning them of the designs of the Indians, and desiring them to leave an answer and some things which he was in want of at a spot designated. The answer and the articles required were accordingly sent back, to the amazement of the Indians, who took him with more certainty for a magician, not understanding how the paper could speak. They now led him about as a spectacle among the tribes on the banks of the Rappahannock and Potomac; and when they returned to the chief's place of abode at Pamunkey, they "entertained him" with a specimen of what they could do in the way of conjuring. He gives the following account of the ceremony, which took place before their idol, to whom he feared they meant to sacrifice him.

"Early in the morning a great fire was made in a long house, and a mat was spread on the one side as on the other; on the one they caused him to sit, and all the guard went out of the house, and presently came skipping in a great grim fellow, all painted over with coal mingled with oil, and many snakes' and weasels' skins stuffed with moss, and all their tails tied together, so that they met on the crown of his head in a tassel; and round about the tassel was as a coronet of feathers, the skins hanging round about his head, back, and shoulders, and in a manner covered his face; with a hellish voice and

a rattle in his hand. With most strange gestures
and passions he began his invocation, and environed
the fire with a circle of meal; which done, three
more such like devils came rushing in with the like
antique tricks, painted half black, half red, but all
their eyes were painted white, and some red strokes
like Mutchato's along their cheeks; round about
him those fiends danced a pretty while, and then
came in three more as ugly as the rest, with red
eyes and white strokes over their black faces; at
last they all sat down right against him, three of
them on the one hand of the chief priest, and three
of them on the other. Then all with their rattles
began a song, which ended, the chief priest laid
down five wheat corns; then straining his arms and
hands with such violence that he sweat and his
veins swelled, he began a short oration; at the conclusion they all gave a short groan, and then laid
down three grains more. After that, began their
song again, and then another oration, ever laying
down so many corns as before, till they had twice
encircled the fire; that done, they took a bunch of
little sticks prepared for that purpose, continuing
still their devotion, and at the end of every song
and oration they laid down a stick betwixt the divisions of corn. Till night, neither he nor they did
eat or drink, and then they feasted merrily with the
best provisions they could make. Three days they
used this ceremony, the meaning whereof they told
him was to know if he intended them well or no.
The circle of meal signified their country, the circles
of corn the bounds of the sea, and the sticks his

country. They imagined the world to be flat and round, like a trencher, and they in the midst. After this they brought him a bag of gunpowder, which they carefully preserved till the next spring to plant as they did their corn, because they would be acquainted with the nature of that seed."*

After some weeks the captain was taken to a place on the York River where Powhatan, the chief werowance, or "emperor" as Smith calls him, of the country was, though he had several residences, then holding his rude court. "Here more than two hundred of those grim courtiers stood wondering at him, as he had been a monster, till Powhatan and his train had put themselves in their greatest braveries." When at last introduced into the presence of the Indian prince, he found him a tall, stern old man with grey hair, and, what was rare in the natives, a slight beard. Dressed in a robe of racoon skins with the tails hanging down, he sat before a fire upon a raised seat covered with mats like a bedstead, with one of his wives on either hand. Along the sides of the house were arranged in rows men and women, whose finery was certainly of a kind to make some impression on a stranger. Red paint seemed to be their main notion of full dress. The women were tattooed on their faces and limbs with figures of beasts and serpents. Strange headdresses were the fashion, and necklaces of copper or white beads. Both sexes wore ornaments in their ears, sometimes a dead rat tied by the tail,

---

* Smith's "General History," i., 160.

sometimes a live snake half a yard long, which would twist about the neck and face. The down of birds, and the feathers skilfully woven into a mantle, were among their decorations; the dried hand of an enemy also was used in this style of costume, where, as Smith says, "he is the most gallant that is the most monstrous to behold."

The entrance of the captain was hailed with a great shout; and now his story begins to savour somewhat of those romances of chivalry which may be suspected of colouring his recollections. A savage queen brought him water to wash his hands, another waited on him with a bunch of feathers instead of a towel, and he was invited to partake of a feast, just as Sir Percival or Sir Gareth might have been on arriving at a castle. But the conclusion of this courteous entertainment was that, after a long consultation, Powhatan ordered him to immediate death. Two great stones were brought in, to which he was dragged and obliged to lay his head upon this rude block. The brawny executioners raise their clubs to beat out his brains. Another moment, and the whole course of the colony's history is changed; when just in the nick of time Pocahontas, the king's favourite daughter, rushes forward, throws her arms round the captive's neck, and declares that they shall kill her before they harm him.

Such is the pretty tableau over which grave historians are now inclined to shake their heads.*

---

* In the Portuguese narrative of De Soto's travels a similar story is related of Juan Ortiz, captive among the Indians of Florida. An Indian chief's daughter, named

The weak point of it is that in Smith's "True Relation," written at the time with the facts fresh in his mind, he says not a word about these dramatic circumstances; and other contemporary accounts are equally silent. Many years afterwards, when Pocahontas had visited England and excited considerable interest in royal and other circles, he gave this version of the story, adding her to the number of ladies who so signally and unexpectedly befriended him in his adventures; but it is, to say the least of it, strange that he should have only then recalled such a remarkable feature in his career. He speaks of her as being at this time twelve or thirteen years old; but in another part of his narrative he mentions her later on as a child of ten, an age at which she was scarcely likely to be so susceptible of such a warm interest in her father's enemy. Another of the settlers reduces this celebrated girl from a noble minded Indian princess to an impudent little hussy with no more grace or dignity than a London arab; she is described as hanging about the fort, and turning head over heels for the amusement of the settlers.

In such a work we need go no further into this disputed question. This much is certain, that Powhatan was induced to spare his prisoner's life, and that Pocahontas was henceforth a good friend to him, and rendered the English important services on more than one occasion.

Milly, is said to have played the same part to a captive American in 1817.

The chief, whose own rank did not prevent him from being skilled in various kinds of handicraft, informed Smith that he should be kept to make hatchets for himself and toys for his daughter. The worthy captain probably proved not very handy at such occupations; and in spite of Powhatan's professions still did not think his life worth much so long as he remained in the hands of these capricious savages. His alarm must have been strongly excited when, two days afterwards, he was taken to a great house in the woods, and there set down upon a mat by a fire and left alone. While he was perhaps trying to recollect whatever prayers were within the compass of a soldier of these days, Powhatan was disguising himself " in the most fearfullest manner he could"; then presently a hideous din was made behind a mat hanging across the building, which was drawn aside, and enter the chief, " more like a devil than a man, with some two hundred more as black as himself."

But all this ceremony was only the prelude to informing him that he was now about to be set free. The king despatched him with an escort of twelve men to Jamestown, requesting a gift of two guns and a grindstone, in return for which he would give him a tract of land and treat him henceforth as his own son. Smith thought this unexpected news too good to be true, and as his savage conductors accompanied him through the woods was in hourly fear that they still meant to put him to some cruel death. But still his fears were not justified. In the morning they brought him safe to the fort, where his presence was much needed, for, as usual, he found that his companions had fallen out; the strongest were preparing to run away with the pinnace, which again they were only prevented by force from doing.

Smith took care to treat his Indian guides well, and offered to keep his promise as to the two guns and the grindstone, which then they found too heavy to be moved, and ran away half dead with fear when he loaded a demi-culverin with stones and sent them crashing among the frozen branches of a tree. He managed, however, to get them back, and loaded them with such presents as were likely to please the taste of Powhatan and his wives and children. The good result of this liberality was soon seen, for now Pocahontas and her attendants began to bring them provisions regularly, without which they had again been in danger of starvation.

These marks of friendship, and the accounts which Smith brought of Powhatan's power and apparent goodwill, went far towards increasing his own influence and encouraging the handful of sickly men who, weakened by the loss of more than half their number, living from hand to mouth, and quarrelling with each other from day to day, were the ambassadors of European civilization in that part of the world. A party among them were yet so moved by hatred of their active comrade that they plotted to have him executed, pretending that he was answerable for the death of the two men who had been killed by the Indians when he was taken prisoner; "but he quickly took such order with such lawyers that he laid them by the heels till he sent some of them prisoners for England." John Smith was indeed a man to make enemies, as well as to have his own way, ready not only with "store of saker and musket shot," and "the hazard of his life" upon occasion, but also most outspoken in his contempt for that worthless class among the emigrants, who, "being for the most part of such tender education and small experience in martial accidents, because they found not English cities, nor such fair houses, nor at their own wishes any of their accustomed dainties, with feather beds and down pillows, taverns and alehouses in every breathing place, neither such plenty of gold and silver and dissolute liberty as they expected, had little or no care of anything but to pamper their bellies, to fly away with our pinnaces, or procure their means to return for England." It was scarcely a happy family which was established in the peninsula of Jamestown; but it would not be John Smith's fault if they did not stick by one another and make the best of what looked like a bad business.

III.

By this time the settlers had gained some knowledge of the main features and capacities of the country in which they had cast their lot. It was an undulating district of soft rich soil, thickly covered with trees, oak and walnut the most common, and by a dense undergrowth of weeds, except on the course of the many streams that intersected it, where were found swampy meadows and little clearings in which the natives had grouped their wigwams of branches and mats. Very different were these aboriginal inhabitants from the Indians who in later days, having learned to use the white man's arms, proved the terror of the frontier settlements, and no less different from the degenerate race among whom European disease and European drink have now made such fatal havoc. They belonged to the family of Algonquin Indians, and were scattered into small tribes, so small that a hundred fighting men was an unusual number, taking name from the rivers on which they dwelt, under werowances or chiefs who owed obedience to Powhatan, the king of the country lying between the James and Potomac rivers. The tribes for whom his authority was a bond of union seem to have numbered in all not more than eight thousand souls, spread over as many square miles. Even if all their forces could have been concentrated, the colony would have found little difficulty in protecting itself from them; a few well armed Europeans were always able by a resolute resistance to set hundreds of these naked warriors to flight. Smith himself, as we have seen, kept two or three hundred of them at bay. A few dogs were sometimes thought to be a sufficient guard against the natives. They were unacquainted with the use of iron; their weapons were arrows pointed with stones or bones, and wooden clubs, with sometimes deer-horns or long sharp stones set across the end in the form of a pickaxe; with sharp shells or pointed reeds they scalped their defeated enemies. Their dress was mainly the skins of beasts, and they delighted much in gaudy and fantastic ornaments. They were well proportioned and not ill looking; the men were accustomed to let their hair grow long on one side, but to be shaved on the other for greater freedom in the use of the bow. They excelled not so much in bodily strength as in fortitude, endurance, and the cunning called forth by the conditions of their struggle for existence. Rude notions of justice and honour prevailed among them, and Powhatan, both by his rank and his force of character, had undisputed power over the lives and liberty of all his subjects. They worshipped hideous idols, to which they gave the name Okee, but which the orthodox English took for a representation of the devil; they were also observed to pay a peculiar reverence to the sun. They lived partly by the chase, partly on the fruits and vegetables which grew wild so abundantly in their seasons, and partly by rude husbandry, the drudgery of which, as usual among savages, fell upon the women and children. Where a settlement was to be made for a time they destroyed the trees by burning the bark round about their trunks, grubbed up the weeds, and planted their corn, which with little further trouble, save that of constant weeding, yielded a plentiful crop in the rich mould. But with their improvident habits they were often in great want, and were utterly incapable of utilizing the resources of a country that to the eye of such a man as Smith plainly needed nothing but industry and orderliness to turn it into a garden. The woods abounded with game, the rivers with fish; fowls, sheep, horses throve here as well as at home; even in its uncultivated state fruits, known and unknown, rotted on the earth; many saleable commodities could in time be produced, and there was promise of minerals, not indeed of gold, but of iron and perhaps copper. "So then," Smith wrote home with a burst of natural enthusiasm, "here is a place, a nurse for soldiers, a practice for mariners, a trade for merchants, a reward for the good, and, that which is most of all, a business most acceptable to God, to bring such poor infidels to the knowledge of God and His holy gospel."

In the meanwhile the colonists were not forgotten by the company at home. As soon as it was known that they had succeeded in making a settlement, two ships were despatched with supplies and nearly a hundred fresh emigrants, all most eager to make their fortunes and too ignorant that neither in the Old nor the New World were fortunes to be made without toil and self denial. A considerable proportion of them, this time, were artisans and labourers, but there were still so many "gentlemen" as to remind us of that famous army which consisted of four and twenty men and five and thirty pipers! One of these ships was driven out of her course by bad weather; the other, commanded by Captain Newport, arrived safely soon after Smith's captivity. Right glad were the colonists to see their countrymen, and not less to find their fare improved by a taste of the fleshpots of England. But now they had some cause to wish to be delivered from their friends. The sailors, being allowed to trade with the Indians, dealt so liberally and carelessly that, whereas Smith's influence had been able to fix a low price for provisions, before long a pound of copper would not buy what had been sold for an ounce.

There is an amusing description of a scene of barter between a party of the English and Powhatan, who received them with great state and many expressions of goodwill, but showed a very keen eye to the main chance, for all his barbarous habits and royal rank. Captain Newport, being minded apparently to play the great man, was about to allow himself to be cheated into buying corn at an exorbitant rate in the useful commodities which he had brought with him, when Smith pulled out and carelessly displayed a few blue beads, which at once attracted the notice of the savage monarch. Seeing his admiration, the captain affected that he could not part with them, " being of a most rare substance of the colour of the skies, and not to be worn but by the greatest kings in the world. This made him half mad to be the owner of such strange jewels; so that ere we departed, for a pound or two of blue beads we brought over my king for two or three hundred bushels of corn, yet parted good friends." Powhatan's brother was also supplied with the same ornaments, which thus came into such estimation that only the chiefs and their families ventured to wear them.

This satire on the follies of the Old World was soon illustrated in a way less advantageous to the welfare of the colony. The gold fever broke out under the auspices of Newport and Martin, who was the weak minded president's chief counsellor. Several goldsmiths and refiners had accompanied this expedition, for in England it was still believed that such a rich country must abound in gold. To Smith's indignation, all useful work now came to a stand still, while the deluded colonists did nothing but search for gold among earth in which some shining particles had been observed, and with which they insisted on loading the ship instead of with marketable articles. And yet at this time fresh misfortunes had deprived these poor men of common comforts. By an accidental fire the little town, thatched with reeds, and the wooden walls of the fort were burned down at the very coldest season of the year; arms, bedding, clothes, and stores were destroyed, and the much enduring preacher lost his little library.

The sailors stayed for more than three months, consuming the provisions which they had brought, and encouraging in their idleness and folly the shivering, half starved colonists, taken up with wild hopes of sudden wealth. When a great deal of time had been wasted "to fraught a drunken ship with so much gilded dirt," which of course proved perfectly worthless, all honest and sensible men were glad to see Newport and his crew return to England, carrying with them Wingfield and another who had assumed high sounding titles and made themselves ridiculous by an attempt to introduce the ceremonies of English government among a community where a

little common sense and right feeling were more
required than a whole cargo of "admirals, recorders,
interpreters, chronologers, courts of plea, and justices
of peace." Ratcliffe, the sickly president, taking
very little trouble except for his own comfort, and
his friend Martin still dreaming of nothing but gold,
Captain Smith, seconded by a certain Mr. Scrivener,
in whom he seems to have found a kindred spirit
among the new arrivals, applied himself to rebuild-
ing the town and planting the fields. They were
thus engaged when the other ship arrived, after
being given up as lost, bringing plentiful supplies
and a captain who behaved better to the colonists.

By this time the gold mania had greatly subsided,
and Smith was able to get this ship reladed with
cedar. The company at home, so greedy of wealth,
had also even then a belief that the west of
Virginia opened upon the South Sea; so, partly to
gratify them with good tidings in default of gold,
and partly perhaps to get rid of Smith's bust-
ling activity for a time, it was proposed that he
should set out upon a fresh expedition of discovery,
and sixty men were given him whom he exercised
and disciplined to some purpose, as was soon proved.
The inconstant savages had again become troublesome; Powhatan, believing himself defrauded in
trade, began to harass the colonists, so that they had
"sometimes peace and war twice in a day," and the
president, who seems to have been a bit of a coward
and was also fettered by instructions from home not to
make war on the Indians, allowed this state of things
to continue till "by chance they meddled with

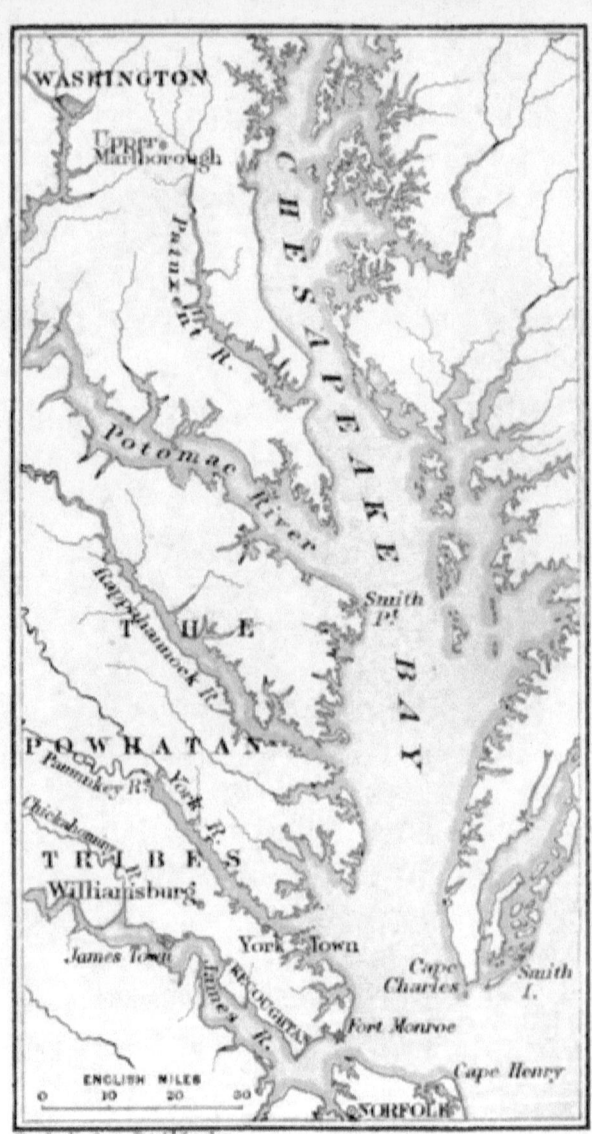

Captain Smith." He at once proceeded to teach their treacherous neighbours a lesson, imprisoned some, whipped others, and so terrified the rest, though without loss of life, that Powhatan soon sent Pocahontas to sue for peace. Having thus brought them to such subjection that, it is said, they were afraid of his very name, he prepared in earnest for his great expedition.

At the beginning of June the ship, which also carried Martin and his golden visions back to England, took Smith and his companions, fifteen in all, as far as Cape Henry, where in an open barge they launched out into the unknown waters of Chesapeake Bay. Crossing the mouth, they discovered an island which received and has retained the name of Smith. Upon Cape Charles they fell in with some Indians carrying long lances headed with bone, who spoke the language of Powhatan, and welcomed the strangers; their chief is described as "the comeliest, proper, civil savage we encountered." They gave such an account of the shores of the bay that the explorers were eager to proceed. Reference to the map will show that this enormous inlet is locked in by a long peninsula, the neck of which is between the mouth of the Susquehanna river and the Delaware bay. It was up the west bank of this tongue of land that our adventurers now coasted, passing by many rivers and uninhabited islands, suffering once from want of water, and once obliged by bad weather to run on shore, after hardly being able to bale the water out of their frail craft. But they repaired the sail with their shirts, and soon made for the other shore, where after some tacking about they entered the majestic Potomac, seven miles broad at its mouth, and traced its course as high as they could, much marvelling at the goodly wooded valleys and hills in which now for the first time echoed the report of firearms.

All this is narrated in the most matter of fact way, with only a hint that this handful of men, most of them inexperienced in the sea, and all of them undergoing toil and hardship that might have made even sturdy sailors grumble, did not always show the same spirit as their intrepid leader. Often they fell in with the natives, once in such numbers as to be taken for thousands, and their reception was not always friendly; but they did not lose a man. The captain used to begin by desiring the Indians to lay down their bows and arrows, and to exchange hostages; after which the Englishmen would condescend to accept food, furs, and whatever else they had to give; and if they did not at once fall in with his terms, a few bullets never failed to bring them to reason. In one case a tribe is said to have been set on to betray the expedition, by the instigation not only of Powhatan but of the discontented faction at the fort, who bore a grudge against Captain Smith; let us trust that here he was mistaken. A danger of another kind is also recorded. The waters were found to abound with fish, so thick and so close to the surface in some places that "for want of nets we attempted to catch them with a frying pan, but we found it a bad instrument to catch fish with." On one occasion the boat being left aground by the ebbing tide among shoal water, they saw many fish among the reeds, and Captain Smith amused himself by nailing them to the ground with his sword. If he had known the nature of the stingray he would not have meddled with it so incautiously. As he was drawing one off his sword it struck its formidable notched spine into his wrist. The only mark left was a little blue spot, but immediately he felt agonizing pain; in four hours his arm became so swollen and his sufferings so great that he was believed to be on the point of death. By his direction his grave was dug on an island close by, and he was preparing for his end like a brave man. But to the joy of all "it pleased God by a precious oil Dr. Russell at first applied to it when he sounded it with probe, ere night his tormenting pain was so well assuaged that he eat of the fish to his supper"—like a practical philosopher that he was!

This Dr. Russell was a physician. There was no surgeon with the party; so it was thought desirable to return to the fort in case further medical assistance should be required, and no doubt they were all glad of any such excuse for repose. The captain's wound must have soon ceased to give them any uneasiness, for when on the 20th of July Jamestown was sighted, the crew were in such good spirits that they played the trick of dressing up their craft with painted streamers, so as to make her look like a Spanish frigate and frighten their friends at the fort.

As usual, however, the colonists were found to be

in no mood for joking. The new comers were all ill, and the rest were full of complaints against the pride and selfishness of the president, who was now deposed and his place offered to Smith. But the hero of the hour had a greater mind for adventures than for honours. He handed over the government to his friend Scrivener, and after a rest of four days set off again, eager to finish his exploration of this great gulf which, as they fondly hoped, might lead them into the waters of the South Sea.

With a crew of twelve men this time, most of them his companions in the former voyage, and having exchanged the physician for a surgeon, he now penetrated to the head of the bay. On the way back he fell in with seven or eight canoes full of Massawomeks, a fierce tribe dreaded by their neighbours. The little crew seemed likely to be hard put to it, for only half of them were able to stand, the rest, new comers unseasoned to the country, being sick. But the sick men lay down in the bottom of the barge; their hats were put upon sticks, and the others, each with two guns in his hands, presented a bold front to the enemy, who first retreated, then returned to visit them peaceably and to give presents, though they could only converse by signs, for these tribes had a different language from that of the Powhatan confederacy. Showing fresh wounds, they gave it to be understood that they had been at war with another tribe called the Tockwoghs, whose seat was near the head of the eastern shore of the bay; and Captain Smith must needs make the acquaintance of these people, who conducted him to a rudely fortified town and entertained him with songs and dances. They were noticed to possess weapons of iron. From them, through an interpreter who spoke the Powhatan language, he heard of a still more formidable tribe called the Susquehannahs, above the head of the bay; and as his boat could not carry him up to them, he sent a civil message desiring them to pay a visit to him, which they did to the number of sixty, bringing presents of food, arms, tobacco pipes three feet long, and much savage finery.

His account of this tribe is one of the passages which make us suspect our captain of seeing things sometimes through a romantic haze. He describes them as a race of giants; one of them measured three-quarters of a yard round the calf of the leg; their voices were deep and resounding; they were clothed fearfully in the skins of bears and wolves, the ears standing up on each side of the wearer's head, the face and teeth hanging on his breast; their weapons were equally formidable in size. Nevertheless they seemed to be a simple and friendly race. They were much impressed with the ceremony of prayer and a psalm, which it was the custom of the explorers to have every morning, and were not to be prevented from worshipping Smith as a god as well as enlisting him for their ally and protector.

If there be any surprise at the unexpected ease with which Smith made his way among so many and so warlike savages, it must be known that, thinking everything fair in discovery as in war, he made use of policy as well as of force; in plain English, he told stories. These tribes were at constant war with each other, and he was able to gain the favour and respect of each by declaring that he either had just conquered their hereditary enemies or was willing to assist his new friends with these irresistible engines of his. The presents received he exhibited as trophies to his next acquaintances, and could have found no better letters of introduction. In ascending the river Rapahannock, he fell in with an Indian called Mosco, whom, from his thick black beard, they took to be of French origin. He was able to suggest to them another use that some of these presents might be put to. From the Massawomeks they had received some light targets, made of twigs woven together so tightly that no arrow could pierce them. These they set up round the sides of the boat by way of a bulwark, behind which they laughed at their ease while passing through a bombardment of a thousand arrows. In the same part of the expedition we meet with a touch which, almost for the first time, recalls the conventional Indian of modern novelists. They were passing by what they took for thirty or forty little bushes fringing the stream, till suddenly a volley of arrows rattled against the targets, and each bush was found to be a warrior hidden behind a screen of branches.

Thus, fighting and feasting by turns, carrying away everywhere, either sticking in their targets, or at the bottom of the boat as tribute, enough arrows to make a bonfire; no sooner off with the old ally than on with the new; informing themselves of the position and strength not only of the tribes which they encountered, but of those farther inland; surveying the islands and inlets of the bay, naming the various points after the members of the crew or after Smith's early patrons; penetrating the country as far as their boat would carry them up the chief rivers; marking the limits of their discovery by setting up crosses and cutting their names on the trees, they travelled three thousand miles in three months, and on the 7th of September arrived safe at Jamestown, where they found affairs thriving under Scrivener as well as could be expected. And Smith, who was not noted for excessive modesty, had now good right to boast in comparing his explorations with the cruel raids of the Spaniards: "Tell me how many ever, with such small means as a barge of twenty-two tons, sometimes with seven, eight, or nine, but at most twelve or sixteen men, did ever discover so many fair and navigable rivers, subject so many several kings, peoples, and nations to obedience and contribution, with so little bloodshed."

IV.

A few days later Newport again returned, bringing seventy emigrants, two of them women, and letters patent formally appointing Smith governor of the colony. At last the right man was put into the right place, and he consented to take the direction of affairs, in which he had almost all along been the mainspring of activity. Still he was far from being master, except by the force of his character. The majority of the council were against him, and he was hampered by the most absurd orders from the company in London. These gentlemen, living at home in ease, began to get impatient at not yet receiving some tangible returns for their outlay; and they now gave the colonists to understand that no further supplies would be sent them unless they did one of three things, instead of returning a beggarly account of "*ifs* and *ands*, hopes and some few proofs." They must find a lump of gold for Newport to take back; or they must ascertain the existence of that South Sea which was still believed to be close at hand beyond the Alleghany mountains; or they must discover one of the settlers left in Virginia by Sir Walter Raleigh, who had disappeared but were supposed to be still alive somewhere. They were also required to set to work at once making pitch, tar, glass and potash; and a band of Poles and Germans were sent to instruct them in these arts, which would have been all very well, as Smith says, if they had not enough to do already in making good their position among the Indians and procuring food. But the silliest of all, in his eyes, was an order to crown Powhatan as an emperor. Having taken possession of this chief's country, the company thought it only right to take him under their patronage, and secure his goodwill by this mighty honour and by some costly presents suitable for a European prince, whereas he would have been as well pleased with a "plain piece of copper."

Captain Smith was evidently in a very ill humour at these orders from men who knew nothing of the difficulties he had to contend with; but it was not for the governor to set an example of disobedience, and he proceeded first to carry out that part of the company's programme relating to the coronation of Powhatan. A most comical ceremony it must have been! At first the savage potentate showed himself very suspicious of the unknown honour which it was proposed to confer upon him, and declined altogether to come to the fort for this purpose; so Newport, Smith, and fifty men had to go to him at his chief residence at Werowocomoco, and there Powhatan was solemnly crowned emperor over the scattered tribes of his dominions, the population of which would have just filled a good sized market town. We may easily imagine that they had "much ado" to get on him the scarlet mantle and other fine clothes which had been provided for the occasion, and he would not let himself be invested in them till assured that they would do him no harm by one of the Indians who had been taken to England and brought back by Newport. "But a foul trouble there was to make him kneel to receive his crown; he, neither knowing the majesty nor meaning of a crown, nor bending of the knee, endured so many persuasions, examples, and instructions as tired them all." At last they contrived to push him down by the shoulders, and three of them, no doubt bursting with laughter, clapped the bauble on his head. Then a salute was fired, which made his savage majesty jump up in a great fright, not understanding that this was done in honour of the ceremony.

The new made emperor did not show himself imperially munificent. After all this grandeur he presented the English with nothing but his old cloak and shoes, and about seven or eight bushels of corn. In every way the company seemed to have sent their regalia to a bad market; for when once Powhatan had got over his suspicions of these strange honours, Smith declares that the effect of making so much fuss about him was to give him a greater notion of his own importance, and proportionally to lower in his eyes the power of the people who put such a value on his goodwill.

It must be of course remembered that the company in London were looking at the relations between the Indians and the colonists from a point of view which was creditable to them. Like good Englishmen and Protestants they were horrified at the cruelties which the Spaniards had become notorious for inflicting upon the natives of countries conquered by them. They were honestly anxious to make friends with the Indians of Virginia, and to bestow upon them the blessings of civilization in return for doing a little violence to their vague rights of property. A question of morality arises in all such attempts at colonization, which it is not easy to solve with a clear conscience. John Smith took another view of the matter. He was certainly not a cruel nor a bloodthirsty man; but his disposition was much more practical than sentimental, and he stuck fast upon the plain fact that if you force yourself on a race of ignorant and warlike savages, you must be prepared to deal with them by the only argument they can understand. After taking possession of their lands, he held, you might expect sooner or later to have to defend your proceedings by force ; and the more clearly you showed them as soon as possible that the force was on your side, the better it would be in the end for all parties. If left to himself, he would probably have got the troubles with the natives over in a short and sharp but effectual fashion; whereas the shilly-shallying policy of his predecessors and successors led in the end to a great loss of life on either side. The sword is not to be lightly played with, but it is often least dangerous in the most determined hands.

In spite of Powhatan's assurances that there was no sea beyond the mountains, Captain Newport, jealous of Smith's success as a discoverer, took no less than a hundred and twenty men, and set off up the river to do a little discovery on his own account. This small army, more than half the whole numbers, had with them a barge sent out for the purpose, which could be taken to pieces and carried over the mountains. When they got to the falls near Richmond they did in fact go forty miles on foot, and visited some of the Monacan Indians, who "neither used them well nor ill"; then they gave it up as a bad job. It is well seen that Smith was not at the head of this party. On the way home they wasted their time searching for mines of gold and silver till they came to be in want of food, for the Indians had hid their corn in the woods, and would neither trade nor fight, but, to get rid of their visitors, told them a cock-and-bull story about some ships having come to attack Jamestown. So home they went, no richer and little wiser than when they started, and Smith was proved to have been in the right again.

While they were away the president had of course not been idle. No sooner were the new emigrants landed than he set agoing the manufactures desired by the company, and led a party of thirty or forty into the woods to cut down trees, make boards, and learn to bear the hardships of their new life. Here is a touch worthy of record: " all these things were carried so pleasantly as within a week they became masters, making it their delight to hear the trees thunder as they fell; but the axe so often blistered their tender fingers that many times every third blow had an oath to drown the echo; for remedy of which sin the president devised how to have every man's oaths numbered, and at night for every oath to have a can of water poured down his sleeve, with which every offender was so washed (himself and all) that a man should scarcely hear an oath in a week." Some apology is made to the spirit of the age for this labour; it is not to be supposed, we are told, that the president and these gentlemen were to be looked on as common hirelings because they cut down trees; they themselves came to consider it almost an amusement. And then, as in more modern colonial experiences, it was observed that when gentlemen did strip off their fine coats and put their hands to work in earnest, they were of more use than the so called labourers, who probably grumbled all day long for want of the beef and beer of Old England, though most likely they had left home because they were too idle or too incapable to earn bread and cheese. Most of them indeed, though called labourers, are said to have been serving men, either out of place with good reason, or having emigrated with their masters, all equally "ten times more fit to spoil a commonwealth than to begin one." The English peasant has many good qualities, but among them is not the faculty of adapting himself easily to new circumstances, or putting a good shoulder to the wheel when taken out of the ruts of his humdrum life.

But no man with a grain of shame or sense in him could have idled when their leader was setting such a good example. A right republican president was Captain Smith. The only sign of aristocratic state about him which we get a hint of is a certain "page," whom he turned to the excellent use of leaving him among a tribe of friendly Indians to learn the language. A strange school for Master Samuel Collier, who had perhaps not run away from home to be set learning languages, but whose master had no need of any page to bear his train or fill his cup! He as little cared for ease and dignity himself as he would tolerate shirking in others. His predecessor had been building himself a "palace," but on Smith's coming to power this was at once stopped as a "thing needless," and rather the church was repaired, the fort strengthened, and sheds were erected for stores. A palace forsooth for the governor of a set of starving tatterdemalions! It would be well for the world if at all times it had more of such governors, with such an honest title to rule. Let lords, fops, courtiers, fools, and the like

delight their empty heads with silks and satins, and
titles and trifles; let them swill and gorge on the
fruit of other men's labours till they grow so bloated
that the earth will no longer bear them, and they
have to go at last to the same lodging as the
hungriest beggar. It may all be right enough;
there are a great many things in this life of ours
which a soldier of fortune does not get time to
understand clearly; but this he knows, and no man
shall say him nay, that John Smith has come into
the world to do some work for which it will be the
better and not the worse, and you had liefer come
between a lioness and her whelps than hinder such a
man from whatever he takes in hand. The work in
hand now is to make a garden of this useless jungle,
to tame these treacherous cruel savages for their
own good as well as ours, to lay firmly the foundations of a colony that shall in time leaven the whole
continent with the blessings of knowledge and industry. By —— (he can scarcely refrain from an oath)
it is a great work, fit to rouse even a rough soldier to
something like enthusiasm; and you contemptible
humbugs who brag about being gentlemen, and you
not less contemptible fellows who give yourselves
out for workmen, were well to make up your minds
that there is a man here who can do it and will,
Heaven helping him. If you agree with him, second
him as you can, obey him in all due service, you
shall find him a good master, cheery, hearty, somewhat rough tongued and hot tempered perhaps, but
without guile or pride, and asking none of you to
share dangers where he does not lead the way. But

if you contradict him when he knows he is right, if you talk nonsense or play the fool, if you waste the public means or refuse to take your share of the common burden, if you are a chattering, loafing, complaining, plotting, fainthearted lump of selfishness and gluttony—why then, take care what you are about, or you may repent having got in the way of the new president, who as yet has no time to make long winded laws and gloomy prisons, and despises you too much to do more than send you off howling to England with a kick and a redhot bit of his mind, but whose patience will some day come to an end; and then the patron saint of useless humbugs have mercy on you, for there is a whole forest of gallows hard at hand, and at its lowest ebb the colony can afford enough rope to hang a dozen such drivellers.

This, we gather, was Smith's notion of governing, and whatever its shortcomings, it was not far from what was wanted in the circumstances. There was nothing of the tyrant in him; he seems to have been a right favourite with the men who served immediately under him in his daring expeditions; but the stay-at-homes could not appreciate his sturdy character, and were so jealous of the influence he had gained by this more than by his nominal rank, that they proposed he should become a stay-at-home also, pretending that the duties of his office were of the sedentary kind so much affected by European potentates. He must not leave the fort without the consent of the council! Smith has few words to waste on such an absurd proposition; it seems to him that these men would rather "hazard a starving than his pains should prove so much more effectual than theirs." The great want of the colonists was a constant supply of corn; their demands on the Indians were beginning to be answered by alternate insolence and deceit; Powhatan's policy was evidently to starve them out of the country. No good came of these expeditions which Smith did not accompany to keep the deluded idiots from grubbing in the earth wherever they thought to see a glittering stone; he must go himself and bring his dusky majesty to reason.

But first the ship was to be got rid of, "that removing tavern," where every one was welcome who had money to spend or accusations to make against the president. Was it not enough for the idle vessel to be a focus of discontent, but the sailors must truck their plentiful victuals with the Indians, giving butter, cheese, beef, pork, whiskey, beer, biscuit, oatmeal, and oil, for furs, wild cubs, and other commodities and curiosities, when the settlers were hard put to it to buy corn at a fair price! Nay more, they had confederates within the walls, who stole tools, arms, and powder, by wholesale, to carry on the same infamous trade. Smith had never read Fenimore Cooper's works, but he knew well that if once these savages got accustomed to the use of firearms it would be harder to deal with them. And Captain Newport, instead of restraining his men, made himself the ringleader of the opposition, and seemed likely to tell such tales to the company at home that Smith had a good mind to keep him for a year in the colony, so that he might "learn to speak of his own experience" and not to slander those whose difficulties he neither understood nor helped to lighten.

At last the ship was sent off, carrying specimens of the new manufactures, and also a most remarkable letter to the company, containing a few of the president's opinions, set forth in such terms as must have caused the highly respectable merchants to open their eyes, and no doubt puzzled them in places as to what the captain precisely meant.

Having thus, like a true Englishman, relieved himself by a good growl, like an Englishman he tackled again manfully to his work, and was off to the frozen wilds, in the midst of the short but severe winter of Virginia, digging away the snow at night and drying the ground with a fire, then putting down a mat on which they "lay very warm," sheltered only by another mat to keep off the biting wind. Yet it was observed that those who did not shrink from such hardships were in better health than the rest. Not much corn however was to be had, for love or money; so now Smith began to think of paying Powhatan in his own coin. He proposed to surprise him and take his provisions, whether he would or not, to the horror of the virtuous council, among whom even Scrivener, late his *fidus Achates*, was now accused of disaffection. But "no persuasions could persuade the president to starve," and it was all the more necessary to attend to the housekeeping, since the first marriage had just taken place in Virginia, the happy man being one John Laydon, and his blushing bride Anne Burras, a waiting maid, who had come out with the last cargo of emigrants.

Powhatan's evil genius now led him to play into the hands of the English leader. He sent to offer a shipload of corn if they would, in return, build him a house and give him a grindstone, fifty swords, a few guns, a cock and a hen, some copper and beads. Here was an opportunity of doing business in some way or other, so the president set off forthwith, taking the pinnace, two barges, and forty-six men.

From the fort to Powhatan's residence was not more than a day's journey by land, but by water it was necessary to go round into the bay and ascend the York River. The year was going out with such boisterous and cold weather that the travellers had to stay and "keep Christmas"* with a friendly tribe, near the mouth of the James River, where they "were never more merry, nor fed on more plenty of good oysters, fish, flesh, wild fowl, and good bread; nor never had better fires in England than in the dry, smoky houses of Kecoughtan." They also quartered themselves for two or three days upon another less well disposed tribe, by way of teaching them civility; and it was a fortnight before they arrived at Werowocomoco. Here the river was frozen half a mile from the shore;

---

* They did not leave till the 29th December, so that "keeping Christmas" was probably a way of expressing what their descendants call "having a good time."

but to save time Smith went on in one of the smaller boats, breaking the ice, till the tide left him fast; then he encouraged his companions to struggle to shore, middle deep, through the frozen ooze, a trial which had almost been the death of one of them. They put up at the first houses they came to, and Powhatan soon sent them plenty of bread, turkeys, and venison. But when he arrived, and the question of trading was discussed, difficulties soon arose. Powhatan would sell his corn for nothing but guns and swords, which the English thought dangerous tools to put into the hands of Indians. Then he complained of their coming armed, as if for war rather than trade, and declared that his people were afraid to bring in their corn unless the merchants would lay aside their weapons.

Next day this wrangling was continued, and Smith could do no business except getting ten quarters of corn for a copper kettle which struck the chief's fancy. They passed a great deal of time in making fine speeches, which are fully reported in the fashion of the classical authors, according to their general drift, for we cannot believe that a shorthand writer was present. Powhatan begins quite classically by setting forth, like Nestor, that he had seen three generations of men, and might be expected to know what he was about. "Think you I am so simple," he says, "not to know it is better to eat good meat, lie well, and sleep quietly with my women and children, laugh and be merry with you, have copper, hatchets, or what I want, being your friend, than be forced to fly from all, to lie cold in the woods, feed upon acorns, roots, and such trash, and be so hunted by you that I can neither rest, eat, nor sleep, but my tired men must watch, and if a twig but break, every one crieth, *There cometh Captain Smith?*" To all this the captain's answer is that fine words feed no mouths; let the chief waste no time in talking, but bring out his corn, or they will find a way to get at it. As for their arms, they always wear them, and there's an end of it; and if Powhatan is so averse to fighting, the English rather enjoy it than otherwise, so he had best mind what he is about. Smith suspects that the chief is trifling with him, to gain time for his braves to come up; in return, he himself plays the same game, and has the breaking of the ice pushed on, that his boats may come to the shore and a stronger force of men be landed. Then Powhatan steals off, leaving the captain held in talk by two or three women, and presently he is aware that the house is beset in which he is with only one of his comrades. They burst out; Smith fires his pistol; the Indians fly in every direction and tumble head and heels over each other; and thus the Englishmen make good their retreat to a party of eighteen men already landed.

Powhatan, seeing that his attempt had failed and that another boatful of men was coming ashore, now sent an "orator" to make his excuses and to appease the white chief by a bracelet and a chain of pearl. He persisted that his people stood in fear; if they could only trust that no harm was meant them, they would come and load the boats with corn.

The Indians kindly offered the Englishmen to take charge of their arms, so that no one should steal them, if they would lay them down. The English proposed an amendment, that the Indians should lay down their arms, which they agreed to when they saw the matches being cocked, and hastened to carry down corn in baskets on their backs. But the tide ebbed and left the boats stranded; so the English returned for the night to their former quarters.

A good watch they kept through the night, and not without cause. For through the dark woods came stealing Pocahontas, who with tears in her eyes told them that her father was plotting to surprise them, and was bent on having Smith's life. Provisions were about to be brought to the house, and if the bearers could not contrive to kill them with their own weapons while they were at supper, they might look to be set on by all her father's forces. She refused to accept any reward, and went secretly as she had come, after begging them to fly. But Smith and his comrades had not come there to fly; they only looked to the matches of their pieces, and waited for what would happen.

Sure enough, within an hour came eight or ten lusty fellows, carrying into the house great plates of venison and other victuals, and showing a strong inclination to remain while the Englishmen sat down to supper. They pretended that the smoke of the matches made them sick, and suggested that it would be polite to put them out. We can hear John Smith's scornful laugh! He told them bluntly

that he knew very well what they wanted to be at,
and after making them taste all the dishes, as a
precaution against poison, sent them off with a
message to Powhatan that he might come as soon
as he pleased, for they were quite ready for him.
Other spies soon came prowling about the house,
while the Englishmen took their supper with their
guns lying handy, but no serious attempt was
made to disturb them. Thus both parties wakefully
passed the night, till it was high water and Smith
was able to regain his vessel, taking leave of the
Indians with hollow pretences of friendship on both
sides.

His next visit was to Pamunkey, the seat of Powhatan's brother, Opechancanough. Landing with
fifteen men he marched up to this chief's house,
and in a somewhat peremptory manner invited him
to trade. Opechancanough and some of his people
soon appeared with plenty of bows and arrows and
very little of any other commodities. Next day,
however, he promised to bring more supplies, but
what he brought next day was several hundreds of
armed men, who surrounded the house in which
were Smith and his little band. Some of the Englishmen showed alarm, but not so their leader. It
was his friends rather than his enemies that he was
afraid of, for he knew that if he caused a slaughter
of these savages the council would find fault, and
the company in England would look upon him as
an oppressor. Besides, he would only succeed in
frightening away all the Indians into the interior of
the country, and no more supplies could be got from

Smith seizing Opechancanough.

Page 127.

them. In this difficulty he proposed to Opechancanough a single combat for a stake of corn on one side and copper on the other. But the wily chief had no fancy for such an encounter. Standing before the door of the house with forty or fifty of his chief men, he tried to draw Smith out to receive a great present which they pretended to have brought for him. "The bait was guarded by two hundred men, and thirty lying under a great tree, that lay athwart as a barricado, each with his arrow nocked ready to shoot," so the president was wisely cautious, and ordered one of his men to go out and see "what kind of deceit this was." The man refused, whereupon Smith, wrathful at his cowardice, rushed out, caught Opechancanough by his long scalp lock, clapped a pistol to his breast, and dragged him among his people, who were so astonished and overawed by this bold treatment of the sacred person of their chief that they not only made no attempt to rescue him, but were induced to throw down their arms. Then Smith, still holding the chief fast, rated them soundly, vowing that he had put up too long with them, that if they shed a single drop of English blood he would exterminate their nation, and that if they did not choose to freight his ship with corn he would load it with their dead carcases.

This vigorous language had such effect that they now crowded back unarmed, bringing their corn and other commodities. But when the president, tired out by his watchfulness and exertions, went into the house to take a sleep, they thought again to have surprised him. Forty or fifty men, armed with clubs and swords, rushed in, with a larger force behind to back them up. John Smith had almost been caught napping. Luckily the noise awoke him; he sprang to his feet, snatched up his sword and target, and charged with a few men upon the dusky mob, who ran out faster than they had entered. "The house thus cleansed," it was thought well to keep the chief and a few of his old councillors as hostages; and of course they had many fine speeches to excuse this last attempt. So the rest of the day was "spent with much kindness," and presents were given on each side.

The Indians, however, were not at the end of their resources. They still seemed to wait for opportunity and courage to attack the strangers, and above all to kill Smith. Indeed he and some others had reason to believe themselves poisoned; but they were quit for a fit of sickness, and the man suspected of bringing the poison was treated no worse than by being beaten and kicked like a dog. At last, partly to get rid of their visitors, and partly from the fear that more men were coming from the fort, the natives brought in liberal supplies. In parts where it was evident that they themselves were suffering from scarcity Smith did not press them; but after visiting several tribes, he contrived to get his ship pretty well loaded.

Though he had set out meaning to deal fairly by way of trade, on his return he fully intended to surprise Powhatan and cut off his stores, by way of punishment for this king's treachery. Powhatan however, warned in time, had fled to the woods, carrying away or hiding all his provisions. The people left behind showed themselves unfriendly, but the president did not molest them, seeing "there was nothing now to be had, and therefore an unfit time to revenge their abuses." And besides there was good reason for his returning home without delay.

While Smith was dealing with Opechancanough and had already enough trouble on his mind, a messenger, who with the greatest difficulty had passed through Powhatan's country, brought him news that his deputy Scrivener and some of the other chief men had been accidentally drowned by the upsetting of a boat. This misfortune he carefully concealed from his companions till the business of victualling was done; but he would probably have lost not a day in hastening back, if he had known all that was taking place in the fort.

Some Germans had been sent to Powhatan to build him a house in the European fashion. These men, won over by the king's promises, were induced to betray the colony, and resolved to cast in their lot with the Indians. While waiting for a favourable opportunity of declaring themselves, they managed by means of confederates in the fort to steal upon such a scale that when Smith returned he found most of the tools and a large part of the arms gone into the hands of the Indians.

This system of theft still went on, and it was long before the manner of it could be detected. The savages, encouraged by the treacherous Germans, and by finding the dead bodies of Scrivener and

K

his companions, began to be emboldened in their attempts against the settlement. Captain Smith himself narrowly escaped an ambush which was laid for him near the fort, and, as he was walking alone, had a desperate encounter with a chief called the king of Paspahegh, who was, so to speak, the landlord of the colonists, as it was on his territory that they had taken leave to settle. This Indian, seeing the captain unprovided with firearms, was about to shoot him with an arrow. Smith instantly grappled with him. He was strong enough not only to prevent the Englishman from drawing his falchion but to drag him into the river, where they wrestled in the water till Smith got his adversary by the throat and nearly strangled him, so that the chief, surrendering, was led to Jamestown and put in fetters.

One of the Germans was also arrested about this time, and the president having now strong reason to suspect their treachery, sent to ask Powhatan to give up the others in exchange for the king of Paspahegh. The answer returned was that the Germans were remaining of their own accord; and soon the prisoner found means to escape. After this Smith went to war with his tribe, burning the chief's house, taking their boats and their fishing tackle, and killing some six or seven; an amount of devastation which might well contrast favourably with the cruelties that the Spaniards would not have spared on such an opportunity. The Indians indeed appealed to his practical turn of mind, pointing out that if he drove them to extremities it would be easy for them to leave the country, whereas, as friends, they would be able to supply the English with corn. Upon this consideration he made peace, and was not further molested by that tribe.

Another band of Indians, the Chickahominies, had now to be dealt with, who under colour of peaceful trading proved to be arrant thieves. By a strange incident Smith made a wholesome impression of awe upon their superstitious minds. Two brothers had been apprehended upon suspicion of being concerned in stealing a pistol. One was sent to fetch the pistol back within twelve hours, or else his brother should be hanged. Meanwhile the president, who could be goodnatured as well as stern, took pity on the poor naked wretch in the dungeon, and by way of making what would probably be his last hours on earth as comfortable as possible, sent him some victuals and a dish of burning charcoal, being as ignorant as his prisoner of the deadly effects of the fumes of charcoal in a confined space. When before midnight his brother returned with the pistol, the prisoner was found stifled and to all appearance dead. The other broke forth into such pitiful lamentations that Smith, though scarcely supposing that the man could be recovered, offered to do his best to bring him to life if they would give up stealing. By the use of spirits and vinegar the body was actually restored to consciousness, and the Indian saw his brother awake in such a dazed and terrified condition, half sensible and half intoxicated, that he seemed to have gone mad. Of this malady also

Smith, with more assurance, promised to recover him, upon promise of their good behaviour. He was laid down by a fire, and when he had slept off the effects both of the carbonic acid gas and of the brandy, rose like a new man, and departed with his brother to give out among his people that the great Captain Smith could not only kill but make alive again.

The arms and ammunition had still continued to be conveyed into the hands of Powhatan, and the German deserters were instructing his men in the use of them. But before long an accident happened which made them somewhat cautious. They were drying a bag of powder by a fire upon the back of a cuirass, and either the metal grew hot. or a spark flew out, for the powder exploded, blew two or three of them to pieces, and scorched the rest so that "they had little pleasure any more to meddle with powder." And Powhatan and his people soon concluded that the terrible strangers who handled such things securely were better as friends than foes. Bringing presents they desired peace, and not only returned many stolen articles, but for a time sent all thieves to the fort to be punished by Smith himself, though it is possible that they looked on his punishments as lightly as Topsy regarded Miss Ophelia's whippings. Flayings and burnings were their own mode of execution, and at the king's command an offender would kneel and without a cry allow himself to be beaten with cudgels by two men on the bare back till he fell senseless on the ground. It is satisfactory to learn that though the treacherous Germans escaped punishment for a time, they came to no good in the end by their conduct. Some time afterwards two of them had their brains beaten out by order of Powhatan, who declared that if they betrayed their old master they were as likely to prove false to him.

Peace being thus secured for a time, the colonists were able to devote themselves to work. They went on with their attempts at manufacturing, dug a well, built houses, made nets and wires for fishing, and planted thirty or forty acres of ground. They reared a number of pigs; and five hundred chickens were soon running wild in the woods. Two block houses were also built, one on an island commanding the approach by the river and one on the neck of the peninsula, as a guard against the Indians. In all these labours Captain Smith was sore vexed by the idleness of many of the emigrants; but he stoutly declared that whoever did not work should not eat, and by punishments, encouragements, and example succeeded in producing a certain degree of activity among the most slothful of these lotus eaters.

This was all the more necessary, as after three months the corn in store was found to be half rotten, and the rest of it almost consumed by a plague of rats that had also come over in the ships and established a more prosperous colony of their own. Now the settlers had enough to do in bestirring themselves to look for food. The main body caught fish and gathered roots and herbs, which enabled them to tide over this scarcity, though not without such discontent that the president had to threaten

with the gallows some who had a mind to run for
Newfoundland in the pinnace. Some were sent
down the river to live on oysters. Some were
billeted among the Indians, who now stood in too
much awe of Smith to do them any harm. Encouraged by this, a few of the soldiers tried to play
the lord in the wigwams, expecting to enjoy idleness and plenty, but were much disgusted to find
that their red-skinned hosts took a leaf out of their
own captain's book, and insisted that their guests
should work for their living, on refusal appealing to
Smith himself, who supported them and punished
his men. This is an example of his fair dealing
towards the natives, "of whom," he said, "there
was more hope to make better Christians and good
subjects than the one half of those that counterfeited
themselves both."

v.

Such was the state of things among the colonists
in the summer of 1609, when a fleet of seven vessels
was descried advancing up the river, which at first
they took for Spaniards, and made preparations for
defence. The new comers, however, proved to be no
Spaniards, but friends who brought more disaster to
the colony than any armament of honest enemies.

In England the company and the nation were not
yet disheartened by the long train of misfortunes
which had attended the settlement in Virginia. It
was still believed that the enterprise might be carried
to a prosperous issue; and the political notions of
the age caused it to be thought that a change in the
form of government was the main thing needful to

redress the evils under which the colony was suffering. It had yet to be learned that good men can make a good government, but that no form of government can manufacture good men, the real want on these teeming western shores. So the company obtained from the king a new charter, transferring to them full powers of legislation and executive, in virtue of which they appointed an excellent nobleman, Lord Delaware, as governor and captain-general for life, with a lieutenant, an admiral, a high marshal, a general of horse, and other officers with high sounding titles to make up for their want of the experience of plain John Smith. Under these distinguished auspices the public interest in colonisation was revived; money was subscribed; willing emigrants came forward; and in the month of May nine ships and five hundred people were despatched with Sir Thomas Gates, Sir George Somers, and Captain Newport, invested jointly with a commission to assume the government till Lord Delaware was able to come out in person.

Unfortunately these three dignitaries embarked in the same vessel, along with their credentials, their instructions, and the best of the provisions. This vessel was driven from the company of the rest by bad weather; and the new government of Virginia was wrecked upon the Bermudas, where, very much against their will, they spent the main part of the next year in building two small ships, and paving the way for an offshoot colony on these islands. Another of the fleet was lost in a hurricane; the rest arrived safe, as we have seen, but scarcely

sound after so much bad weather, bringing
Captain Smith's old enemies, Martin, Archer, and
Ratcliffe *alias* Sicklemore in command of a motley
crew, "wherein were many unruly gallants, packed
thither by their friends to escape ill destinies," and
already prejudiced by report against a governor so
strict in enforcing law, order, and industry.

It may be imagined in what danger the colony now
was of being thrown into anarchy. The new comers
loudly declared that Smith's rule was at an end;
but the lawful authorities might be at the bottom of
the sea for all that was known of them. Smith was
not willing to give up the colony to mere disorder;
and the best of the new emigrants, seeing his worth,
agreed to support him in maintaining his position
for the meanwhile, and imprisoning some of the most
turbulent and factious of his opponents. Nevertheless, when his year of office was at an end, he resigned the presidency to Martin; but that worthy
had at least the sense to know his own unfitness,
and at once gave it up again to Smith. The post
indeed was not one to be coveted. Not content with
trying to seize the stores and to usurp the government, some of this disorderly rabble must needs
destroy the good understanding that had been
established with the Indians, by stealing their corn,
robbing their gardens, beating and imprisoning
them, and then of course had to call upon Smith
for aid against the resentment called forth by these
acts of oppression. What with mutinies within,
attacks from without, complaints from the natives,
new delusions among the English about gold

mines and the South Sea, he had his hands full of vexations, when an accident happened to him which at last forced this brave man to abandon his post.

He had been up the river to settle the quarrels and repair, as far as possible, the errors of a branch colony that had been seated near the falls. On his return, while sleeping, he was terribly burned by the accidental explosion of a powder bag, "which tore the flesh from his body and thighs, nine or ten inches square, in a most pitiful manner; but to quench the tormenting fire frying him in his clothes, he leaped overboard into the deep river, where, ere they could recover him, he was near drowned."

In this state he had to travel a hundred miles without surgical aid. Arriving at Jamestown, though unable to stand, and almost out of his mind with pain, he attended to the business of government as well as he could. An important matter on hand was the trial of Ratcliffe, Archer, and other malcontents, who, it is said, fearing the result, sent a man to murder the president in his bed. If the story be true (which, we should hope, was rather due in part to poor Smith's distracted mind) the heart of the would be assassin failed him, and he was unable to discharge the pistol. The president's old comrades in arms were eager to take the lives of his enemies; but revenge was never part of this hero's character. His resolution began to give way under all these mental and bodily sufferings. He scarcely expected to live; at the best his injuries would prevent him from that ceaseless activity by which he had hitherto secured the welfare of the colony ; pain, ingratitude, and uncertainty combined to make him lose heart. The ships were to leave for England next day. He suddenly determined to return with them, and did so, coming home as poor as he had gone.

He left the settlement, however, in a state of comparative prosperity, which there was every reason to believe would have gone on increasing under his management, for "it was his ill chance to end when he had only learned how to begin." Besides five or six outposts and branch plantations, the fort at Jamestown was in good repair, and afforded safe and sufficiently comfortable habitation. It was built in the form of a triangle of strong palisades, with an outwork at each corner in the shape of a half moon, where also were the gates, guarded by cannon. Along the inside of the walls fifty or sixty houses were arranged in the same shape, built of boards plastered with clay, roofed with bark, and hung with mats after the Indian fashion. The space in the middle was called the market place, where stood a storehouse, a guardhouse, and a church sixty feet long, presently to be adorned with pulpit and pews of cedar and a black walnutwood communion table. There were twenty-four pieces of ordnance, three hundred muskets,* plenty of ammunition, pikes, swords, and other weapons, as

---

* These stores were not always of the best quality. Smith says that tradesmen would take a share, value £12 10s., in the company, to have the privilege of furnishing the settlers with inferior articles, unsaleable at home. Jobs and "rings" were not unknown in the "good old times," it would appear.

well as clothes, nets, and tools of all sorts, seven horses, pigs and fowls by the hundred, some goats and sheep. The community had also seven boats, a good store of commodities suitable for Indian trade, and a newly gathered harvest; so now, if ever, they were in a condition to be left to themselves, and to spare a little time for wrangling and idling.

But almost immediately they had too good reason to regret their folly and the loss of John Smith's clear head and busy hand. His authority had been left in the hands of Percy, brother of the Earl of Northumberland, who was himself sick, and had to compete with "twenty presidents and their appurtenances," self elected. Under this distracted rule soon ensued the darkest days that had yet befallen the plantation, where idleness, selfishness, and incompetence had now freedom to do their work.

When the Indians learned that the man who had been at once their conqueror and protector was gone, they were no longer restrained from attacking the settlers. They destroyed the boats, killed the hogs, and drove away the deer from that part of the country. The settlement at the falls had to be abandoned, after half its numbers had been cut off. Ratcliffe and thirty men fell into the snares of Powhatan, and were slain almost to a man, one only escaping, and a boy being saved from death by Pocahontas. Another band, sent out to trade for corn, ran away and turned pirates. The rest, harassed by constant attacks, learned when too late the worth of him against whom they had lately clamoured as an oppressor. Provisions began to fail; no supplies were to be had from the natives, and the stores were wasted by theft as well as by the greed of the new officers. This period was long known in the annals of the colony as "the starving time." The survivors were reduced to live on roots, berries, acorns, mushrooms, and the like; starch became a luxury among them; the skins of horses were eaten; and it was even said that they devoured human flesh. A dreadful story indeed came to England that one wretch had killed his wife and eaten her; but this proved to be a case of ordinary murder. The criminal was burned alive.

Thus within six months their numbers, which at Smith's departure amounted to nearly five hundred, were brought down to sixty miserable souls. Even these were like to perish in a few days when, in the spring of 1610, Gates and Somers, with their company of one hundred and fifty, arrived at last from the Bermudas, where in the meanwhile they had been undergoing sufferings and dissensions of their own. The long-boat of their wrecked ship, while fresh craft were being built, had already been sent to Virginia to seek help from the helpless colony there, but was never heard of again.

A helpless remnant was all they found of those hundreds who scarce more than a year before had left England along with them in such high hope. A lethargy of despair appeared to have fallen upon the survivors. Rather than crawl out to gather the firewood that lay rotting on the earth around them, they had torn down and burned their own cabins;

there was little care then for the defences and public buildings. So when the new comers eagerly landed, expecting to be welcomed with joy and abundance, their dismayed eyes were met by the sight of broken palisades, open gates, doors off their hinges, rusty guns, empty and half ruined houses, among which still moved a few pale and hollow eyed wretches, with but energy enough to complain and accuse. Well for them that they had not already fallen an easy prey to the savages!

The two knights lost heart at such a prospect. Nothing but death seemed to flourish on this fatal swamp. All the grain remaining, dealt out in scanty rations, would only support them for a fortnight. Now it was agreed by all that the plantation must be abandoned as a hopeless attempt. Crowded into their small and frail craft, the emigrants, old and new, embarked for Newfoundland, trusting there to find English fishing vessels which would help them home. They were scarcely to be prevented from setting fire to the fort where they had suffered so much. Without a tear they bade farewell to this unblessed spot.

But now occurred one of those timely incidents which give such a dramatic cast to the early history of Virginia. As they drop down the river, they fall in next morning with a boat, the vanguard of a new expedition. Lord Delaware, the governor, has come with three ships and abundance of supplies. At once the fickle sky of their fortune is changed from cloud to sunshine. The outgoing vessels turn their heads, and all make again for the fort, where they arrived before the Indians had learned their departure.

On the 10th of June the lord governor landed to the sound of trumpets, attended by a gallant guard of halberdiers in red cloaks, and several gentlemen of rank. He then proceeded first to the half ruined church, which it was among his earliest cares to have restored and decorated from day to day with fresh flowers. After service he read his commission and addressed the colonists, warning them against the faults that had hitherto been their bane, and announcing his intention henceforth to enforce order and industry.

New strength now quickened the pulse of the revived settlement. It seemed to be the hand of God that had thus punished them for their sins and yet ever marvellously preserved them from utter destruction. The English nation were plainly in earnest about this work, albeit it had as yet brought little but loss and misery. The English spirit rose to the task, and, forgetting all past discouragements, again girded itself to strive with the forces of the wilderness.

VI.

For a few years the record of John Smith's life is almost blank for us. Rewards and fame in that reign were not for such as he, who, at the best, had only been ruling a crew of starving ragamuffins that the country was well rid of, and, if his enemies spoke true, was a violent, boasting, firebrand of a fellow, wholly careless of proprieties and respectabilities. We can but speculate as to where and with whom he lived, when he reached England and the surgeons had set him on his legs again. It is possible that he saw and had speech of many of the great men of the day, who might well be curious to learn something of this colonial experiment on which he had so much to say. He certainly appealed to the patronage of Lord Bacon, who may from his information have taken almost every line of that essay in which the great writer insists that "it is a shameful and unblessed thing to take the scum of the people and wicked condemned men to be the people with whom you plant; and not only so, but it spoileth the plantation; for they will ever live like rogues, and not fall to work, but be lazy, and do mischief, and spend victuals and be quickly weary, and then certify over to their country to the discredit of the plantation." At the Mermaid Tavern Smith may have drunk a cup of sack with Shakspeare himself, and narrated to the mighty bard his own tale of

> . . . most disastrous chances,
> Of moving accidents by flood and field,
> Of hairbreadth 'scapes i' the imminent deadly breach,
> Of being taken by the insolent foe,
> And sold to slavery; of my redemption thence,
> And portance in my travel's history.

And the child Milton may have listened with eager wonder to the reminiscences of the man who had visited the East as well as the West, and with his own eyes had seen the steppes of Scythia and the "cany wagons light" of barbarous hordes. Who knows? This we do know, that his faith in the results of colonial enterprise continued unshaken, and that he laboured heart and soul to persuade his countrymen that the rich might multiply their wealth and the poor find ease and plenty in the New World, not from fabulous Golcondas and Eldorados, but by the prosaic yet profitable occupations of agriculture, fishing, trade and shipbuilding. No poet ever desired to find a publisher more earnestly than Smith sought to find patrons who would help him to prove the truth of what he said, by giving him means to forward discoveries and plantations.

It will be remembered that the area destined for colonisation in the first years of King James's reign lay between 34° and 45° north latitude, that is, from the south of Virginia to the middle of the present state of Maine. Two companies were formed, one at London, the other at Plymouth. To the first was granted the right of settling the southern half, with what success we have seen. The north was set apart for the West of England adventurers, and a small colony had been sent out, which however soon abandoned their settlement at the mouth of the Kennebec, and returned with a woeful tale of the ruggedness of the soil and the severity of the climate. The attempt was not repeated till Smith, meeting small encouragement from the London company which owed so much to him, offered his services to the promoters of the other enterprise. He made a voyage of exploration to their territory, the coast of which he carefully surveyed and gave it for the first time the name of New England, where-

as it had hitherto been called North Virginia or
Canada. So successful was this voyage in a business
point of view, and so glowing an account did
its commander bring back of the capacities of the
neglected country, that fresh interest was awakened
in the schemes which he had so much at heart.
Sir Ferdinand Gorges, Raleigh's old friend, and
other men of property backed him up, and he
twice set out for New England with the view of
planting a small colony. But once the bad weather
drove him back; and the second time he was taken
prisoner by a French privateer, from which he made
one of his wonderful escapes in an open boat.

Such hardships our adventurer was accustomed
to, but he could ill brook the vexations and delays
with which his plans now met. Just as a modern
projector might advertise in the newspapers, he
wrote a book on New England and caused two or
three thousand copies of it to be printed, distributing
many to the trade corporations of London, to
invite the aid of moneyed men. "Near a year,"
he says, "I spent to understand their resolutions,
which was to me a greater toil and torment than
to have been in New England about my business
but with bread and water and what I could get
there by my labour." It was no longer doubted
that profit could be made out of the proposed
enterprise; the question now was who were to
share those profits, while honest Smith thought
mainly of the glory of the nation and the gain of
mankind. Disputes arose between the two companies;
parliament showed its dislike towards the

exclusive privileges which the king proposed to confer; private adventurers durst not move in the matter, for fear of encroaching on the royal patent. Thus, before anything was done, New England had already been founded by the Pilgrim Fathers. John Smith had no great faith in the firmness of this foundation. Though he hated greed, he was not above ordinary business considerations of profit and loss, and taking a plain view of average human nature, declared: "I am not so simple to think that ever any other motive than wealth will ever erect there a commonwealth or draw company from their ease and humours at home." There were some depths of human nature which the clear headed captain had not yet sounded, as we shall see in time. He himself, after freely spending time and money, got no profit for his pains but the empty title of Admiral of New England. He might have known that the best work in the world is done for nothing.

But while occupied with abortive schemes for the settlement of New England, we may be sure that Smith never ceased to follow with warm interest the varied fortunes of his old friends and foes in Virginia, to whom we now return for a time.

Lord Delaware was soon driven from his post by sickness, and died in attempting to return to it. After him came a succession of governors, who were far too frequently changed for the welfare of the colony. The experience of past disorders had seemed to render good government necessary, and severity was our ancestors' idea of good government. A terribly Draconian code of laws was proclaimed to keep the settlers in order; they were looked upon as the servants, almost as the slaves, of the company, and subjected to the most rigorous martial discipline of the age. Their morals and theology were provided for as strictly as industry and orderliness. Every one on arriving in Virginia had to satisfy the minister that he had been duly instructed in the principles of religion, and if he was found wanting must submit to be taught and catechised on pain of whipping. It was death to speak against God, the king, or the Bible. Whoever failed in reverence to a preacher was to be whipped three times, and to ask forgiveness publicly in church. Prayers were read twice a day, and must be attended by all; staying away from church on Sundays was punished, the first time by stoppage of the offender's allowance of provisions for the week, the second by a whipping in addition, the third by death. The Indians were protected against all but authorised attacks and encroachments. Death was denounced against robbery, perjury, desertion, private trading with the Indians, even against such a fault as killing any tame beast or bird imported into the colony. Twice a day the drum beat in the fort to call the labourers out to their work, from six till ten, and from two till four; and if any one failed to answer the summons his skin must pay for it. The cooks and bakers who prepared the food were threatened with the loss of their ears upon any negligence or dishonesty. Laundresses were to be whipped if they stole or changed the linen entrusted to them, and also if they washed within forty feet of the

palisades or threw out suds into the enclosure. The
soldiers were enjoined to present such an example
of virtue as might be rather expected from
angels; death was the punishment for feigning
sickness, having private converse with Indians,
being absent from duty; and quarrelling, duelling,
gambling, swearing, and the like were prohibited
under such penalties as whipping, lying tied head
and heels together, which seems to have been a
favourite punishment of the time, or " passing the
pikes," by which we may understand something
like running the gauntlet. The intention of all
these regulations was good, but their provisions
were so rigorous that it is impossible they could
have been thoroughly executed. They were effectual
however in repressing mutinies such as had vexed
John Smith so often, and also unfortunately in
getting a bad name for the colony, as a place of
penal servitude rather than of exciting adventure,
a reputation not mended by the reports of sundry
knaves and dastards who found their way home to
England. In the plays of the period Virginia was
reviled and ridiculed, and its name began to pass
for a proverb in much the same sense as that of
Botany Bay did in later times.

In spite of this, however, emigration still went
on, for the population of England was so large as to
try its resources, and during the inglorious reign of
James there was no war to act as an outlet for restless
spirits. The company continued to take a lively
interest in their venture, and funds were raised by
means of public lotteries, which produced a con-

siderable sum, till after few years they were put a stop to by parliament. Fresh supplies were sent out; new plantations were started in the interior of the country; a small settlement which the French had ventured to make in New England was attacked and destroyed without ceremony; the Spaniards made no serious attempt to disturb their rivals, as it was feared they would have done; and the dominion of the colony seemed to be established as well as extended. John Smith began to feel a little jealous of the boasting reports which were now sent home by his successors. All their discoveries, he declared in his rough style, were but "pigs of his own sow," and no more wonderful, after he had opened up the way, than it would be to go from Billingsgate and discover Greenwich, Gravesend, and Margate.

These growing encroachments, as may be supposed, were not yet acquiesced in by the Indians; and collisions still occurred between them and the settlers, who were annoyed rather than checked by such opposition, and provoked more and more into making might the law of right. Again Pocahontas, this time against her will, played an important part in bring about a better understanding. Captain Argall, who brought out a batch of emigrants in 1612, hit upon the device of kidnapping the Indian princess and holding her as a hostage. By a bribe of a copper kettle, a precious treasure in native eyes, he induced an old Indian to entice her on board his vessel, then sent a messenger to her father, declaring that she was only to be ransomed by his surrendering certain English deserters, along with arms and tools which had been stolen from the colonists.

In answer to this Powhatan hesitated, procrastinated, and lied, for "he loved both his daughter and our commodities well." An expedition was sent against him, but still nothing was settled; and as the English had to return to plant their fields, he had a respite till they should have leisure to turn their ploughshares back into swords.

In the meanwhile an unexpected and important turn was given to the relations between the two races. John Rolfe, an English gentleman of good character, fell in love with Pocahontas, and she with him. They were married, with the full approval of the governor on one side and of her father on the other; and Powhatan not only entered into amity with the colonists, but was the means of bringing about a peace with the Chickahominy Indians, who consented to become subject and tributary to King James, their eight chief men being in sign thereof invested with the title of noblemen, and supplied with insignia of their high rank, in the shape of a red coat, a copper chain, and a copy of the royal portrait.

This marriage proved a not less happy than fortunate one. Pocahontas, now styled the Lady Rebecca,* learned the English language tolerably

---

* Her real name is said to have been Matoax or Matoaka, which the Indians changed, from a superstitious fear that if the English knew it they might be able to do her a mischief. She is also mentioned as having still another alias.

well, became a sincere convert to Christianity, and grew "formal and civil," according to the then accepted models of civilised behaviour. In 1616 she accompanied her husband to Europe, where she was received with curiosity, admiration, and cordiality by the good society of London, and was specially distinguished by the king and queen. But she liked the smoke of the city so little that she soon removed to Brentford. Here, to her joy and surprise, she again met her old friend, Captain Smith, whom she had been taught to believe dead, and was much vexed that he now approached her with an air of distance and reserve, which he had some ado to explain. It seems that King James, in his respect for the sacred blood of kings, had no mind that Powhatan's daughter should be treated familiarly by his subjects; he is even said to have been jealous of Mr. Rolfe's alliance with a royal family and suspicious of this residence at Brentford, where perhaps he remembered that two kings were proverbially licensed.

So Smith treated her Indian royal highness with due reverence, and loudly sounded forth the praise of her conduct towards him. But as he was on the point of setting out upon one of his voyages to New England, he did not see much of his former benefactress, and next year at the very beginning of her voyage home she died at Gravesend, leaving one son, from whom some of the chief Virginian families were afterwards proud to claim their descent.

This untoward event did not alter Powhatan's friendly conduct towards the English. He was too well satisfied of their power to make any further attempt at resisting it. It is related that he sent his son-in-law to England to number the population, who, on his arrival at Plymouth, provided himself with a long stick and tried to keep count by notches on it of all the men he met, but, as may be supposed, grew very soon "weary of that task," and came home to report that one might as well try to count the stars in the sky, the leaves on the trees, and the sand on the seashore. The year after his daughter's death Powhatan also died, and according to the custom of this people, was succeeded by a younger brother of whom we hear little more than the name, and are not sure how to spell even that. Another brother, with whom we are better acquainted, Opechancanough, appears now as the most active spirit among the Indians. He had always hated the intruders, and though for a time he dissembled, soon proved that his disposition was unchanged. It began to be suspected on both sides that no union between the two races was possible, and that only the extermination of one or other power could put an end to constant bickerings, injuries, and reprisals.

With many ups and downs, however, the colony continued to struggle on towards prosperity. An important step had been taken when, instead of obliging the settlers to work solely for the common stock, each man was given a small plot of land to make the best of for his own advantage, and the right of private property was found the surest stimulant to industry.

In 1619 Sir George Yearley came out as governor, with instructions to abolish the severe code by which the colonists had hitherto been restrained as if they were soldiers in presence of the enemy, and to substitute the free laws of England. An assembly was also summoned with power of making laws; the germ of American independence was latent in this provincial parliament. Measures were taken to promote education and to convert the Indians to the Church of England, which was declared to be the established religion of the colony. Industry was at last turned into a profitable direction; the settlers, after wasting much energy on the manufactures protested against by Smith and on the cultivation of vines and the rearing of silkworms, found that tobacco would pay them far better and more quickly. Tobacco was therefore cultivated with such zeal that at Jamestown even the streets and market place were planted with it. The "sotweed" became the staple of Virginia, and for long served as its currency.

Though the climate and the hardships of Virginia had been so fatal to former emigrants, in the year 1619 we find that more than twelve hundred new settlers were landed. Among these were a consignment of "ninety young women to make wives," which is a good sign of the plantation's taking root. The price of a wife was from a hundred and twenty pounds of tobacco, according to merit and the state of the market. Emigrants who could afford to pay their passage were rewarded at once by a grant of land. Those who were sent out at the company's expense had to give their labour in return for a certain time; later, they were assigned as apprentices to private planters, becoming free after a term of years. This was the origin of a system which led to great abuses. The condition of apprenticeship showed a tendency to become a more degraded state of servitude, in which the bondsman might be transferred from one master to another like a head of cattle. Criminals began to be transported; the troubles of the civil war led to the custom of consigning political prisoners also to this fate; and convict labour was thought a convenient and profitable way of advancing the colony. Worse, there were found miscreants who made a trade of kidnapping, or "spiriting" as the old phrase was, young people and selling them to the planters. Many a poor mother's child has disappeared thus, to toil for years under the hot sun of Virginia, and never to see his friends or be heard of again at home, in these days when neither the police nor the post office were such active institutions as they are now. Bristol and Aberdeen were notorious for this nefarious practice, which, so late as the middle of last century seems to have been carried on almost publicly, and sometimes was even connived at by the magistrates.

The seeds of another evil, which in our own times was to bring forth fatal fruit, were introduced into the colony also in 1619, when twenty negro slaves were brought by a Dutch ship and sold to the planters. God grant that America is at length washed clean of that sin by so much of her best blood!

There were plainer signs which made men like John Smith shake their heads over the prospects of the young colony, for all its growth and flourishing. The colonists were now dispersed on separate plantations, extending over a hundred and forty miles. They had ceased to entertain fear or even caution towards the Indians, who visited them freely, went in and out of their houses, and were welcomed as guests and friends. Nay, they were actually becoming expert in the use of the arms neglected by the English. They were sometimes employed to shoot game; such laxity appears to have been winked at, and it was even debated whether the natives should not be authorised to use firearms, as a bait to convert them to Christianity. One preacher of the muscular Christian school had little attention paid to him when he complained that his missionary efforts were unsuccessful, and would be, till a few of "their priests and ancients had their throats cut." It was rather considered, and rightly, that kindness was more likely to win them over to the true faith. This conduct towards the Indians was more creditable to the hearts than to the heads of their conquerors. Having passed some time without any serious fighting, the English allowed themselves to be off their guard; and beneath all this fair show of friendship lay the hatred of a cruel and treacherous race, forcibly deprived of their own and seeing their power grow less from day to day. On the 22nd of March, 1622, their real sentiments were displayed in bloody characters.

A plot was formed to fall upon the settlers on

that day, at the same hour, and massacre them to a
man, after having lulled them into security up to the
fatal moment by extraordinary pretences of alliance
and goodwill. Luckily, the night before, a converted
Indian betrayed the design to the man he was
appointed to kill, who lost no time in hastening
to Jamestown to inform the governor. Thus at
many of the chief settlements the English were
found prepared, and their enemies retired without
striking a blow. At more than thirty places, however, the messengers of death were received without
suspicion. Entering into the houses, they eat,
talked, and traded with the inhabitants, till they
found some safe opportunity of discharging their
treacherous task. Close upon three hundred and
fifty persons were thus murdered, men, women, and
children. Some were slain in their houses with
their own weapons, so suddenly that they saw not
by whose hand the blow was given. Some were
enticed forth and assassinated in the woods. Some
were taken unarmed at work, and speedily pierced
with arrows, and their brains dashed out by clubs.
Houses were burned, property was destroyed, and
the bodies of the victims were mangled with unspeakable barbarity. None were spared; the pious
benefactor of the natives met the same fate as their
oppressor. Instructed by familiarity with the settlers' habits, the savage ingenuity had so well con-
certed its plans that few of those taken by surprise
were able to save themselves in flight. Only when
the least resistance was possible the Indians showed
themselves as cowardly as cruel. One wounded

man set a band of them to flight with an axe. At another place a boy discharged a gun at random, and that was enough to protect him. A party of Englishmen took refuge in a half built house, and successfully defended themselves with axes, spades, and brickbats. One small family had what appeared a miraculous escape. At a plantation near them seventy-three persons were butchered; yet it was two days before this little household even heard what had happened.

Though the Indians thus failed of their full intent, the blow was a disastrous one for the colony. The panic stricken planters hurried to concentrate themselves in a few spots, leaving, for the most part, their fields unsown, their vineyards to be trampled down by wild animals, their cattle to be killed or driven away by the enemy. Terror and uncertainty paralysed all enterprise for a time, and many now left the colony, despairing of its future. But the moral effects of the massacre were even worse. As soon as the English recovered from their surprise, their first thoughts were of reprisals. A reaction of feeling took place; men blamed themselves for the kind policy by which they had tried to convert their savage neighbours, who were now spoken of as beasts and fiends, unworthy of pity or justice, by those who little thought that in the days of their grandchildren their own civilised island would behold a similar scene of horror enacted in a Highland glen. Revenge was now their text, and the missionary work of throat cutting found full favour. The cruelties of the Spaniards were significantly referred to, and no longer with horror. Some even said that this bloody day would do more good than harm to the colony, since now they need no longer trouble to keep on good terms with the Indians, but might destroy them by all means possible, and take their houses and clearings, which were the best spots in the country.

Such unchristian lessons were soon put into practice. The colonists assembled in bands, and fell upon the natives, killing, burning, and destroying in their turn. These attacks were repeated, and thus revengeful feeling was kept up on both sides. In 1644 the Indians planned and carried out another massacre, at which time Opechancanough was killed, having lived to a very great age. But the increasing numbers of the colony at last put it beyond the power of the Indians to do them serious harm, though ever and again the conquered race harassed their conquerors by the robberies, frays, and surprises which have afforded such a theme for fiction. It was long before the advancing frontiers of civilisation ceased to smoulder with the embers of mutual hatred; even in our own days we have seen a flicker of the flame that once burned so fiercely.

In England the news of the massacre of 1622 called forth horror and sympathy; aid was sent at once to the suffering colonists. Now John Smith again appears upon the scene; though the best of his life is gone, he is as ready for work and danger as when he was a beardless boy. We find him making an offer to the company to go out and reduce the savages to subjection, if he might have a body of a hundred and fifty men as a sort of police force with which to scour the country. The answer was that the company could not afford the expense of such an armament, though it was suggested that they would be obliged to him if he would do the business at his own charges, allowing them to have half the pillage. So little even yet did these gentlemen know of the country that they undertook to govern, in which, as Smith told them, he would not give twenty pounds for all the pillage that was to be had in twenty years. Industry and not pillage had ever been the ground of his faith in the prosperity of Virginia.

But soon the power of governing was taken away from this corporation. Commissioners were appointed to inquire into the causes of so much misfortune, and they did not neglect to take advantage of Smith's sagacity and experience. He gave the reasons which we have seen him urging all along, and also some practical suggestions for the reformation of the colony; the main thing necessary in his opinion being "sufficient men of any faculty," but on the other hand to "rectify a commonwealth with debauched people is impossible."

The result of this investigation was that Virginia was transferred to the crown of England, though retaining its popular assembly, with the rights of which the Stuarts either did not think it worth while, or soon had their hands too full at home, to meddle. And here we leave it and its colonists, as Smith ends his history, "to the trial of time . . .

praying to that great God, the Protector of all goodness, to send them as good success as the goodness of the action and country deserveth, and my heart desireth."

The last few years of Smith's life were spent in writing, editing, and publishing his works; he even travelled about distributing them. His whole heart was thrown into this work. He used to call the colonies his wife and children. Their undeveloped riches was his constant text. No task, so his sermon ever ran, could be more profitable, honourable, and religious, than that of bringing their boundless wastes and wild inhabitants within the pale of civilisation. Adam and Eve, he declared, were the first planters, and Noah was the second to set the same example. What could be more glorious than for a prince thus to extend his dominions? How could our fellow men be better served? Was it not a work pleasing to Heaven to spread that light of truth with which England had been blessed? By such appeals he sought to stir the age into some share of his own enthusiasm, and with his pen, as before with sword and axe, laboured to clear the forests of the New World.

Besides his books on Virginia and New England, and the story of his adventures in the four quarters of the world, he wrote a "Sea Grammar," for the instruction of young sailors. He is said to have been engaged on another nautical work when he died in 1631, at the age of fifty-two, having seen a colony after his own model begun by the Puritans in New England, to whom he heartily wished success, though he doubted if they had regard enough for bishops.

The career of this worthy may seem to have been too long dwelt on; yet the importance of his services can scarcely be over estimated. He may have been somewhat given to blowing his own trumpet when no one else undertook that duty, and, as we have seen, there is reason to suspect that his imagination sometimes led him astray in that account of his "True Travels in Europe, Asia, Africa, and America," but this is not so certain as that, neither during his life nor since, has he had among his countrymen the meed of fame and credit which is honestly due to him. The more one knows of him, the more one comes to like the rough and ready hero, as well as to respect him for what he did. As men go, he was a fine fellow; compared with other discoverers who had the same trials and temptations, his character seems nothing less than noble, and we may well wish with his rhyming panegyrist that there were "many such *Smiths* in this our Israel." He had his faults like the rest of us, but in his faults and in his virtues he was what we are perhaps too complacently accustomed to consider as a typical Briton, on the whole a good specimen of the race that has contrived to conquer half the world, not always with the loftiest intentions, but not often with the most unsatisfactory results. If he made enemies he had also friends who knew him thoroughly, and could speak warmly of him as one "that in all his proceedings made justice his first guide, and experience his second, ever hating baseness, sloth, pride, and indignity more than any dangers; that never allowed more for himself than his soldiers with him.; that upon no danger would send them where he would not lead them himself; that would never see us want what either he had or could by any means get us; that would rather want than borrow, or starve than not pay; that loved action more than words, and hated falsehood and covetousness worse than death; whose adventures were our lives, and whose loss our deaths."

THE PILGRIM FATHERS.

I.

The advance of enlightenment in the civilised world may be compared to the process of discovery and colonisation, in which we have seen how men, sometimes illustrious, more often humble and unknown, had to sacrifice comfort, health, life itself, to the arduous and perilous task of clearing the ground for their more fortunate successors. Crowded cities now hide the swamps that once steamed with deadly vapours; rich fields cover the wildernesses where the first turners of the sod pined with hunger. The roots of our moral culture, as of this prosperity, have been watered with blood and tears.

We Englishmen of to-day find ourselves in such a position that it is hard for us to realise some of the conditions under which men lived in the past. Every man among us may now think freely and speak his mind. Every man may worship according to his conscience, none daring and few caring to make him afraid. The general good is recognised as the object of our laws; class and sect may no longer have a hand in them. In this state of security we are too prone to forget the toils by which the path to it was hewn and beaten smooth, and too seldom bethink ourselves that these are the grass-grown graves of martyrs which we find so easy to our feet.

The rights and immunities that we enjoy so carelessly we owe to men who won them in tortures and labours, in prison and exile, at the pillory and the stake, as well as on the field of battle. For their courage and perseverance we cannot be too grateful. It were good for us if we oftener turned to the story of their sufferings, and learned from them so to play our part as to hand down the gift of life richer and freer to our posterity.

Ten generations have not come and gone since the English Puritans were in the forefront of the battle of humanity. Their name is with some still a word of opprobrium; their doctrines are not now in fashion; but only the ignorant and thoughtless can sneer at what they veritably did. That, like their contemporaries, they entertained many erroneous notions, we must admit. That they were not pleasant companions for men of a less thoughtful and stern temper, we may well believe. That they cultivated some absurd peculiarities of appearance and behaviour, we have heard more than enough; we know also that some of the peculiarities which offended their enemies are the ordinary habits of our own time, when we should find the lace and lovelocks of the Cavaliers far more ridiculous and unmanly than the short hair and sober garments of the Roundheads. That they did not fully understand their real principles, and while giving their own blood in the cause of religious liberty were so inconsistent as to turn the sword against other seekers of the truth, is but to say that they were men, and men of an age in which only here and there a sage such as Milton, or an enthusiast like Fox, had begun to comprehend the true idea of freedom. But it would be foolish to deny that they were, as a body, men of singular strength and courage, who have wrought many of their opinions into the texture of our national life, and communicated to the spirit of all our churches something of their characteristic zeal. Work like theirs cannot perish; time destroys only the prejudices and errors which blind and hinder such men. The nasal twang of the Puritan saints, all their narrow-minded austerities and ludicrous applications of Scripture, have vanished or are vanishing like the smoke of a furnace; but all the brighter glows that part of them which abides with us, and the clearer is the lesson of their earnestness and simplicity and reverence for the eternal. Though their name and memory were wholly to pass away, their influence would still be with us. And so long as our world is what it is, and not what it ought to be, we cannot do without men who in the Puritan spirit will face its afflictions and wrestle with its oppressors.

The Reformation affected the Church of England in a manner which could not be satisfactory to those who had at heart the principles of the one and the purity of the other. It was brought about by the selfish policy of the king rather than by the enlightened judgment of the people, and the main change which it introduced at first was the substitution of the royal for the papal supremacy over conscience. Timid well-meaning men, crafty time-serving men, men who were indifferent to all religion, and men who were so careful of their religion that they feared to destroy it in the process of reformation, in short, the mass of the people, accepted more or less willingly the arrangements made and altered from time to time by the capricious and narrow mind of Henry VIII. Whoever openly controverted whatever doctrines the theological Bluebeard chose to set his seal to was disposed of by burning or otherwise, and thus he trusted to preserve that superficial uniformity of opinion which is so dear to a certain order of intellect.

Yet, even before the days of Wickliffe and ever since, there had not been absent from our national life a strong undercurrent of feeling against priestly assumption and the corruptions of the Church of Rome. This feeling now found expression through reformers who yearned after the simplicity and purity which they found in the Bible, and would make no terms with the ceremonies and doctrines by which its lessons had been overlaid. Such men were in no mood to accept the partial and inconsistent reforms given to the church at the arbitrary will of any sovereign; still less would they submit to the reactionary measures on which Queen Mary staked her crown. The fearful persecution which ensued could not silence them. Those who died at the stake but lighted a candle which has never been put out. Those who lived sought an asylum among their brethren on the continent, where, embittered by exile, they listened eagerly to the teachings of the most advanced reformers, and became more zealous to make a radical change in the church of their native land.

At the death of Mary the exiles flocked back to England with their increased hatred of Rome, and found their countrymen, horrified by the epoch of cruelty which had just gone by, in a mood to give more friendly welcome to the new ideas, for which every martyr had been worth a thousand arguments. If they hoped much from Elizabeth they were disappointed. This princess proved as little disposed as her father to abate the claims of the royal supremacy over the church, and no less lukewarm against the unreformed features of its ritual. Had her reign been a period of profound peace, the victory of religious liberty might have been delayed for a century. But its foreign enemies played their game so badly that queen and people were driven together into an attitude of opposition, and the cannon of the Armada itself secured the safety of English protestantism. Still, however, the sovereign was jealous of all dissent from the established forms of religion. Persecution was relaxed in her reign, but not abandoned. Compared with the reign of her sister, it was an age of mercy; compared with the reign under which we now live, it was an age of intolerable oppression. Suspension, fines, imprisonment, sometimes even death, were the reward of those who went too far, as well as of those who did not go far enough, for the royal pleasure. Such persecution was effectual only in irritating without overawing the sufferers, and the cause in which they suffered struck deeper root and flourished more vigorously for this pruning. Elizabeth and her ministers were helpless against the spread of the new leaven. Long before she died, sick and weary of life, it was recognised that a large and influential section of the church and the nation had adopted that cast of opinions and morals which now became known as puritanism. The word explains itself; it is a name befitting those who in all times have been moved to seek, not so much to be better than their neighbours, as to be better than themselves, and from the contemplation of their own imperfect nature have risen to a higher conception of true goodness.

James I., brought up in the keen protestant air of Scotland, might well have been expected to favour the extreme anti-Romanist party in his new dominions. But the education of this weak and vain prince proved to have had a far different effect; he was so disgusted by the austere religion forced upon him by his fellow countrymen that he at once showed a dislike to the kindred sect in the south, and drew closer to the obsequious bishops who declared, when his majesty was pleased to exhibit in the controversy the learning of a pedant adorned by the manners of a bully, that he spoke by the special assistance of the Holy Spirit! Besides, his love of power sharpened his wits to the apprehension of a new danger. This wisest fool in Europe had reason in his maxim, "No bishop, no king." The men who had so long suffered from the abuse of royal power had naturally grown aware of the iniquity of such abuse, and religious and political discontent became involved in one agitation. The Puritans were no longer a sect, but a powerful party, whose demands began to be more open and urgent. The breach was widening year by year; moderate counsels gave place to extreme views on either side. On the one hand was the royal and episcopal power, more and more asserted and enforced; on the other stood the growing strength of the people and the most pious members of the church, more and more aroused to the danger of that power and determined to lessen it. Ignorant of the force of the storm that was gathering against his notions of government, James thought to oppose it by the petty inquisition of such courts as the Star Chamber and the High Commission. He could not have taken better means to foster the cause which he hated. Sympathy with the victims went to swell the popular discontent. The severities exercised against the Puritans were most useful in winnowing from among them all whose motives were not sincere, or whose spirits not resolute, and thus providing a picked body to carry the standard of reform against all odds. It was the boast of the people of Massachusetts that three kingdoms had been sifted to afford the choice seed from which they sprang, which was again sifted in exile as it had been in persecution. For some of the oppressed, beginning to despair of peace and liberty at home, were at last driven to seek them once more abroad in a country which had just rendered itself illustrious by a gallant struggle for civil and religious freedom. Republican soil was again found congenial to anti-sacerdotal principles; New England was born at Geneva, and cradled in Holland.

As is usual in such movements, a division had not failed to make its appearance in the ranks of the reformers. The Puritans, it must not be forgotten, were still members of the Church of England. While they deplored its corruptions, they had no wish to withdraw from its communion, believing that all the nation should belong to one religion, and that the state had a clear right to prescribe the terms of unity. But twenty years before the death of Elizabeth, there had appeared a sect with less regard for the ordinances of man and more bold intention to attain the purity after which all the party aspired. This sect in time grew into the powerful body of the Independents; but at first it was a small and despised faction of obscure men, spoken of contemptuously as "Brownists," from one of their leaders who little deserved that honour, as "Barrowists," from another who suffered martyrdom under Elizabeth, or as "Separatists," because they cut themselves loose from the bonds of the state church and did not hesitate to worship in illegal conventicles. The Puritans long looked upon these proceedings with grave disapproval; and the position of the two kindred parties towards each other was much like that of the Ritualists and the Romanists among ourselves. In time indeed the principles of the Separatists carried it over the scruples of the Puritans, so that the two parties are often identified under the latter name. But so long as their common enemies were in power the more thoroughgoing party of course bore the brunt of the persecution. It was they who now turned to Holland as their fathers had turned to Switzerland and Germany, for a refuge from oppression.

It was in the northern part of England that this sterner temper prevailed. At the beginning of the seventeenth century, about the time when Bartholomew Gosnold discovered Cape Cod, there gathered round a village near the borders of Lincolnshire, Nottinghamshire, and Yorkshire, a little congregation which covenanted to follow humbly the teachings which, as they believed, they found in the word of God. Mr. John Robinson, a young Cambridge man, became the pastor of this flock, among which were not many rich nor mighty nor learned, but which was strong in the spirit that bound them together in such adverse days. They were mostly young men of the rank of peasants or small farmers. For some time they made shift to worship as much as possible in private, and to bear the penalties of nonconformity with patience. But soon they found their position intolerable. "For some were taken and clapped up in prisons, others had their houses beset and watched night and day, and hardly escaped their hands; and the most were fain to fly and leave their houses and habitations, and the means of their livelihood. . . . Seeing themselves thus molested, and that there was no hope of their continuance there, by a joint consent they resolved to go into the Low Countries, where they heard was freedom of religion for all men, as also how sundry from London and other parts of the land, that had been exiled and persecuted for the same cause, were gone thither and lived at Amsterdam and in other places of the land."

It was in 1607 that this resolution was taken, but it could not be immediately carried into execution. What they meditated was accounted by the government a crime, and it was necessary to wait, to bribe sailors, to steal away in secret. Once, after hiring a ship at a high rate, they were betrayed, robbed and imprisoned. Again, while embarking from a desolate common, a company of horse and foot came upon them; a few men who had already gone on board were carried away without clothes or money, and saw their wives and children once more seized, without being able to help them. The magistrates, who acted thus upon instructions from the king's council, seem to have been rather ashamed of their task, and showed what favour they could to these unfortunate people. In the end, all perils and difficulties were overcome, and by one way or other the little band safely reached the country which they desired. They now began to call themselves Pilgrims, confessing that they sought no country on earth but that from which they might best make their way to heaven.

Most of the exiles came from small villages, and did not fail to be impressed by the wealthy towns and strange habits and manners of the foreign people among whom they now found themselves.

But they had little opportunity for idle curiosity; these travellers were poor, and must at once look about for the means of gaining a bare subsistence, with all the disadvantage of ignorance of the language and inexperience for the most part of such handicrafts as would enable them to settle together in some town. Their first year in Holland was one of trials and privations. When all the members of the congregation had come over, they removed from Amsterdam to Leyden, where they contrived to support themselves by various occupations, such as weaving, silk dying, and printing. Their honesty and industry soon became so conspicuous that they found ready employment and were much respected by their Dutch neighbours. At the end of twelve years the magistrates of the city declared that no complaint had been made against any of these English settlers.

Yet now, when they seemed to have lived down the worst of their troubles, certain reasons induced them to think of removing once more to found across the Atlantic an asylum for their oppressed co-religionists. They could only maintain themselves in Holland by incessant toil, which was already bringing premature old age upon some of them, and deterred many of their friends who in other circumstances would have been glad to join their community. They were anxious to secure a more favourable lot for their children and to educate them as Englishmen, apart from the bad examples which had already led many astray from the severe manners of their parents. War was on the point of breaking out between Spain and Holland, and in its chances they knew not how much longer they could count on security. Their enemies declared that they were restless to find themselves now unpersecuted and unnoticed; and there is a sense in which this charge may have a tinge of truth. Those who have led a stirring life do not easily settle down to a monotonous course of commonplace drudgery; the Pilgrims had been fiercely tried in spiritual tempests and conflicts, and they might well feel a vocation for further adventures in the cause to which they had engaged their lives. One of their main objects in going to America was the spread of the gospel among the heathen. All the early colonists, as we have seen, made the same profession; in this case there is least reason to doubt that it was sincere.

After some hesitation, for the dangers were known and weighed, it was decided by the majority to go. The next question was, in what part of America should they seek their settlement? Some proposed the rich regions of Guiana, which Sir Walter Raleigh had made famous among his countrymen; others, the shores of Chesapeake Bay, where an English colony, as we know, was already struggling into prosperity. But in the one case was objected the fear of the Spaniards; in the other, the uncongenial character of their own countrymen, by whom they might be persecuted in America as at home. Finally they chose the northern part of Virginia, now beginning to be called New England, where several attempts had been made, but no colony had yet succeeded in establishing itself. To this quarter their thoughts were naturally directed, not only because they would be in less danger of interference there, but because their adopted fellow citizens were beginning to take an interest in it.

Since the Pilgrims came into Holland, Henry Hudson, voyaging in the Dutch service, had discovered the noble river which bears his name, had sailed along the many miles of tall cliffs now known as the Palisades, steered safely through the grand gorges of the Highlands, passed by the wooded banks of West Point in their early autumn glory and by the ridges of the Catskill mountains, run aground at low tide, as river steamers will still do in some of the shallower reaches, and had succeeded in ascending about as far as Albany. He found the natives "very civil" and generally willing to barter tobacco and skins for cheap European commodities. His masters were too good men of business to lose a chance of profitable trade with the West as well as the East Indies, so they soon established trading posts in the vicinity of Manhattan island, upon which was built the town called at first New Amsterdam and now celebrated as New York.

The Pilgrims had then to consider how means might be provided for the long voyage and to support themselves during the first months of their settlement. The West India Company, which had just been formed among the Dutch, were willing to transport them to the banks of the Hudson; but terms could not be agreed upon, for the leaders of the congregation stipulated for conditions which showed that, for all their enthusiasm, they had a shrewd eye to the chances of the proposed enterprise. Their main hope was that the London Virginia Company would send them over, and that the king would grant a charter, securing them in the exercise of their religious liberties in the New World. For this purpose protracted negotiations were carried on, and for a time with some prospect of success. The English company also were ready to engage the services of men who had proved themselves of no ordinary stamp. The king considered their demands, and in all respects but one had reason to be satisfied with their declarations of loyalty. They refused to admit the ecclesiastical authority of bishops; and it was to episcopal counsellors that he submitted their petition. Naturally it was refused. Unable to procure a distinct promise of toleration under the royal seal, the Pilgrims could only hope that their proceedings so far from home would be winked at by the government. After all, they thought it better to put their trust in God than in princes. They reasoned that if the tyranny of the bishops looked across the Atlantic, "though we had a seal as broad as the house floor, there would be means enough found to recall or reverse it." So they ceased to seek for any formal promise; and the only document of the kind held so important by colonists in these days, which they acquired, was a patent taken out in the name of a person who did not accompany them. This was therefore useless and worse than useless to their designs, as we shall see in the end.

At last, weary of delays, the agents of the Pilgrims in London entered into an arrangement on their behalf with about seventy merchants and other men of business, who agreed to subscribe for a greater or less number of shares in the undertaking. The services of each emigrant were to be reckoned as a single share of ten pounds, besides what he might contribute from his own means to the joint stock. Most of the funds were of course furnished by the "adventurers," as they were called, who did not adventure their persons. For seven years the partnership was to continue, at the end of which all profits and effects were to be equally divided among those who had given work and those who had given money, according to the number of their shares. The colonists were in the meanwhile to be supported out of the common property.

These were hard terms for one party, seeing that the danger of death and privation was as great as the prospect of profit from the fishing and fur trading for which New England was now becoming known in the commercial world. The arrangement gave rise to frequent disputes and difficulties, and the result proved that "those who adventured their money were no great gainers, yet those that adventured their lives in carrying on the business of the plantation were by much the greatest sufferers."

The Pilgrims were too poor to haggle. They accepted the conditions now offered them, and rather less than half of the congregation, "such of the youngest and strongest as freely offered themselves," made ready to set out at once. They numbered over a hundred souls, including some women and children, and were to be accompanied by Elder Brewster as their religious teacher. The larger half were to remain at Leyden with Mr. Robinson till the settlement had been fairly established and funds provided for the transport of them all. It was some years before this consummation could be attained.

On the 22nd of July, 1620, the voyagers embarked at Delft Haven. Their brethren accompanied them to the port, where they renewed their solemn covenant and took leave of each other with psalms and floods of tears. Their pastor gave them a parting charge, the language of which deserves to be well marked. No preacher less deserved to be called a bigot than he who, after passing through the trial of persecution and the greater trial of spiritual eminence among such a flock, was wise and humble enough to charge them by God and His blessed angels to follow him no further than he followed Christ. "I am very confident," he said, "the Lord has more truth and light yet to break forth out of His holy word." He bewailed the condition of the reformed churches, which had come to a standstill in religion, and would go no farther than the instruments of their reformation. Luther and Calvin were great men in their day, yet they penetrated not into the whole counsel of God; and their followers who stuck upon the letter of their teaching had missed its spirit. But he besought the Pilgrims to be ready to receive whatever truth might be revealed to them, for it was not possible that the Christian world should have come so lately out of such thick antichristian darkness and that full perfection of knowledge should shine forth at once. In the same spirit this conscientious dissenter, who has been so unjustly accused of manifesting a factious and sectarian spirit, advised them to seek union with the Puritan conformists, now that they were about to be so placed that the causes of disunion would be removed, and expressed a hope that some other pious minister might join them before his coming, for the flock that had two shepherds was not endangered but secured thereby. "Words," well says an historian, "almost astonishing in that age of low and universal bigotry then prevailing in the English nation, wherein this truly great and learned man seems to be the only divine who was capable of rising into a noble freedom of thinking and practising in religious matters, and even of urging such an equal liberty on his own people."

The Speedwell hoisted her sails, and, firing a salute with their muskets and three pieces of ordnance, the emigrants saw the shores of Holland sink out of sight, and were borne by a fair wind to Southampton. Here they found the Mayflower, the larger of the two ships which had been hired to transport them across the ocean.

In a fortnight these vessels set out. But before they had gone far the crew of the Speedwell either found or pretended that their ship was unfit for such a long voyage. They put into Dartmouth for repairs, then proceeded. When they had reached the open sea the Speedwell's men were again dismayed, so they had to put about once more and return to Plymouth. Here the smaller ship was dismissed, and a few faint hearted persons withdrew from the enterprise. The rest, numbering in all about a hundred, were now embarked together on board the Mayflower, which after these delays at last set sail on the 6th of September, her passengers little thinking how famous their voyage was to become.

"What a shoot was that," exclaims a writer whose style speaks his name, "which England, carelessly, in quest of other objects, struck out across the ocean, into the waste land which it named *New* England! Hail to thee, poor little ship Mayflower of Delft Haven—poor common-looking ship, hired by common charter party for coined dollars—caulked with mere oakum and tar—provisioned with vulgarest biscuit and bacon! yet what ship Argo, or miraculous epic ship, built by the sea gods, was other than a foolish bumbarge in comparison! Golden fleeces, or the like, these sailed for, with or without effect. Thou, little Mayflower, hadst in thee a veritable Promethean spark, the life spark of the largest nation on our earth: so we may already name the Transatlantic Saxon nation. . . . Honour to the brave and true! They verily, we say, carry fire from heaven, and have a power that themselves dream not of."

Any voyage in these days had hardships which would appal the cabin passengers of our generation. The fathers of New England experienced more than

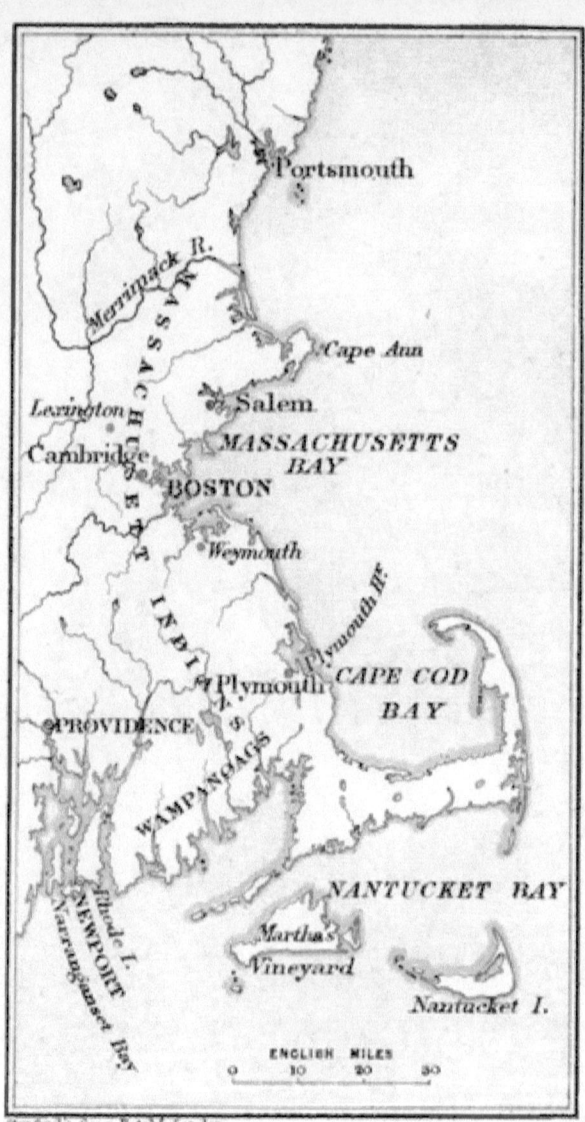

their share of such hardships. Crowded into one vessel, badly provisioned, buffeted by rough weather, they had need to play the man at the very outset of their undertaking. One died during the passage, and one child was born. It was two months before they sighted land at Cape Cod, the most prominent and singular feature of the New England coast.

Their intention had been to settle near the Hudson River, and thither the vessel directed its course. But at this late season of the year the storms and shoals of the coast were not to be rashly encountered; they were all eager to get on land; so they resolved to bear up to the north and return to Cape Cod.

II.

A glance at the map will show how Massachusetts got its familiar name of "the Bay State." Almost all its rugged coast is bent into one great bay, the northern point of which is Cape Ann, originally christened by Captain Smith Cape Trabigzanda, after his Turkish patroness, while on the south Cape Cod stretches, in the shape of a sickle, nearly a hundred miles into the ocean, and curls its narrow point round a vast natural harbour where the largest navy in the world might ride safely. Into this harbour, on the 11th of November, 1620, crept the weather-beaten Mayflower, and the pilgrims fell on their knees and blessed the Lord, who had delivered them from all the perils and miseries of the ocean and brought them to the land where, as they trusted, they might at last dwell in peace and be free to serve Heaven as their conscience bade them.

Yet their worst troubles might have seemed only about to begin. Even in summer the aspect of that coast is little inviting to strangers; and the voyagers of the Mayflower found the severe winter of New England setting in, and saw their new home with its most cheerless looks. By the shore were bare heaps of drifting sand; beyond, sombre woods. No human habitation met their eyes. They could expect a welcome only from wild beasts, or from as wild savages, who, so far from entertaining them with the kindness shown to Paul by the barbarous people of Melita, might prove "readier to fill their sides full of arrows than otherwise." Behind was the ocean, cutting them off from their friends and their country. Before them was this wilderness, full of untried dangers, in which the sailors were urging them to find a settlement without delay. These sole allies were already hinting at a desire to be rid of them; then the little band must shift for themselves as best they could, in the rigours of that season, and five hundred miles from the nearest dwellings of civilised men. Only the firm faith and high purpose of the Pilgrims could have given them courage to face such prospects. Well for them that theirs was no ordinary fortitude, which now, and throughout their coming trials, did not fail them and made theirs no ordinary history. We have seen what sort of tale must be told hitherto of almost all these pioneer settlements, a tale repeated most accurately by a writer of our own day, who is describing what took place within the time of men still living: "things went smoothly enough as long as the business of the colony was mainly confined to eating the provisions that had been brought in the ships; but as soon as the work became real, and the commons short, the whole community smouldered down into chronic mutiny." We are to see how the men bore themselves who came to the New World to seek first the kingdom of God and the true riches, and why the American Republic rightly dates its history from "that English settlement which," says Cotton Mather, "may, upon a thousand accounts, pretend unto more of true English than all the rest." He wrote when Old England and New England were still one.

Two of the chief persons of the company, Bradford and Winslow, kept a minute record of their proceedings from their arrival, and we may well follow every footstep with interest. Their first measure was to hold a meeting on board the Mayflower, and draw up an instrument, "solemnly and mutually, in the presence of God and one another," constituting themselves a civil body politic, and promising obedience to whatever just and equal laws might be made for the general good. This constitution was signed by forty-one men, the rest being women and children; and Mr. John Carver was unanimously elected governor. Some such legal machinery seemed necessary, as there had been signs of unruliness and dissension only natural among the vexations of the long sea voyage. But it is to be noticed that the power of punishment had not to be exercised for four months, after which a certain John Billington was "convented before the whole company, for his contempt of the captain's lawful command, with opprobrious speeches," for which he was adjudged to have his neck and heels tied together, but was forgiven for this first offence upon humbling himself and craving pardon. Three months later the second offence was committed by two servants, who fought a duel and wounded each other, whereupon they are "adjudged by the whole company to have their head and feet tied together, and so to lie for twenty-four hours without meat or drink; which is begun to be inflicted, but within an hour, because of their great pains, at their own and their master's humble request, upon promise of better carriage, they are released by the governor." This absence of crime, and mild government, contrasts most favourably with the condition of other settlements, where we hear of assizes, hangings, and whippings, almost from the beginning of their history.

It was Saturday when the ship anchored in Cape Cod harbour. A boat was sent to land, to fetch wood and water, and a favourable report of the country was brought back, but no natives had been seen. Next day was probably kept quietly on board. On Monday "our people went on shore to refresh themselves, and our women to wash, as they had great need." There are touches of homely fact in this heroic record. The Pilgrims feasted on shell fish, and made themselves very ill by this indigestible nourishment. They saw great whales playing in the harbour, and regretted that they had no means of catching them and making three or four thousand pounds worth of oil; their piety was of no such colour as to blind them to fair chances of profit. But their greatest complaint was of the cold. Unfortunately, the water was so shallow that they could not get to land without wading a bow-shot or two, and this helped to bring on the severe colds and consumptions which carried off so many during the winter.

Their desire was to set out at once to examine the coast and find a good place for their plantation. But the shallop in which this journey must be made was found so much in need of repair that it was more than a fortnight before she was out of the carpenter's hands. Some of the bolder spirits, impatient of this delay, proposed to explore by land; and a party of sixteen men, armed with musket, sword, and corslet, set out under the famous Captain Miles Standish.

Marching in single file by the seashore, they soon saw a small party of Indians with a dog, who "ran away with might and main" at the sight of them, and hid themselves in the woods. The English followed on their trail till nightfall, when they halted and camped out round a fire. There were reasons for both the scarcity and the shyness of the natives, which were to be explained in time.

"In the morning, so soon as we could see the trace, we proceeded on our journey, and had the track until we had compassed the head of a long creek; and there they took into another wood, and we after them, supposing to find some of their dwellings. But we marched through boughs and bushes, and under hills and valleys, which tore our very armour in pieces, and yet could meet with none of them, nor their houses, nor find any fresh water, which we greatly desired and stood in need of; for we brought neither beer nor water with us, and our victuals was only biscuit and Holland cheese, and a little bottle of aquavitæ, so as we were sore athirst. About ten o'clock we came into a deep valley, full of brush, woodgaile, and long grass, through which we found little paths or tracks; and there we saw a deer and found springs of fresh water, of which we were heartily glad, and sat us down and drunk our first New England water with as much delight as ever we drunk drink in all our lives."

Continuing their journey, they now came upon marks of recent habitation, ground that had evidently been tilled, then new stubble, and a spot where a house had stood, and where was lying a great kettle seeming to have belonged to a ship. A little farther on were the remnants of an old fort. By a creek lay two canoes. What most puzzled the explorers was the appearance of certain heaps of sand, one covered with old mats, and having rude household utensils laid upon it. Turning up the earth they found a bow and arrows rotting underneath, and rightly guessed that these heaps must be graves, which they wisely resolved not to disturb further, lest they should offend the natives. But soon the look of a freshly turned mound tempted them to dig again, and this time they found that they had hit upon a granary: two baskets of corn had been buried here, according to a common custom of the Indians. After consultation they resolved to take the kettle and as much of the corn as they could carry away, and to satisfy the owners as soon as they should present themselves, which in due time was done. "So we took all the ears and put a good deal of the loose corn in the kettle, for two men to bring away on a staff. Besides, they that could put any into their pockets filled the same. The rest we buried again; for we were so laden with armour that we could carry no more."

Soon afterwards they again halted for the night, making a great fire and a barricade to the windward of them, beside which shelter they slept in the rain as best they could, three men standing sentinel in their turn, "while five or six inches of match were burning." This hint as to the way of telling how time passed shows us that their guns were still the old matchlocks. We soon hear occasionally of a "snaphance" or firelock among them, but this improved form of weapon had not yet come into general use.

All these little details help us to form a picture of the men and to realize the circumstances under which they did such great things in such a matter of fact way. No doubt Defoe had studied their story, and perhaps borrowed from it more than one hint for his "Robinson Crusoe." He could well fancy their astonishment when they found this kettle of European make, almost as significant a discovery for them as was the footprint on the sand in that celebrated tale which reads as much like a true history as the narrative of the Pilgrim Fathers might sometimes be taken for a cunningly wrought fiction. For the Pilgrims themselves, the kettle of corn slung between two men must have borne a homely resemblance to the grapes which the spies of Israel brought back from the land of Canaan.

Next day they started homewards, after looking to their pieces, which would not go off because of the wet. As they wandered through the woods and could not find their way, they had another proof of the existence of these inhabitants who kept themselves so invisible; one of them found himself caught by the leg in a trap set for deer. Game seemed to abound; partridges and wild fowl rose and flew from their advance, and they "saw three bucks, but had rather have *had* one of them." At length they came in sight of the ship and fired off their guns as a signal for the boat to come on shore. "And thus we came both weary and welcome home."

When the shallop was ready, another visit was made in it to the place where the corn had been found, to which they gave the name of Cornhill. Further search there and in the neighbourhood disclosed more Indian corn and a bag of beans, so that they got about ten bushels of grain to serve them for seed. They ascribed it to "God's good providence" that they had found the corn on their first journey, for now the ground was covered with snow, and so hard frozen that they had much ado to "carve" it with their cutlasses, then to "heave" it up with levers, as they had neglected to bring mattocks and spades. The weather looked so unpromising that the shallop went back; but a party remained here to make further search for the Indians, of whom they could see nothing but their graves.

Next morning they followed certain tracks into the woods, and came upon a beaten path two feet broad. Here they lighted all their matches and looked sharply about them, expecting every moment to come upon a village or an ambuscade. But this proved to be only an opening made to drive deer. For five or six miles they traversed the woods, and at last came to another grave, "much bigger and longer than any we had yet seen. It was also covered with boards, so as we mused what it should be, and resolved to dig it up; where we found first a mat, and under that a fair bow, and then another mat, and under that a board about three quarters of a yard long, finely carved and painted, with three tines* or broaches on the top, like a crown. Also between the mats we found bowls, trays, dishes, and such-like trinkets. At length we came to a fair new mat, and under that two bundles, the one bigger, the other less. We opened the greater and found in it a great quantity of fine and perfect red powder, and in it the bones and skull of a man. The skull had fine yellow hair still on it, and some of the flesh unconsumed. There was bound up with it a knife, a pack needle, and two or three old iron things. It was bound up in a sailor's canvas

---

* Prongs.

cassock and a pair of cloth breeches. The red powder was a kind of embalmment, and yielded a strong but not offensive smell; it was as fine as any flour. We opened the less bundle likewise, and found of the same powder in it, and the bones and head of a little child. About the legs and other parts of it was bound strings and bracelets of fine white beads. There was also by it a little bow, about three quarters long, and some other odd knacks. We brought sundry of the prettiest things away with us, and covered the corpse up again. After this we digged in sundry like places, but found no more corn nor anything else but graves."

While they were thus searching, and disputing whether this embalmed corpse was that of an Indian chief or of a European, two empty wigwams were discovered, and for the first time they saw the homes and furniture of the people who were either to be their neighbours or their enemies.

"The houses were made with long young sapling trees bended, and both ends stuck into the ground. They were made round, like unto an arbour, and covered down to the ground with thick and well-wrought mats; and the door was not over a yard high, made of a mat to open. The chimney was a wide open hole in the top, for which they had a mat to cover it close when they pleased; one might stand and go upright in them. In the midst of them were four little trunches* knocked into the

---

* *Truncheons*, slight poles of hard wood. This rude gridiron was in use among the natives of various parts of America.

ground, and small sticks laid over, on which they hung their pots and what they had to seethe. Round about the fire they lay on mats which are their beds. The houses were double matted; for as they were matted without, so were they within with newer and fairer mats. In the houses we found wooden bowls, trays and dishes, earthen pots, hand baskets made of crabshells wrought together, also an English pail or bucket; it wanted a bail, but it had two iron ears. There was also baskets of sundry sorts, bigger and some lesser, finer and some coarser. Some were curiously wrought with black and white in pretty works, and sundry other of their household stuff. We found also two or three deer's heads, one whereof had been newly killed, for it was still fresh. There was also a company of deer's feet stuck up in the houses, harts' horns and eagles' claws, and sundry such-like things there was; also two or three baskets full of parched acorns, pieces of fish, and a piece of a broiled herring. We found also a little silk grass and a little tobacco seed, with some other seeds which we knew not. Without was sundry bundles of flags and sedge, bulrushes and other stuff to make mats. There was thrust into a hollow tree two or three pieces of venison; but we thought it fitter for the dogs than for us. Some of the best things we took away with us, and left the houses standing still as they were."

It was now getting late, and the tide was going out; so they hastened down to the shallop and returned to the ship. They regretted not having brought some beads and such wares which they might have left in the houses in sign of amity. Though necessity obliged them to help themselves in the absence of the owners, they had no wish to take this corn or anything else of value without making full compensation; and we may imagine that after all they had seen, mere curiosity made them more and more anxious to fall in with these natives, who so persistently kept out of the way.

Some difference of opinion now prevailed among the emigrants as to whether they should settle on Cape Cod, or seek a more favourable situation. The weather was so bad, and they were suffering so much from sickness, that many of them were anxious to spend no more time in deciding; but on the 6th of December some volunteers went in the shallop to make a further examination of the bay. It was bitterly cold, three or four of them were ill, the spray froze on their clothes and made them like coats of iron; it was long before they could round a point which lay not a furlong from the ship. But these bold men persevered in their undertaking, and coasted for several leagues without seeing the mouth of any river. Running water was the thing which they were most desirous to find, as they prudently reflected that ponds might be dried up, and do not seem to have thought of sinking a well. At last they saw some Indians who were cutting up a grampus on the shore, but who as usual ran away at their approach. Landing with some difficulty on a sandy flat, they passed the night, their lodging "such as it was" being only a few miles from the fire by which the Indians were encamped.

Next morning they divided, some going by sea and some on shore, noting that it was "a level soil, though none of the fruitfulest." The latter party followed the footsteps of the Indians on the sand and were led by them into the woods, where they came upon a great burying place, fenced round in part like a churchyard and containing graves of various sizes and degrees of pretension. Near were some empty wigwams, and ground that had been planted, but not that year. How could it be that the natives had withdrawn, as if to make room for these new comers!

At night they met the shallop, gathered firewood, made a barricade, and gladly gave themselves to rest, for they were weary and faint, having eaten nothing all day. About midnight there was an alarm, which made them spring up and fire a couple of muskets, when the noise which had disturbed their sentinels ceased suddenly and was supposed to have been nothing more than the howling of a pack of wolves. But in the morning twilight as they were breakfasting, with their arms for the most part laid on the shore at some little distance, this sound once more rang through the woods, and they knew it for the terrible war whoop. "They are men! Indians! Indians!" cried one of the company, running in, and in a moment the arrows were whistling about their ears. Thus taken by surprise, the Englishmen were in some danger. Some had to dash out under fire to fetch their arms; Miles Standish and three others who had theirs ready flew to the barricade, and let fly two shots; three more were fired from the shallop; the rest of the men on board were heard calling for a light to kindle their matches. One snatched a burning log from the fire and ran with it to them, "which was thought did not a little discourage our enemies." The dim light added to the confusion. The Indians kept under the cover of the trees, whereas the English were exposed beside the blaze of their fire. But Captain Standish behaved with great coolness. He ordered his men not to be in a hurry to fire; and there they stood taking careful aim and starting out of the way of the arrows, till at last Standish himself, it is said, shot the chief in the arm as he exposed it in reaching to his quiver; whereupon he gave an "extraordinary cry" and they all ran away. Carefully posting a guard over the shallop, the English followed for a quarter of a mile, and when they abandoned the pursuit raised a hearty cheer and fired two shots to proclaim their triumph.

Thus ended this "First Encounter," the name of which was given to the place. None of the English were hurt, though some coats hanging up on their barricade were riddled with arrows. They might well say that Providence had once more interfered for their protection. But they seem, taking into account the time and circumstances of the attack, to have shown great courage, and courage of that ready "two o'clock in the morning" order, which Napoleon declared to be so rare among men. It was soon to be seen that no curled and swaggering gallants had such stout hearts as these Puritans.

After giving thanks to God, they got into the

shallop and sailed along the coast with a fair wind. But now they had to do with the elements, worse enemies than the naked savage. It began to snow; the wind rose; the rudder was broken, and they were scarcely able to steer with two oars; while night drew on, and the sea was running rougher and rougher. In this strait they came to Plymouth Bay, at the mouth of which, as they were making all sail to enter, a fierce gust tore away their mast and they were almost lost in a cove full of breakers. But the waves carried them into the landlocked harbour, where they landed upon a little island and spent the night on it in the rain, keeping good watch against Indians. In the morning they found it to be uninhabited, so they stayed here for a day to dry their things and rest. The next day was the sabbath, which they passed in religious exercises.

On Monday the 10th of December they sounded the harbour, which proved excellent for shipping. They marched into the land, and found cornfields, brooks of running water, and all that they desired for a convenient situation. So they returned to the ship with the good news of their success, and it was resolved to settle in this bay, to which the name of Plymouth was given in grateful recollection of the English port that had been the last halting place of their voluntary exile.

The spot where the Pilgrims are said to have first stepped ashore may well have become an object of enthusiasm to their descendants. Poetry and eloquence have cast a halo round that rough stone which saw the beginning of such great things. In various towns of the Union are reverently treasured the smallest fragments of—

The Plymouth Rock, that had been to their feet as a doorstep
Into a world unknown—the corner stone of a nation!

III.

Plymouth, or Patuxet as the natives called it, is a tract of sandy hills and woods where pinetrees are the most common, picturesquely interspersed with streams and basins of water. The soil, which the Pilgrims found already cleared to some extent though not occupied by the Indians, is favourable to the growth of maize, and a strip of richer land runs between the hills and the sea. But the main attractions were the fishing promised them by the bay, and "a very sweet brook" and "delicate springs of as good water as can be drunk."

Two days before Christmas the settlers went on shore and began to fell timber for their building. The houses were laid out in two rows upon the slope of a hill which commanded a wide prospect by sea and land; on the top was made a platform for the ordnance, and in time the position was fortified by a palisade. Each family was to have a separate house and plot of ground, proportioned to its size. The single men attached themselves to one or other of the families, which then numbered nineteen, and every party laboured at its own house, having drawn lots for the situation. Now the woods rang with the sound of axe and saw; some made mortar and some gathered thatch. But the work went on slowly; the ship was obliged to lie a mile and a half from the shore, and the weather was sometimes so rough that communication was impossible. Rain and frost, sickness and fear of the Indians, hindered the builders, and they were seldom able to work more than half the week. The largest building, a "common house" twenty feet square, was being roofed when it unfortunately caught fire through a spark flying into the thatch, and those on board the ship feared that the savages had fallen upon the settlement. Not long after a little house built for the sick was set on fire in the same manner; so early was America establishing its character for conflagrations. Another day a violent storm threatened the safety of the frail erections as well as of the ship. The worst of the winter had passed before the Pilgrims and their stores were securely under cover.

In the meanwhile we have several small incidents chronicled, which are not without amusing features. Two men lose themselves and are obliged to sleep out in the snow, lightly clad, and armed only with the sickles with which they had been cutting sedge. Through the night they hear, as they imagine, the roaring of two "lions," and make ready to hurry up a tree. Their companions go in search of them, and believe them to have been cut off by the Indians; but next day they return in such a state that one of them has to have the shoes cut off his swollen feet. A few days afterwards this poor fellow hobbled out to "use his lame feet," and two of the "lions," now seen to be wolves, ran upon a little spaniel dog which

accompanied him. John Goodman, such was his
name, threw a stick at one of them, whereupon they
ran away but presently came back and "sat both
on their tails grinning at him a good while; and
went their way and left him." Before this a sharp
boy called Francis Billington had from the top of
a tree discovered the lake which is still known by
his name, "the Billington Sea." This Billington
family fills in the early records of the colony a place
quite disproportionate to its merits. The father
was the first person who had to be punished, as
before mentioned. Ten years later, he also enjoyed
the distinction, such as it was, of being the first
man hanged by the Pilgrims; so it is right to
explain that he did not belong to the original congregation, but was one of a few who "shuffled in"
among them during their detention in England.
Another of his sons soon gave a great deal of
trouble by wandering into the woods, and requiring
to have an expedition sent after him to get him out
of the hands of the Indians, who came upon the boy
when he had been living for five days on berries, and
seem to have treated him kindly enough. He was
all "behung with beads" when his friends found
him, whereas he rather deserved to be decorated
with stripes. He was probably the young Billington who had nearly been the destruction of the
whole colony while the Mayflower was lying at
Cape Cod. In his father's absence "he had got
gunpowder, and had shot off a piece or two, and
made squibs"; and these pyrotechnic performances
he carried on beside an open barrel of powder half

full, with part of the contents lying scattered about the cabin, so that it was a wonder the ship was not blown up. Fancy the destinies of New England at the mercy of such a mischievous little monkey! But the greatest events of history may often have hung upon as small a hinge. And if any of us feel the character of the Pilgrim Fathers too solemn and lofty to excite our friendly interest, we shall not be ill pleased to think that they had among them troublesome urchins who liked to climb trees and play with powder, and girls who no doubt may have preferred dolls and skipping ropes to the catechism.

These are but occasional lights upon a sombre picture. There is little trace of complaining, yet it is plain that the settlers suffered terribly. Their living was as poor as their lodging. On Christmas day, of all days in the year, they found their beer at an end and had to content themselves with water, unless when the sailors, who seem to have been better provided, gave them a treat. Drinking water in these days was looked on as a sign of little less than destitution. It is hard to imagine how they lived at all. The shell fish which abounded in the bay seems often to have been their chief resource, and some of us know by experience that "clam chowder" is a more toothsome than wholesome diet. Their little store of corn had to be husbanded for seed. They thought it worth while to commemorate the feast days when such delicacies as a goose or a dried neat's tongue fell to their share, or when one of them shot an eagle which eat "like mutton." They had already been weakened by the long voyage and by bad provisions on board ship; now consumption and scurvy made sad havoc among them. Fortunately the winter seems to have been unusually mild for that country, or not one of them might have lived to tell the tale of their troubles, which they insist on less than on their mercies.

In the most matter of fact way it is recorded that nearly half their number died before the winter was out, and that at one time only six or seven were able to attend to the sick. Tradition says that the graves of the dead were levelled and corn planted over them, to conceal their losses from the Indians. But after all this suffering, when the Mayflower returned to England in April, not one of the Pilgrims sailed in her; they were not the men to turn back after putting their hands to the plough. John Smith, who rather despised the " Brownist " colony, was fain to confess that they showed wonderful patience and endurance.

Though the Indians still kept aloof from friendly intercourse, there was reason to believe that they did not view the settlement with indifference. The smoke of their fires could often be seen, and they could be heard moving through the woods. Some tools which had been left by the workmen at a little distance from the houses were taken away during the night. The colonists began to grow uneasy and to look to their defences. On the 17th of February they held a meeting to establish some military organization, and Miles Standish was formally appointed their captain. As they were thus consulting, two dusky forms appeared upon the top of a hill, not a quarter of a mile off, and made signs to them, whereupon the new captain proved his courage by going out to meet them with a single companion. He laid down his musket in their sight and tried to bring them to a parley, but they fell back and joined a band which were lying behind the hill. It was clearly desirable to have the " great ordnance " mounted without delay. So the sailors brought on shore and helped to drag up the hill this formidable artillery, which seems to have consisted of one six pounder, a *saker* as it was called in those days, a *minion* or four pounder, and two *bases*, which modern warriors would think little better than popguns. The other firearms were carefully seen to, for the wet weather had injured them. Our heroes were of that order who trust in God but do not forget to keep their powder dry. Even when they went to church they marched in military order, summoned by beat of drum; and cannon were mounted on the roof of the building. Happily, however, the attack expected at this time did not take place.

Spring brought brighter days, in a double sense. In the beginning of March there were glimpses of fine weather; the birds sang cheerily in the woods; and for the first time the Pilgrims were visited by a thunderstorm. The 16th was a fair warm day, and they had again come together to hold the meeting for military organization, which we have seen adjourned upon the alarm of Indians. Again, by a curious coincidence, their deliberations were interrupted. A tall naked Indian walked boldly up to the village, passed through the houses, and came straight among them, exclaiming "*Welcome Englishmen!*"

How great must have been their surprise and delight to find that this man could speak broken English, which he had picked up among the fishermen on the coast! He had evidently acquired some familiarity with English habits, for he asked for beer, but was as well pleased to get "strong water, and biscuit, and butter, and cheese and pudding." The settlers were in a mood to make much of their new friend, whose name was Samoset; and he for his part seemed willing to prolong his visit even longer than they cared to keep him, fearing that he might be playing the spy. They dressed him in a "horseman's coat," and spent all afternoon interrogating him. Now for the first time was explained the mysterious conduct of their Indian neighbours and the deserted state in which they had found that part of the country.

For three or four years a mysterious pestilence had been raging along the coast of New England. Whole districts were depopulated. Some tribes became almost extinct. The Massachusetts, it is said, were reduced from 30,000 to 300 fighting men. A traveller found the forests strewn with skulls and bones so thickly as to recall the name of Golgotha. Patuxet, where the Pilgrims had settled, was one of the many places from which men, women, and children had been swept away. The superstitious

Indians connected this calamity with the appearance of a comet, which in Europe also had seemed to presage some dire event. The God-fearing Puritans conceived with awe that the inscrutable power of the Almighty had verily cleared this land of its natural inhabitants to make room for the chosen race who should fulfil the destinies of Heaven. Disease had done for them the work which elsewhere had to be done by the sword. How would they have given thanks with trembling, if they could have foreseen that this fearful mortality was but the warning of that fate by which the Indian tribes have dwindled and perished before the path of the higher race!

The work of godless man too was now disclosed. This neighbourhood had already been visited by an English trader named Hunt, who had treacherously kidnapped a number of the natives and carried them away to sell for slaves. The cruel selfishness of this villain had made white men odious and feared among the Indians; hence their holding aloof from the new colony. If strength and courage had not been wanting to them, they would probably have attempted to slaughter these innocent settlers in revenge for the injury done by their countryman.

Such was Samoset's information, and the Pilgrims were able most heartily to assure him that they were no man-stealers, and, giving him presents, sent him to invite their neighbours to trade and intercourse. This friendly treatment had soon the desired effect. The Indians began to pay visits, which were not always very well timed. The first call was made by some half a dozen "proper men," whose dress of skins recalled the Irish, while their complexion seemed like that of the gipsies. Unfortunately they came on the Sabbath day, and not only sang and danced, but proposed to trade, to the scandal and perplexity of their grave hosts, who got rid of them as politely as possible and asked them to come again. This marks the strictness of Puritan principles; for to establish a friendly understanding with the natives was a matter of the utmost importance to them. Probably indeed some misunderstanding was caused on this occasion, for the Indians did not return according to their promise; and their next visit had a semblance of reconnoitring with hostile intent. Strange to say, the English were for the third time attempting to bring their military meeting to a conclusion, when for the third time they were interrupted by the appearance of scouts close to the village. And next day they met again for the same purpose, but had scarcely been an hour assembled before Samoset arrived, bringing another Indian called Tisquantum or Squanto, who on more than one account was most welcome. He was the only surviving native of Patuxet, who could therefore grant the new comers the just title which it was their desire to obtain to the land on which they had settled. He was also one of the very men who had been stolen by Hunt. Fortunately this buccaneer had not been able to carry out his intention of selling his victims in Spain. They had been set at liberty through the intervention of certain pious monks; and Squanto had found his way to London, where he lived for a time in the house of a merchant in Cornhill, and learned to speak the language after a fashion. He would seem to have been well treated, for being now returned to his native country he willingly sought out the English settlers and henceforth attached himself to their fortunes.

These two came to announce the approach of no less a personage than Massasoit, the chief or sachem of the neighbouring tribe of Wampanoags, who, in fact, soon appeared on the top of the opposite hill, attended by sixty of his braves. At first they hesitated to come nearer, and the English governor was equally unwilling to trust himself among them; but after some parley a hostage was left in their hands, and the Indian chief came over the brook which was the boundary of the settlement, bringing twenty of his men, who, according to the etiquette already established for such occasions, left their bows and arrows behind them. The Pilgrims wondered at the fantastically painted forms of these visitors, and all their Indian stolidity did not prevent them from showing a childlike astonishment at the strange sights, the rumours of which had excited a curiosity not unmixed with fear. The "king," as the English called him, was seen to tremble as he sat beside the governor upon a couch of state, hastily improvised out of a green rug and three or four cushions. There may have been other reasons for this discomposure. After mutual embraces his white brother had called for "strong water," and drunk to him, and then he had taken a good pull at the cup, "that made him sweat all the while after." He is described as a well made man in the prime of life, "grave of countenance and spare of speech; in attire little or nothing differing from the rest of his followers, only in a great chain of white bone beads about his neck; and at it, behind his neck, hangs a little bag of tobacco." On his bosom he wore a long knife hanging in a string. His face was painted a dull red, and all his head was oiled, so that he "looked greasily."

The claims of hospitality and curiosity being satisfied, the parties proceeded to business and soon agreed to the terms of a treaty, which were:

1. That neither he nor any of his should injure or do hurt to any of our people.

2. And if any of his did hurt to any of ours, he should send the offender that we might punish him.

3. That if any of our tools were taken away when our people were at work, he should cause them to be restored; and if ours did any harm to any of his, we would do the like to them.

4. If any did unjustly war against him, we would aid him; if any did war against us, he should aid us.

5. He should send to his neighbour confederates to certify them of this, that they might not wrong us, but might be likewise comprised in the conditions of peace.

6. That when their men came to us they should leave their bows and arrows behind them, as we should do our pieces when we came to them.

Lastly, that doing thus King James would esteem of him as his friend and ally.

This agreement being concluded, the king was conducted across the brook, and his brother Quadaquina came in turn to see for himself the remarkable establishment, of which some taste had been sent out to him while waiting, in the shape of refreshments and ornaments. He also was treated with all attention and friendliness. He was evidently not at ease till the guns were put out of sight, but " he marvelled much at our trumpet, and some of his men would sound it as well as they could." So much delighted indeed were some of the Indians with all they saw, that it was found difficult to clear the place of them; and they spent the night in the woods close by, where next day Miles Standish, ever foremost in venturesome affairs, returned their visit, and was hospitably received according to their fashion.

A trade in furs was now opened; and the Wampanoags, anxious to secure the assistance of these powerful allies against the hostile tribe of the Narragansetts, showed every disposition to keep up friendly relations. Squanto remained with the English, and was of the greatest use to them as interpreter.

More hopefully then, they were at last able on March 23rd to settle their military and civil affairs, making such arrangements and passing such laws as seemed desirable in the condition of their little state, and re-electing Mr. John Carver as governor. Unhappily the effect of their early hardships had not yet passed away; death was still busy among them. A month had not ended before they were firing a funeral salute over their honoured governor's grave.

William Bradford was chosen as his successor, and being re-elected from year to year held this office during a great part of his life, though he and others of the chief men would seem to have been so far from coveting power, that it was found necessary to affix a penalty to the refusal of office duly bestowed by the electors.

IV.

The rest of the year passed by uneventfully. Under the genial warmth of an American summer, the Pilgrims recovered their health and enjoyed the fruits and herbs which grew wild around their new home. By excursions among the Indians they extended their knowledge of the country and its people. Several of the chiefs entered into a league with them*, following the example of Massasoit; and when the Narragansetts threatened this chief, the English fulfilled the terms of the treaty by making a successful demonstration in his favour with an army of ten men, who scarcely met with any resist-

---

* They seem to have promised more than friendship, if they understood the terms of the following formal document: "Sept. 13, A.D. 1621. Know all men by these presents, that we, whose names are underwritten, do acknowledge ourselves to be the loyal subjects of King James, King of Great Britain, France, and Ireland, Defender of the Faith, etc. In witness whereof, and as a testimonial of the same, we have subscribed our names or marks, as followeth:

   Ohquamehud.   *Chikkatabak.*
   Cawnacome.   *Quadaquina.*
   Obbatinnua.   *Huttmoiden.*
   Nattawahunt.   *Apannow.*"
   Caunbatant.

ance, and struck panic into the enemy by discharging two pieces at random. A visit to Massasoit showed them that he had more to gain from their friendship than they from his, so great was the misery to which he was often reduced. He was able to treat their two ambassadors to but a single meal, consisting of two fishes, divided among some forty persons. This was the only food they tasted for more than thirty hours. On the night of their arrival, "late it grew, but victuals he offered none, for indeed he had not any." The visitors had to be content to stay their stomachs with tobacco after a long day's walk; and when they retired to rest they were put to sleep six in a bed, "so that we were worse weary of our lodging than of our journey." They were kept awake by vermin and mosquitos, as well as by the barbarous sounds of savage music. Having lain thus two nights with scarcely a wink of sleep, they hastened to get home with all the strength remaining to them after this scant hospitality, fearing that they would fall ill if they stayed any longer. If Rousseau had ever been the guest of an Indian king, he could scarcely have written his glowing encomiums of the innocent pleasures and romantic perfections of savage life.

The settlers would not have failed to exert themselves, even if it had not been so evident that they would have to depend on their own exertions. While some traded with the Indians for beaver and other furs, the rest busied themselves in fishing and agriculture. Besides six acres of barley and peas, they planted twenty acres of Indian corn. Instructed by Squanto, they manured the ground after the native manner, with a kind of fish called *alewives*, which in spring crowded up the streams to spawn in the ponds and could be caught by thousands. An excellent harvest was the result. When it was gathered in the governor sent out four men to shoot game, and a thanksgiving festival was held, at which Massasoit and ninety of his men were entertained for three days, contributing five deer as their share of the good cheer.

Things looked so prosperous that the Pilgrims wrote home, warmly urging their friends to join them without delay. They described the country and its inhabitants in high terms of praise. Industry only was necessary to secure a competent livelihood. Men indeed, who looked after "great riches, ease, pleasures, dainties, and jollity in this world," were advised to stay away; but those who did not mind roughing it a little might be assured of a moderate degree of comfort, along with peace and religious liberty, and not without a share of wholesome and honest pleasures, if the greatness of the work, to found a kingdom for Christ and spread the knowledge of the gospel among the heathen, were not enticement enough. As for those who feared the tediousness of the voyage, the danger of pirates, the treachery of the savages, " it were well for such men if they were in heaven. For who can show them a place in this world where iniquity shall not compass them at the heels, and where they shall have a day without grief or a lease of life for a moment?" Whoever still thinks of these separatists as a set of gloomy visionary fanatics, has only to know more of them at this period, to see that their religious zeal was hardened to a most practical temper by qualities now recognised as sturdy manliness and sober common sense.

But the account which they sent home during the summer proved too favourable; and when the second batch of emigrants arrived in November, ill provided with food in expectation of the plenty which had been described to them, they found that another season of dearth had set in, and it was hard work for the colonists to feed their friends when they had not enough for themselves. Not till cattle had been introduced, were they secure from want. Another important step was the establishment of salt works, by means of which they were able to preserve their provisions. It was quite true that at certain times of the year they had plenty, of fruits and fish in the summer, of corn in autumn, of wild fowl when the cold weather began to come on; and if we have never reflected on the economy of civilisation, which by a widespread and complicated machinery provides us regularly and continually with the productions of the earth, we may be surprised to hear such a frequent tale of scarcity among those early settlers in a country abounding with animal life and vegetation. We must remember that at first the colonists lacked experience and means to preserve the food which nature dealt out to them in alternate moods of stint and profusion. The Indians, we have seen, with all their knowledge of the country and cunning in the chase, were often reduced to the greatest distress; and this precarious mode of life had taught them to endure long fits of abstinence, as well as to eat enormously when food came in their way. So the English were yet to find themselves often in the most pressing straits; but they never lost hope, and never failed to be relieved in some manner which they took for a special interposition of Providence. Now a ship passed by from which they were able to buy supplies; now their hunters made a prize and brought back meat to their starving comrades. And throughout their sufferings they were sustained by godly patience and unselfish unity of spirit. If any fainted, there were strong arms to keep him from falling. They breathed courage into each other's hearts by friendly exhortation and appeals to their high purpose and calling. "Now, brethren, I pray you, remember yourselves, and know that you are not in a retired, monastical course, but have given your names and promises one to another, and covenanted here to cleave together in the service of God and the king. What then must you do? May you live as retired hermits, and look after nobody? Nay, you must seek still the wealth of one another, and inquire, as David: How liveth such a man? How is he clad? How is he fed? He is my brother, my associate; we ventured our lives together here, and had a hard brunt of it; and we are in league together. Is his labour harder than mine? Surely I will ease him. Hath he no bed to lie on? Why, I have two; I'll lend him one. Hath he no apparel? Why, I have two suits, I'll give him one of them. Eats he coarse fare, bread and water, and I have better? Why, surely we will part stakes. He is as good a man as I, and we are bound each to other; so that his wants must be my wants, his sorrows my sorrows, his sickness my sickness, and his welfare my welfare; for I am as he is." Such was the genuine homespun doctrine out of which was woven the stuff that wore so well through many a rough winter. Can it be that the men who taught thus and strove to follow this teaching were persecuted as criminals, and driven from a Christian land where Laud and Buckingham were held in honour?

Unfortunately, in the second year the relations of the colony with the Indians became troubled; and much time, that might have been more profitably spent, had to be given to strengthening their position by a palisade and a fort. The Narragansetts had hitherto been wavering in their policy; but in January, 1622, they sent a messenger with a bundle of new arrows, wrapped in a rattlesnake's skin, which the English were told meant a declaration of war. After consultation they returned the skin stuffed with powder and bullets, and this is said to have so terrified the hostile chief that he would not touch it nor allow it to remain in his country. Sincerely desirous of maintaining peace, the Pilgrims thought it best to carry themselves fearlessly in presence of the danger to which they were far from being indifferent, and were not to be deterred from their trading journeys by rumours that the Narragansetts to the south, and the Massachusetts to the north, were conspiring to destroy them. Suspicions were also aroused that their neighbours the Wampanoags were about to prove unfaithful.

The worst of it was that they were uncertain what to believe. They were dependent for information upon Squanto and another Indian, named Hobbamock, who had attached himself to them. These men showed some of the jealousy which is prone to exist between two factotums, and were found contradicting each other, to the serious perplexity of their patrons. It seemed that Squanto had a mind to play the great man in the eyes of his countrymen, on the strength of his position among the English, and tried to use his influence with them for his private ends. He gave out that the Pilgrims kept the plague in their cellars and could dispense it at will; the moral of this fiction of course was that it would be well to be on good terms with one who enjoyed the privilege of such familiarity with these powerful strangers. There was reason to suppose that he aimed at stirring up war against Massasoit, his natural sovereign, hoping to advance himself at the expense of his own people. These designs coming to light, the governor "sharply reproved" him; but the plain truth was that they could not do without Squanto; he was their "tongue," as the poetic diction of the Indians put it. This consideration did not prevent Massasoit from being jealous and angry when he perceived the ambition of his presuming subject. The chief insisted on Squanto being surrendered to him for just punishment, according to the treaty. The governor was at a loss how to answer. He ought to give up the man who had made so much mischief, yet he scrupled to hand over to a cruel death one who had done and could yet do so much for the English. In the end he made some excuse for delay, and the interpreter contrived to make his peace with Massasoit. But before long he fell ill and died, desiring his white friends to pray for him that he might go to their heaven. In spite of his faults he had been a valuable friend to the Pilgrims, and was sorely missed by them, for they seem to have been slow in acquiring the Indian language.

During this summer (1622) news came of the terrible massacre of the English in Virginia, which did not tend to reassure the Plymouth colony as to their own safety. Soon they found themselves exposed to danger in the most unexpected way, by the bad conduct of their own countrymen. A merchant named Weston, one of those who had been forward in promoting their undertaking, seeing it now likely to be pecuniarily successful, resolved to set up a colony of his own, and sent out fifty or sixty persons in two ships, which arrived about the beginning of July. These were adventurers of the ordinary kind, neither professing nor practising the high rule of conduct which was a bond of union to the Pilgrims. Yet the Plymouth men received them kindly and entertained the whole party till they found a settlement for themselves at a place to the north, to which the name of Weymouth was given. The ungrateful guests repaid this hospitality by stealing the corn of their hosts while still green. It was quite clear that they and the old settlers were not likely to get on well together; but the Pilgrims seem to have honestly done their best to help the new comers, trying to make allowance for their moral deficiencies, and fearing that their ignorance and rashness would lead them into trouble.

So indeed it proved. The men who had pilfered from their own friends were not restrained from robbing the Indians, who soon came to Plymouth with complaints of their wrongs. It was less likely that friendly remonstrance would be effectual with these fellows than that the discredit of their doings would be reflected on their countrymen. The English name had hitherto commanded respect; now Weston's colony brought it into ill odour, the effects of which were soon felt both at Plymouth and Weymouth. It was perhaps a pity that the two companies joined in common expeditions to trade for corn; but blood is thicker than water, and fellow countrymen could not be expected to stand aloof from each other so far away from home. It must also be said that there were some honest men in the Weymouth colony, who were not insensible to the reproaches of their neighbours, and tried to put a stop to the ill doing of their associates. The stocks and the whipping post were set up; but, as usual, the fear of punishment was not enough to produce good morals among bad men. One was even hanged for stealing a cap full of corn from an Indian, an example which was wholly useless when the colony was already at the point of ruin. The poor Indians, as might be expected, did not fail to retaliate as they could. They were found stealing, in turn, from the Plymouth people, as well as from the real wrong doers; but Miles Standish carried things with such a high hand that the stolen articles were brought back, and in one instance at least a chief came to say that he had himself punished the culprit.

By March, 1623, Weston's men had eaten all their corn, leaving none for seed. It was in vain they tried to use the credit of the other colony. The Indians would now neither lend nor sell to them. In this strait they proposed to take their corn by violence, as Captain John Smith, we must fear, might not have hesitated to do under similar circumstances. But when they consulted the Plymouth people, the latter strongly dissuaded them from any such attempt. Apart from the sinfulness of it, and the displeasure which would be called forth at home by bloodshed in such a cause, it would be very bad policy for the sake of a temporary supply to destroy the confidence of the Indians for ever. The Weymouth colonists were by this time in such a weak state that they could not but listen to this reasonable advice. As a last resource their governor sailed to the coast of Maine, to seek aid from the English fishing vessels by which it was now frequented. The Pilgrims, though ill able to spare from their small store, gave him provisions for this journey; and during his absence they were obliged to take active steps to save both their neighbours and themselves from destruction. They became aware of this danger through an act of friendly attention shown to Massasoit.

News came that this chief was lying seriously ill, and also that a Dutch ship had been driven on shore beside his dwelling. The Indians were known to attach great importance to the custom of being visited by their friends in sickness, and it was thought right to send some one to observe this kindly custom in Massasoit's case, as well as to communicate with the Dutchmen. So Edward Winslow, one of the chroniclers of the colony, set out upon this double duty, with Hobbamock for his guide, and as a companion a certain "Master John Hampden, a gentleman of London, who then wintered with us, and desired much to see the country." It has been supposed that this John Hampden was no other than the celebrated English patriot; but he is a great deal more likely to have had a namesake of a roving disposition than to have been absent from his post in parliament when such great affairs were on hand in Old England.

On the way the three travellers heard that in both objects of their journey they were frustrated. The Dutch ship had got off, and Massasoit was reported to be dead. The Indian guide freely gave way to his grief, for the attachment of these people to their chiefs was often as sincere and affectionate as any advocate for the Divine right of kings could have desired. The English were grieved on a more selfish account. This chief had stood their friend, but if he were dead they feared his people might be moved by other counsels; indeed his probable successor, Conbatant, was known to be ill disposed towards them. They thought it best, however, to go boldly on, hoping to be able to conciliate the goodwill of the new sachem, though after all that had passed between them it was possible he might desire rather to do them a mischief. "Leaving the event to God," they made straight for the lion's den, Conbatant's own house, whom they found not at home, but were kindly entertained by the *squaw sachem*, his wife.

Here they heard that Massasoit was still alive, though his death was expected every moment. As soon as they received this news by a messenger whom they had sent to inquire the truth, they hastily went on to the chief's house, where they arrived at night, and found themselves not too late to assist at a most noisy deathbed.

The house was so full of people that the new comers could scarcely make their way in. Round the patient had gathered all the *pow-wows* of the neighbourhood, an order of men who among the Indian tribes exercised the double functions of priest and physician. These ignorant impostors were called in to conjure out the evil spirit which was believed to possess the sick man. This duty they performed by dancing and yelling frantically around him, hideously disguised in paint and feathers; they were accustomed to throw their limbs into the most horrible contortions, to strain their eyes almost out of the sockets, to sweat, to foam at the mouth, till they were exhausted by the violence of their exertions, which they would keep up for hours, while the spectators surrounding them with admiration joined in the chorus of their yells and shrieks.

Sometimes they would administer herbs, stroke or chafe the afflicted part, or pretend to suck out the ailment; but these maniacal spells were the chief feature of their treatment, and Winslow and his companions found a band of them in full swing, "making such a hellish noise as it distempered us that were well, and therefore unlike to ease him that was sick."

With all their superstition the Indians had much respect for the wisdom of the white men. The pow-wows brought their din to an end, and Winslow was allowed to approach the bed. The old chief held out his hand and faintly bade him farewell. But the visitor, though he knew little of physic, thought something might still be done for the sick man's comfort at least, and addressed himself to play the doctor after a more sensible fashion. Putting a little piece of "confection of conserves" upon the point of his knife, he forced it through Massasoit's teeth, and the chief swallowed the juice of it, to the delight of those about him. Winslow then made the usual inquiries as to when the patient had last slept, eaten, and so forth, looked at his tongue, found it so much swollen that he could swallow nothing, washed out his mouth, got down a little more of the confection, and dissolved some in water, which the sick man presently drank. This slight nourishment wrought a wonderful improvement; the chief, to the astonishment of those who had given him up for lost, began to recover his sight, his voice, and his appetite. Winslow sent off a letter to the plantation, desiring that there might

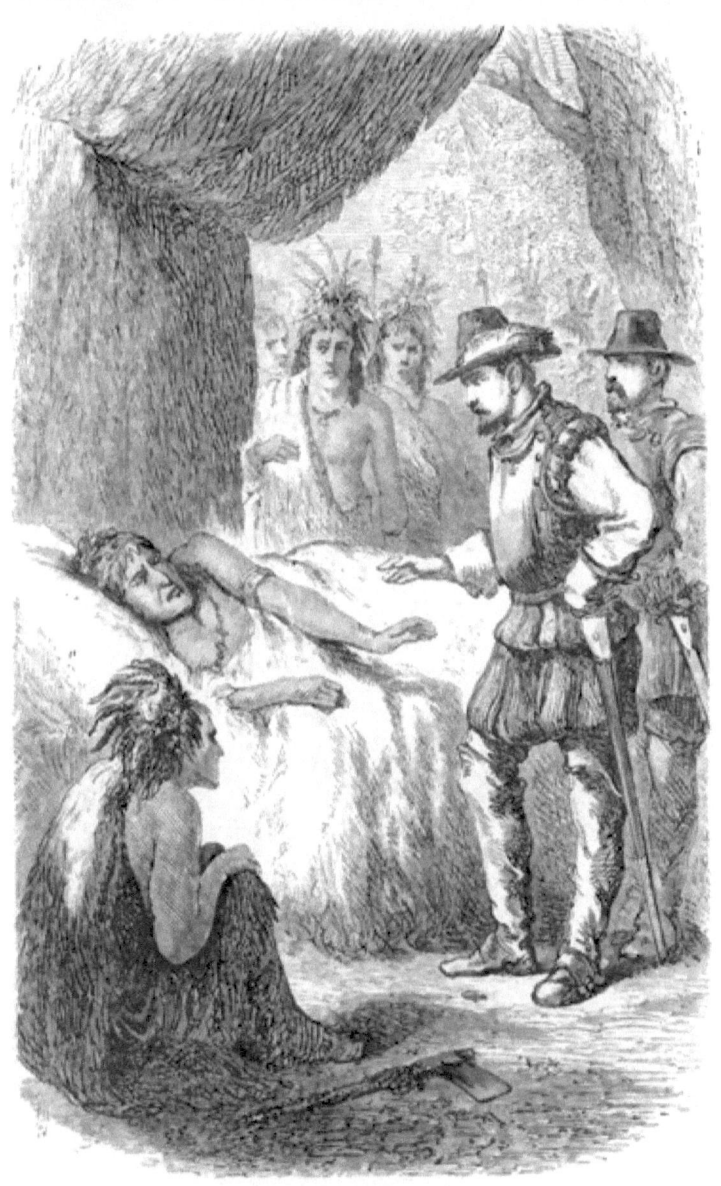

The Sick Chief.

Page 220.

be sent at once a bottle of drink, some chickens, and other articles of food suitable for invalids, and whatever physic their surgeon might think to be indicated by the symptoms described.

In the morning Massasoit was so much better that he was calling out for broth, such as he had once tasted at Plymouth. His English visitor was as little of a cook as of a physician, but he did his best with corn, strawberry leaves, and sassafras root, boiled in a pipkin, of which concoction the patient drank a pint, and desired a duck or a goose to follow. Winslow succeeded in shooting one, and Massasoit, disregarding all advice, ate so greedily that he made himself sick, and his nose burst out bleeding, which among the Indians was held for a sure symptom of death. Yet by care and nursing he now recovered rapidly, and when the chickens arrived desired that they might be kept for breeding, as his stomach no longer required to be tempted by such dainties.

This unexpected cure did not fail to send up the credit of the English, nor was the boldness of two men in trusting themselves among the Indians without good effect. In the warmth of his gratitude Massasoit revealed that the Massachusetts were plotting to rouse the other tribes to fall upon the strangers in both colonies. He himself, he said, had been solicited to join this conspiracy, but had refused; and he now advised his friends, if they valued their safety, to anticipate the blow by attacking the main instigators of the intended mischief, and striking terror into the rest before they could move. With this important information they returned home.

The warning was not too early. At this very time, as was afterwards known, Captain Miles Standish had a narrow escape of being murdered while on a journey. He owed his safety to the fact of the weather being so cold that he could not sleep all night, but kept moving about the fire, so that the would-be assassin had no opportunity of taking him unawares. His death was to have been the signal for an attack upon his companions.

If the Indians meant fighting they were right to begin by an attempt to cut off the doughty commander of the Pilgrims' little army. Miles Standish was a veritable man of war, of the John Smith stamp, rather than like the grave and scrupulous men with whom he had cast his lot. He had been a soldier in the Low Countries, and there had made the acquaintance of Robinson's congregation, whose high character he seems to have respected while he was unable to enter into their religious zeal. It is said that he never became a member of the church in the service of which he played such a valiant part. The Pilgrims, while owning their obligations to him, had to confess with sorrow that the old Adam had much to do with his prowess. "A little chimney is soon fired; so was the Plymouth captain, a man of very little stature, yet of a very hot and angry temper." He nearly came to blows with a company of his own countrymen, who landed on Cape Ann and took possession of a fishing stage, claimed by the Pilgrim colony. So we need not expect to find the short choleric captain showing much meekness or forbearance towards the Indians in the complications which were now to be dealt with.

On March 23rd was held the annual court meeting of the colony, the year for business purposes being then considered to begin on Lady Day. By this time the governor had received further information of the intended treachery, and he laid the matter before the whole company for their decision. It was indeed a difficult question to reconcile the principles of the gospel of peace with the steps that seemed demanded by consideration for their own safety. "We knew no means to deliver our countrymen and preserve ourselves, than by returning their malicious and cruel purposes upon their own heads, and causing them to fall into the same pit they had digged for others; though it much grieved us to shed the blood of those whose good we ever intended and aimed at, as a principal in all our proceedings."

In the end the meeting came to the wise conclusion that this was not a matter for public debate, and left the responsibility of taking hostile operations in the hands of the governor, his assistant, and the captain. They resolved that the latter should go to Weymouth, warn the colonists of their danger, and, as it was impossible to deal with the Indians except by stratagem, should feign friendly intentions till he had an opportunity of judging of their designs and effectually punishing them; he was specially empowered to take the head of a certain Massachusett brave, named Wituwamat, "a notable insulting villain, one who had formerly imbrued his hands in the blood of English and French, and had often boasted of his own valour and derided their weakness, especially because, as he said, they died crying, making sour faces, more like children than men." For this service Captain Standish was to take as many men "as he thought sufficient to make his party good against all the Indians in the Massachusett Bay." Eight men was the number which he thought sufficient, and he refused to take more, fearing lest the enemy might be alarmed and not give him a fair chance of coming to blows with them. Reluctantly and considerately this measure had been determined upon; its execution was well left in the hands of one who would be sure to carry it out with vigour and decision.

Before the little army set out, one of the Weston colony came with a most lamentable account of the state of his companions, who were now suffering the worst results of their idleness and improvidence. They had separated into three companies, with scarcely any powder and shot left, and were living wherever they could get the least scrap of subsistence. Some had run away to live among the Indians; the rest seemed to have lost all self respect, and from threatening and contempt had come down to a helpless condition, in which they submitted to be insulted and wronged in their turn by their savage neighbours, to whom many had sold their clothes and hired themselves as servants, and were now on the point of starving from cold and hunger. This was the swaggering band which had sneered at the Puritan colony, declaring that with their wives and children the latter would not be able to defend themselves, and no doubt making great fun of the prayers and sermons of the "saints," who were supposed so unfitted for scenes of peril and adventure. The event must have made the Weymouth planters a little ashamed of themselves, if they had grace enough to be capable of shame.

Arriving at Weymouth by sea, the captain's first visit was to the ship in which Weston's colony had come, and which lay now idle in the creek. He found no one on board, not even a dog was to be seen. Upon firing a musket, however, the master of the ship and some other famished wretches appeared upon the shore, where they had been gathering ground nuts and roots. Their misery seemed to have reached the point of indifference. Unarmed and careless of danger, they were offering themselves an easy prey to the Indians. The captain passed on to the plantation, where the leaders of the party were to be found, and informed them of the cause and purpose of his coming, offering them an asylum at Plymouth, and desiring them to draw together and keep at home, till he had a good opportunity of punishing their enemies. They could not but thankfully acknowledge these friendly intentions, as an earnest of which a pint of Indian corn was served out daily to each of them.

Bad weather and the suspicions which his dissembling did not prevent the Indians from enter-

taining, delayed the opportunity which the captain
desired. But soon, growing bolder, some of the
pineses, or braves, began to come to the plantation,
" where they would whet and sharpen the points of
their knives before his face, and use many other
insulting gestures and speeches." Among these
threatening boasters were the doomed Wituwamat,
and another brave called Pecksuot. The former
bragged of the excellency of his knife, saying
meaningly that by-and-by it should eat but not
speak. "Also Pecksuot, being a man of greater
stature than the captain, told him, though he were
a great captain, yet he was but a little man;
'and,' said he, 'though I be no sachem, yet I am
a man of great strength and courage.'" Little
men are apt to be sensitive to allusions of this
kind; but if Miles Standish's bile was roused, he
swallowed it down for the meanwhile, waiting the
time when he should be able to make a most
effectual example. But he did not wait long.

" On the next day, seeing he could not get many
of them together at once, and this Pecksuot and
Wituwamat both together, with another man, and
a youth of some eighteen years of age, which was
brother to Wituwamat, and, villain like, trod in his
steps, daily putting many tricks upon the weaker
sort of men, and having about as many of his own
company in a room with them, [he] gave the word
to his men, and, the door being fast shut, began
himself with Pecksuot, and snatching his own knife
from his neck, though with much struggling, killed
him therewith, the point whereof he had made as

sharp as a needle, and ground the back also to an edge. Wituwamat and the other man the rest killed, and took the youth, whom the captain caused to be hanged. But it is incredible how many wounds these two pineses received before they died, not making any fearful noise, but catching at their weapons and striving to the last. Hobbamock stood by all this time as a spectator, and meddled not, observing how our men demeaned themselves in this action. All being here ended, he brake forth into these speeches to the captain: 'Yesterday Pecksuot, bragging of his own strength and stature, said, though you were a great captain you were yet but a little man; but to-day I see you are big enough to lay him on the ground.'"

Some Indian women were at the same time taken prisoners. Standish would not allow the least injury to be done them, but he ordered them to be detained for a short time, lest they should convey a warning to their friends. Three more of the enemy were thus taken by surprise and killed, but one managed to escape and give the alarm. The captain, however, took the field with some half dozen men, and, after beating the country for some time, was successful in falling in with a band of those whom he sought. According to the tactics so often to be practised in Indian warfare, both parties made a dash for a hill which lay near them. The English gained this advantage, whereupon the Indians retreated, and in their usual fashion tried to keep up a running fight from behind the trunks of trees. A bold charge soon drove them into the shelter of a swamp, from which they refused to emerge, though the captain stood taunting their chief, and daring him to come out and fight like a man, after all his loud boasting. They stole away through the thickets, where the English could not safely follow them.

As nothing more could be done, the captain now returned home, taking a few of Weston's men, who volunteered to join the colony at Plymouth, while the majority of them chose to go after their leader to the fishing vessels in which they hoped to get a passage home to England. Miles Standish somewhat contemptuously told them that he would undertake to hold their plantation with a smaller number of men than they were, but he gave them food and saw them safely off; no doubt thinking in his heart that the country was well rid of such a helpless and mischievous crew. Thus was this colony broken up within a year of beginning with boasts of their superior strength and worldly wisdom.

When the victorious party came to Plymouth, they found the fort now finished, and the head of Wituwamat was set up on it, after the barbarous custom by which the heads of the Pretender's adherents were exposed on Temple Bar more than a century later. The fort had already been "hanselled" by an Indian prisoner, who for the first time was chained up there on suspicion of having to do with the conspiracy. This man made a full confession of the design, and was released to be sent to the chief of the Massachusetts with a message, desiring him to take warning from what had happened and to deliver up three Englishmen who were still in his hands, else his country would be made too hot to hold him.

For a long time no answer came to this message, the Indians being thoroughly cowed and afraid to trust themselves near the plantation. At last a squaw ventured herself; the English had always been most careful not to maltreat women, who, as they generally served for drudges, now became useful as ambassadors. She, on the part of Obtakiest the chief, expressed great sorrow that he had killed the Englishmen before the governor's message reached him. He was now fain to make his peace, but so little expected to be allowed to do so that he had forsaken his dwelling, and was wandering about from place to place, afraid from day to day of being pursued by the English vengeance. His tribe and their confederates were equally apprehensive. They took to the swamps; they were afraid to plant their fields; and many of them perished from disease and hunger, so that they feared the God of the English was offended with them and would destroy them in His anger.

By this bold blow Miles Standish had secured the colony for many years to come against such a danger as had befallen their brethren in Virginia. But when their pastor at Leyden heard of these martial doings, he found them scarcely consistent with the spirit of the gospel, and desired his flock to think seriously about their captain's readiness with the sword. "He hoped the Lord had sent him among them for good, if they used him right; but he doubted whether there was not wanting that tenderness of the life of man made after God's image which was meet," writes good Mr. Robinson, whose lights were in more respects than one in advance of his age, and concludes: "oh, how happy a thing had it been that you had converted some before you killed any!"

The behaviour and fate of Weston's colony was a lesson not thrown away on the Plymouth people; they saw how such neighbours were likely to be the ruin of others as well as of themselves. They have been blamed for the peremptory manner in which they henceforth got rid of uncongenial spirits who found their way among them. But unity of sentiment was absolutely necessary for the public weal. Their position was a new and undefined one; in strict law they had no right to administer justice. They held their lands, not by a charter from the king, but by a patent in the hands of a company of merchants, most of whom had little sympathy with the religious earnestness of the settlers, but looked on their labours merely as the means of gain. These merchants were unwilling to send over Mr. Robinson from Leyden, and in his stead tried to force upon the colony a minister of "heretical and papistical" views; that is to say, a man favourable to the church establishment, and one indeed whose moral character proved to be no credit to any church. As might be expected, the Pilgrims soon sent him ignominiously about his business. Three heifers and a bull that came over with him "did the land certainly better service than ever was done by him," such was their opinion. He is said to have been almost literally *kicked* out of the colony through a double line of soldiers, who accelerated his progress with the butt ends of their muskets. Content for the meanwhile with the ministry of Elder Brewster, they waited in hopes that their beloved pastor would find means to join them. But before he could see this promised land he died at Leyden; and in 1629 the Pilgrims for the first time chose a minister to their mind. It is a mark of their respect for this office that all this time Brewster scrupled to dispense the sacraments, though he efficiently performed the other services of religion.

This was but one of several inconveniences arising out of their relations with the mother country. Their patent was taken out, as a matter of form, in the name of a Mr. John Pierce, who, when the colony bid fair to prosper, bethought himself of claiming his legal rights, and went the length of embarking with the intention of playing lord proprietary over the Pilgrims. Luckily perhaps for both parties, his first taste of the sea was not such as to encourage him to proceed. He transferred his patent to the whole company, whose rights the colonists were after a time able to buy up, agreeing to pay £200 for nine years, and thus became their own masters. And for the weakness of human nature it was found better to abandon the plan of common labour; each man received a separate piece of ground to be worked at his own risk and profit.

So now the colony and the colonists were practically independent. Slowly but surely they took root in the rugged soil of Massachusetts, and before long saw kindred shoots springing up around them on every side.

The Pilgrim Fathers, it should be remembered, were not the main body who settled New England. They were the advance guard of an army which followed them in a few years, and spread over all the coast while their little plantation did not yet contain more than a few hundred souls. But they have rightly been held in special honour by all the children of their adopted country. In the words of one of the greatest historians of America: "they formed the mould for the civil and religious character of its institutions. Enduring every hardship themselves, they were the servants of posterity, the benefactors of succeeding generations. In the history of the world many pages are devoted to commemorate the men who have besieged cities, subdued provinces, or overthrown empires. In the eye of reason and of truth, a colony is a better offering than a victory; the citizens of the United States should rather cherish the memory of those who founded a state on the basis of democratic liberty, the fathers of the country, the men who, as they first trod the soil of the New World, scattered the seminal principles of republican freedom and national independence."

THE SETTLERS OF NEW ENGLAND.

I.

By this time the northern coasts of America were becoming better known, and men of business began to understand that money might be made here by the prosaic occupations of fishing and fur trading as surely, if more slowly, as from the gold mines of the south. John Smith's constant preaching to this effect was listened to when Englishmen saw how the French traders prospered, for whom the gallant explorers De Monts and Champlain had opened up the shores of the St. Lawrence. The western fishermen, as we have seen, had pushed the limit of their summer voyages to the coasts of Maine; and Dutch ships were also frequenting the harbours of New England, which was soon to find a New Holland rising between it and Virginia.

So now the projects of English colonisation, which for some years had hung fire, began once more to be stirred. The Plymouth company was revived, and to forty persons the king gave away all the land between 40° and 48° north latitude; this patent was signed about the time that the Pilgrims drew near Cape Cod. The holders of it did not attempt to turn it to immediate account by any bold and large undertaking of their own, but hoped to make profit by a tax on the exertions of

more enterprising persons. They tried to make
all fishermen on the coast take out a licence from
them, and to prohibit any settlers who had not
purchased their consent to face death and privation. But the time had come when this system
of monopoly was no longer to be quietly tolerated.
The king supported, but the parliament opposed,
these pretensions of the company, which in the end
gained little for itself and was mainly successful in
hampering private adventure for a time.

The most energetic of all its members was Sir
Ferdinand Gorges, the heir to Raleigh's hopes and
disappointments as he may be called, who had now
spent many years in promoting colonial enterprises
without ever taking part in them himself. Though
he was himself a Churchman, his zeal for colonisation seems to have been greater than his zeal for
creeds, and he helped to procure that the Pilgrims
should not be interfered with. He never ceased to
take a warm interest in New England, of which in
his old age he was appointed governor-general. It
was perhaps as well that he did not then carry out
his intention of visiting it, for his church-and-king
principles could scarcely have harmonized with the
development of the Puritan settlements. Fortunately
also for them, his attention was mainly taken up by
the northern shores, now known as Maine and New
Hampshire, where he laboured to plant colonies
with a perseverance deserving of better success.
He moreover incited the king to trespass upon the
neighbouring territories claimed by France. A
colony of Scotchmen were sent out to take posses-

sion of Nova Scotia, but were not so successful as their countrymen are wont to be abroad. A few years later, war being declared between England and France, a small expedition ascended the St. Lawrence and captured Quebec, where the French had already a small town. Neglected by the home government, they could make no effectual resistance, and for the moment England was mistress of the whole coast as far south as Cape Cod. But before this conquest was accomplished peace had been restored in Europe; Canada was given back, and the great struggle between the two nations on American ground was postponed for a century.

The prosperity of the northern part of New England was long retarded, as we might expect, both by disputes about boundaries between the French and the English, and by the conflicting claims of different patentees and unlicensed adventurers. The coast became dotted with fishing stages and huts, but Gorges found himself disappointed in his efforts to win a rich domain from the wilderness, and, during the period of our narrative, there is little of interest to be recorded about these scattered settlements. The southern part was more fortunate. Near the scene of confusion and failure there was forming in Massachusetts Bay the nucleus of the greatest of the American colonies.

The Puritans, beginning to despair of the prospects of religion and liberty in their own country, had turned their attention to New England. The success of the Plymouth settlement, small as it yet was, had proved that the land could be made to yield a livelihood to men who were of the right stuff. In more than one part of England this example was now discussed, and prominent members of the Puritan party encouraged each other in projects of planting a similar asylum on a larger scale. A corporation was formed, consisting of men of means, experience, and position, who obtained from the Plymouth company a grant of land from the Charles to the Merrimac, where, even before this arrangement was made, a small band was holding the country as "the sentinels of puritanism." These were soon reinforced by a party under John Endicott, appointed governor by the new proprietors, and the town was begun to which the emigrants gave the name of *Salem*, to betoken the peace that they hoped to find there. In the following year, 1629, this party was joined by two hundred more. The next step was an enormous one, which elevated the colony to the rank of a commonwealth.

Charles I., who had now succeeded to the throne, was the last monarch from whom concessions favourable to liberty and nonconformity might have been expected at this period of his power. But whether it was from carelessness, or from a momentary fit of relenting in his ecclesiastical policy, or from a wish to get rid at any price of members of that party which offered such a sturdy and effective opposition to his darling notions of government, or in the design of encouraging the settlement of those regions which otherwise seemed likely soon to fall into the hands of the French or the Dutch, the king, on being applied to for a charter by the new body of adventurers, granted them one containing all that they could desire. They were free to transport to America any persons willing to go, who should thenceforth live under such laws as might be made by themselves, being only not repugnant to the general laws of the realm. Not a word was said about enforcing conformity to the Church. Allegiance to the crown was to be maintained, but all power was put into the hands of a governor, a deputy governor, and eighteen assistants, who were to be elected annually by the members of the corporation.

Charles and his advisers perhaps little thought of the use that would be made of this charter, by which Massachusetts was held, we may smile to read, as belonging by legal fiction to the manor of East Greenwich! Either by chance or design a time was specially named for holding these annual elections, but no place. This gave opportunity to the leaders of the enterprise to conceive the idea of transferring charter, corporation and all, from England to Massachusetts, admitting all worthy emigrants to the freedom of the company, and thus at one stroke establishing the colony as an independent state. So much, they had good legal advice, was within their powers, and when the scheme was mooted the government did not question it.

Here was an unhoped for chance to form a community of choice and harmonious characters. No one could be a member unless admitted by the company, and their aim was and had been to pick their colonists from the best men in the nation.

But why then be content with helping others to this model commonwealth? Such was the question which began now to be agitated among the English Puritans. Many considerations urged them to fly from their native country. The evils and corruptions of the time were grievous to pious souls. The king had entered upon the last stage of his blind career, and many had little hope of success in the contest with his power. The renewed persecutions of the reformed churches abroad were a warning of what might soon be expected at home. These thoughts spread silently, but sank deeply. In the language of one of the Puritan historians, it seemed as if God "served as it were a *summons* upon the *spirits* of His people in the English nation, stirring up the spirits of thousands which never saw the *faces* of each other, with a most unanimous inclination to leave all the pleasant accommodations of their native country, and go over a terrible *ocean*, into a more terrible *desert*, for the *pure enjoyment of all His ordinances.*"

In August 1629 the court of the company voted unanimously to transfer its meetings to New England. A body of men of wealth and education had previously bound themselves to emigrate, if this vote were passed, and they now found no lack of companions willing to give themselves and their all in such a cause. John Winthrop, a Suffolk gentleman of high character and loveable disposition, was elected governor. The winter was passed in preparations for the exodus now determined upon. Funds were collected from sympathisers throughout the country; emigrants of the right kind were sought out; shipping was engaged. In the spring of 1630 Winthrop set sail with eleven ships, having on board the precious charter. During the year more than a thousand persons were transported to Massachusetts. Full twenty thousand are supposed to have arrived within ten years.

This was no obscure enterprise like that of the Pilgrims. The eyes of all England were upon these emigrants, and many wished them God speed as they departed into their voluntary exile. They were a select band in more than one sense. Their numbers comprised not only merchants, farmers and artisans, but scholars, learned divines, men of mark and family, delicately bred women and children. The governor's ship was named after Lady Arbella Johnson, who did not shrink from accompanying her husband, and "took New England on her way to heaven." She died very soon after her arrival, but the early historians of the colony never fail to mention her with respect, for lords and ladies were then no ordinary folk, even among the Puritan forefathers of the American republic.

Nor had these new comers to pass through such an ordeal as so terribly thinned the ranks of the Plymouth people. The main body arrived in summer, when wild strawberries were ripe to regale them as soon as they set foot in their new home. They found friends waiting to welcome them with "a venison pasty" and otherwise. They had cattle and horses, and were far better furnished with means and materials for settling. Yet these too had their share of hardships. It was not easy to provide shelter for so many all at once. Provisions ran short. Sickness broke out. Two hundred died within a few months, and a hundred persons deserted the colony. But now and again they were wonderfully preserved through their season of trial. Tradition has it that the governor was giving away the last handful of meal when a ship came in sight which had been despatched to Bristol for supplies. Though they say little enough about it, these gentle women and these honourable elders, who had a right to think their work in the world nigh done and to look for some share of peace and ease, must have gone through sufferings which would seem terrible to the self indulgent habits of our gilded youth. Colonising on the stern shores of New England was no romantic work of the Paul-and-Virginia kind, but a real struggle for the very necessaries of existence, even under the most favourable conditions.

Hitherto the settlement at Salem had been scarcely more prosperous than two or three others which had been essayed in the same neighbourhood, under the auspices of such men as Gorges and Weston. Now Winthrop removed with the greater part of the people to Boston harbour, and on various points of its winding shore rose little groups of booths and tents, which in time grew into more substantial towns. We need not ask whether these plantations flourished nor can we follow their fortunes in detail. It is well known that, if the Puritans ordered their lives with a main eye to the next world, they proved themselves capable of lending a most serviceable hand in the affairs of this state of being. Theirs it was to show that the way to make profit from America was not to sue for patents and monopolies, and send out worthless fellows to carry on your business for you, but to go yourself, strip off your fine coat, and buckle to work like a man.

It is pleasant to learn that before long the new colonists were welcomed by and formed friendly relations with the Pilgrims at Plymouth. The latter, we know, had been held in some disesteem by their reforming brethren in England. The Puritans had accused the separatists of disaffection to their mother country, which they themselves had left with loyal good wishes and sincere regret. But now that there were no bishops and church establishments to raise questions between them, it was seen that they agreed far more than they differed; indeed, times of trouble and danger had brought the Puritans to view in a different light what they once considered the sin of separation. The independent form of worship and church government was adopted throughout the settlements, and Plymouth and Massachusetts proved to be one in spirit, though it was many years later before they were formally united.

Now prevailed that austerity of morals which has left its mark upon all the Puritan colonies. Among so many there could not but have been a mixture of characters and aims; Mr. Worldly Wiseman and Mr. By-Ends did not fail to slip in along with Greatheart and Faithful; and we hear of "lewd servants" who from the first were a trouble to the grave leaders of the "colony of conscience." But the better, at least the more influential part, were men of real religious principle, who, both by example and precept, insisted on a high moral standard. If the laws made by them appear to us too severe let it be remembered that they legislated for themselves, and invited no one to join them who was not prepared to pass his life under the restraints which they thought wholesome; it is also the case that neighbouring communities voluntarily sought admission into the Puritan commonwealth. On the other hand it must be confessed that some of their enactments can on no plea be defended, but must stand as a beacon to well-meaning men who, getting too much of their own way, are prone to fall into the snare of power and spiritual pride.

The keeping of the sabbath was a main point in their strict system. Preparation for it began on Saturday afternoon, when all labour was to be laid aside and the mind directed to the services of the next day. These services were long, and would have seemed insufferably tiresome to a generation which is said to have lost "the art of listening to a two hours' sermon." Extemporary prayers and discourses and a few monotonous psalm tunes filled up the best part of the day; no one might remain absent under penalties; and strict attention, or semblance of attention, was enforced. There were officers whose duty was to wake the sleepers and to chastise such fidgety young folks as might disturb the congregation. Religious education was chiefly concerned with keeping the children in "great awe," which, if it be an error, is perhaps no worse than the contrary extreme of fond indulgence more in fashion at the present day. The rest of the day was spent in harmony with the tone of these public exercises. It must often have been a sore trial to the little ones. There were few books in the colony in these early days, and fewer "good" books which they cared to read; and the Bible is not always the better liked for being prescribed morning, noon, and night. What a boon it must have been when the "Pilgrim's Progress" reached New England, to vary the dulness of catechising! Games and lively movements were of course tabooed; one of the Puritans' chief quarrels with the king had been anent that Book of Sports by which he tried to encourage a different manner of observing Sunday.

All amusements indeed had been regarded with suspicion by the Puritans, and when they had their way, the ordinary games and sports of the English people were strictly prohibited, both Sunday and week day; cards and dice were banished; maypoles were held an abomination. They had a horror of holidays, which in their eyes savoured of popish superstition. There was plenty of occupation for idle hands, and during the first years of the settlement little leisure was available for frolicking. Industry was exacted from all. Discipline they declared to be as necessary as food or clothing, and the rod appointed for the back of the fool. The servants belonging to the company were divided into families, at the head of each of which was placed a religiously minded person, and a daily register was to be kept of the work done by every member. Other persons who had come over at their own expense, were not so easily dealt with; but they were expected to apply themselves to some calling, and might by no means set a bad example of idleness. Swearing and other signs of immorality were sternly dealt with, and if the offender proved too hardened for correction he was promptly got rid of at any cost. The stocks, the whipping post, and the pillory figured on the common green of the rising townships. Other punishments were used which were severe enough, according to our notions, but not more severe than the inflictions which had in England rewarded such crimes as attending a conventicle or writing a tract. A scold, for instance, would be made to stand in public with a cleft stick on her tongue. A man might be seen with a red letter D hung round his neck for a year, to point him out to scorn as a drunkard. That this rigour was not without effect is testified by a clergyman who, preaching before the Houses of Parliament, declared that he had lived in New England for seven years without hearing an oath or seeing a beggar or a drunkard.

In spite of this praise, we know that Governor Winthrop and others of the chief men had perplexing doubts about the use of "strong waters," though nobody had yet thought of teetotalism. Some of the colonists seemed inclined to abuse these "good creatures" by way of consoling themselves in exile, and the bestial intoxication in which the

Indians too easily learned to delight was a warning not thrown away. The custom of drinking healths was, as leading to excess, soon forbidden by the governor at his own table, and some years later it was abolished by law, " though divers even godly persons were loath to part with this idle ceremony." Here we have the germ of those scruples which led to the Maine liquor law. Tobacco also exercised the minds of the rulers. They did not go the length of absolutely forbidding it, but at first they enjoined that it should only " be taken privately by ancient men," and for " the preservation of their healths." This limitation was found impracticable; but we may be sure the rule was not relaxed so far as to please the present rising generation. Even among the Indians, we are told, though the men took much tobacco, " for boys so to do they account it odious."

Fasting at least was no part of the creed of those worthies, though it might often be perforce included in their practice. They knew how to be in want, but also how to abound; their toils in the keen air of New England made them relish its productions with double thankfulness. Hominy and pork and beans became staple dishes, and good housewives learned to be cunning in the making of these homely dainties for which the country is still celebrated. The orchards of Old England were soon found to flourish here, and the west country emigrants did not fail to bring with them the art of making the cider, which came to be as plentiful in Massachusetts as in Devonshire. And in these old days, before ice water and close stoves had come into use we may guess that New England faces bore small signs of commerce with the fiend indigestion.

New Englanders nowadays have the credit of being uncommonly sharp at a bargain, not to give a harsher name to this characteristic. But such "smartness" was by no means an object of admiration to the founders of their state. A carpenter who had charged an exorbitant price for making a pair of stocks was with grim humour and appropriate justice punished by being made to handsel his own workmanship. Mr. Cotton, one of the chief ministers, took occasion to denounce such notions as "that a man might sell as dear as he can or buy as cheap as he can," and "that as a man may take advantage of his own skill and ability, so he may of another's ignorance or necessity." Here is teaching to ruffle the respectability of Wall Street and our own Stock Exchange, where the golden rule of life is to buy in the cheapest market and sell in the dearest. Believing the Bible, and reading in it how we were to love our neighbours, these stubborn Puritans could not see that it was loving one's neighbour as oneself if one sold him for a hundred dollars what one knew to be worth less; and they would have considered gambling in shares as bad as gambling with dice. The rulers of the colony went so far as to commit the mistake, as it is now considered by political economists, of attempting to regulate prices and profits by law. Traffic was in these days mainly carried on by means of readily marketable commodities, such as corn and beaver skins. Musket bullets passed as farthings. *Wampum*, the Indian money, was also largely used. This consisted of strings of shells, some white and some a dark blue or purple; the latter was twice as valuable as the former, and a fathom of it was equal to about ten shillings. It was not till 1652 that Massachusetts set up a mint, usually considered the privilege of kings, and coined silver money stamped with a pinetree, specimens of which are now treasured among the antiquities of America.

The dress of the Puritans was for the most part unpretentious and substantial, doublet and hose of leather or strong cloth, knitted stockings, stout shoes, high broad-brimmed hats or caps, and plain bands in which starch was held by some extreme fanatics a mark of worldliness; yet, according to our standard of taste, they were not so devoted to sombre colours as they get credit for, presenting though they did a strong contrast to the court gallants who would wear a farm on their shoe strings and a manor on their hatband. In a list of clothes to be sent out to the colony we find mention of a hundred waistcoats of green cotton edged with red tape, and five hundred red knit caps. Nor was a certain display of silk or lace forbidden upon occasion to those whose rank and means were held to justify it, while any one who aped the fashions of his or her betters was liable to be taken sharply to task. In the early days, indeed, when the colonists had to depend upon England for almost everything, dress must have been too expensive to indulge much ambition of this kind, and the women generally wore plain homespun garments in which they pleased their husbands and sweethearts better than if they had been loaded with all the fripperies of a modern New York belle.

Far more important than fine clothes were the arms with which every man must be furnished, swords, pikes, long matchlocks, or the more convenient snaphances, a form of the flint lock now coming into use. Armour for the head, breast, back, and thighs, "varnished all black, with leathers and buckles" is included among the first supplies. But armour was already going out of favour; King James had well said that it not only protected the life of the wearer, but hindered him from doing hurt to anybody else. The settlers soon found the truth of this when they had to do with nimble Indians in tangled brakes and swamps. They began to use instead quilted coats, strong enough to turn an arrow while not so much impeding their own movements, and in time the Indians saved them the trouble of wearing this defence by learning to use firearms.

As for their houses, these were at first huts of earth or of logs plastered with mortar and thatched. When the colonists had time and means to improve their dwellings, many of them erected buildings of brick or stone; but wood still continued a favourite material, and many houses built of it in the seventeenth century are standing to this day. Frequent fires soon made it necessary to forbid wooden chimneys and thatched roofs. Instead of glass, then a luxury, the windows were often filled with paper steeped in linseed oil. Ventilation was not thought much of in the old days, but here it was no doubt sufficiently provided by chinks and cracks. These rude dwellings may have been comfortable enough, at least to the lower class of the colonists, who had been accustomed to no better accommodation at home. If the weather was cold, firewood was the one thing in which most of them had no stint. In hot weather there were the mosquitoes, which could not be so easily guarded against; but mosquitoes seemed a plague more bearable than Laud's pursuivants and apparitors. Those who could stand the climate and the rough work enjoyed excellent health in this new way of life. It must have been the less robust members of the colony whom we find from time to time casting a wistful eye towards sunny Virginia and the fruitful islands of the West Indies.

The following anonymous lines, describing the life of the first settlers, will be found interesting if not elegant. They are also curious as being the earliest known composition of the kind by an American writer.

New England's Annoyances, you that would know them,
Pray ponder these verses which briefly do show them.

 The place where we live is a wilderness wood,
 Where grass is much wanting that's fruitful and good;
 Our mountains and hills, and our valleys below,
 Being commonly covered with ice and with snow;
 And when the north-west wind with violence blows,
 Then every man pulls his cap over his nose:
 But if any's so hardy and will it withstand,
 He forfeits a finger, a foot, or a hand.

But when the spring opens we then take the hoe,
And make the ground ready to plant or to sow.
Our corn being planted and seed being sown,
The worms destroy much before it is grown;
And when it is growing, some spoil there is made
By birds and by squirrels that pluck up the blade;
And when it is come to full corn in the ear,
It is often destroyed by racoon and by deer.

And now do our garments begin to grow thin,
And wool is much wanted to card and to spin.
If we get a garment to cover without,
Our other in-garments are clout upon clout.
Our clothes we brought with us are apt to be torn,
They need to be clouted soon after they're worn;
But clouting our garments they hinder us nothing,—
Clouts double are warmer than single whole clothing!

If fresh meat be wanting to fill up our dish,
We have carrots and pumpkins and turnips and fish:
And, is there a mind for a delicate dish,
We repair to the clam banks and there we catch fish.
'Stead of pottage and puddings and custards and pies,
Our pumpkins and parsnips are common supplies:
We have pumpkins at morning and pumpkins at noon;
If it was not for pumpkins we should be undone.

If barley be wanting to make into malt,
We must be contented and think it no fault;
For we can have liquor to sweeten our lips
Of pumpkins and parsnips and walnut-tree chips. . . .
    (*The rest of this verse is wanting.*)

Now while some are going let others be coming,
For while liquor's boiling it must have a scumming;
But I will not blame them, for birds of a feather
By seeking their fellows are flocking together.
But you whom the Lord intends hither to bring,
Forsake not the honey for fear of the sting;
But bring both a quiet and contented mind,
And all needful blessings you surely will find.

The simplicity here indicated was the general rule in the lives of high and low. Winthrop, who was so often elected governor and was all his life the leading spirit of the colony, set a good example in this way, wearing plain clothes, living temperately, and working with his own hands when not employed on public business. We hear of him travelling about on foot, and acting as minister to a congregation who happened to be without one. His palace was no other than a common frame house, which he soon ordered to be moved and set up at Boston.

This town was originally called Trimountain, from the three hills on which it stands. Tremont Street and the well known Tremont House still recall this name, which was changed to gratify some Lincolnshire men who had a tender recollection of their last view of old Boston Stump. The prospects of the place were at one time so unpromising that grave wags gave it the nickname of *Lost* Town; but Winthrop judged it the best situation for the seat of government, and its growth and fame have justified his choice. At Cambridge, which may now be said to be a suburb of Boston (and a charming surburb it is) the first New England university was founded so early as 1642 with nine students, four years after the first printing press had been established in the country. Thus careful were the fathers of the country for letters and education. At a time when a thorough system of popular instruction was scarcely dreamed of in any European country, they ordered that every township, as soon as it reached the number of fifty houses, should appoint a dominie duly fitted and equipped for the discomfiture of that power which finds mischief still for idle young folks to do and ignorant old ones.

Many such townships quickly sprang up around Boston, at first holding to the inlets of the sea and the course of the large rivers, then spreading themselves more boldly into the interior. The favourite names were the old familiar ones. There were no Syracuses, Troys, and Mugginsvilles in those days; Manchester, Gloucester, Marlborough, Ipswich, Bradford, Salisbury, Exeter, Lynn, Northampton, are but a small sample of the names which testified the unalterable affection of the colonists for their mother country, and still remind both John Bull and Jonathan of what was, and ah! of what might have been.

Nowhere in America does the Englishman feel himself more at home than in this neighbourhood, where his Puritan ancestors made their first dwellings in the wilderness. Of all the great western cities, Boston and its surroundings wear for him the friendliest face and seem to give him the heartiest welcome. After the monotonous magnificence, the pretentious grandeur that weary him with their staring colours, sharp outlines, and painful newness in the square blocks of the enormous mushroom emporiums which it is the American traveller's duty to visit, he comes with inexpressible relief to a town where there are old houses, and crooked streets, and moss-grown gravestones, and ancient elms that have a story to tell, and spots that are kept for ever green, consecrated by the memory of great deeds done on them. Such, at this day, is the city which its inhabitants call the "hub of the universe," and delight to consider as the Delphi of the modern world, whence come the oracular straws that show how the wind of future ages is going to blow. We cannot find fault with this enthusiasm. When we consider what Boston has thought and done for the world, there is no wise lover of his fellow men who will grudge the pride with which its children regard "the dear old three-breasted mother of American liberty." Even its founders might consider themselves citizens of no mean city, in and around which were already seething some of the greatest problems of modern life.

II.

"It was not long before the *Massachusetts* colony was become like an *hive* over-stocked with bees, and many of the new inhabitants entertained thoughts of *swarming* into plantations extended further into the country." Some six years had passed when a band of "worthy, learned, and genteel persons traversed the woods," and settled themselves, after incredible difficulties and hardships, upon the Connecticut river. Other adventurers soon found their way to the shores of Long Island Sound and formed the colony of New Haven; they even spread across the channel and began to dispute the island itself with the Dutch. Thus the pious Cotton Mather might well be moved to break forth, comparing the lot of his own country with that of Israel of old: *"O God of Hosts, Thou hast brought a Vine out of England, Thou hast cast out the heathen and planted it; Thou preparedst room before it, and didst cause it to take deep root, and it filled the land; the hills were covered with the shadow of it, and the boughs thereof were like the goodly cedars; she sent out her boughs unto the sea."*

Such comparisons with the history of the Jews were not confined to metaphor. The leaders of the Massachusetts colony were inclined to cast their politics in an ecclesiastical mould, to take the Bible for their statute book, and to substitute a confession of faith for an oath of allegiance. They did not speak of sending out a colony or of building a town, but of "planting a church" in such and such a place. No one might have a vote who was not a member or communicant of the church; and as admission to this privilege depended on the candidate's both making a public profession of his conversion before all the congregation and privately satisfying the church officers of the sincerity and soundness of his belief, it may be understood that only a minority were church members, and consequently citizens.

This was not pure democracy, and the worst evils might have arisen from such a constitution. When the church rules the state, the interests of both are apt to be in danger. But in more than one instance a national spirit of bigotry has been seen to consist with a lively appreciation of political freedom, and this proved to be the case in Massachusetts. Parties were formed there by religious questions, but the ministers often found that they could by no means have their own way in what seemed to touch the rights of their supporters. Some of these ministers headed what may be called a conservative party, that sought to model the constitution according to Jewish precedents. Now there can be no doubt that the history of the Jews says nothing about popular institutions, and these pious minds were only logical in suggesting that magistrates ought to be elected for life and that something like a governing class should be thus established. The majority of the voters, however, were inconsistent enough to take a different view, having had enough of tyrants who ruled by the most scriptural warrant. They insisted on exercising their power without regard to any principle but the public convenience, and sometimes at the annual elections sent their best magistrates into private life for a time by way of a hint as to the tenure on which they held office. Some of the gentlemen who had been accustomed all their lives to respect from inferiors were not very well pleased at this spirit, and inclined to agree with the ministers. A good deal of jealousy and bickering was caused by such questions, which were warmly canvassed at one time in connection with a great case about a stray sow, where the populace and their deputies took one side, and the magistrates another.

The personal character of Winthrop, who so often served in one office or another, went far towards checking what might in the early circumstances of the colony have proved a dangerous excess of liberty; but it was clearly shown that aristocracy was a plant not likely to flourish upon New England soil. Certain Puritan noblemen who proposed to emigrate were restrained from doing so when they found that an hereditary nobility would not be recognised; and had it not been for a stray lord or knight coming over as a visitor, Young America would have forgot the sound of titles. The ideas of republican government ripened fast among the settlers now that they had come out from the shadow of the English throne. The new colonies of Connecticut and New Haven, being without the limits of the Massachusetts charter, made no difficulty about forming constitutions for themselves; and in the former state the franchise was granted without regard to a religious qualification. This reform was of course only a matter of time in the other states. In all, not only preachers but elders were from the first expressly excluded from civil office, no great deprivation in a community where the pulpit had such power.

But the Massachusetts voters, if they jealously guarded their own civil rights against any encroachment on the part of ministers and magistrates, allowed them to have their will of those who were "without," as the phrase was. To differ from the church in practice or opinion was a liberty by no means to be conceded. While the Puritans instinctively rejected the plain lessons of the Bible as to constitutional government, they zealously enforced principles of legislation which they found in it, and which they did not perceive to be equally unfit for their state of society. Unfortunately it was the Old rather than the New Testament which inspired them, and they regarded the Mosaic law more than the Sermon on the Mount.

Winthrop indeed, than whom no man was more truly religious nor more zealous to maintain a high standard of public virtue, was in favour of a milder rule than pleased his stern associates. "To do justice, to love mercy, and to walk humbly with his God," was the motto with which he undertook office. A story is told of him which well illustrates his character. A poor man was once accused to him of stealing from his wood pile. The governor pretended to be very angry and ordered the man to be sent for. The culprit came trembling, already feeling the lash on his shoulders in the terrors of imagination. "Friend," said Winthrop kindly, "it is a severe winter, and I doubt you are but meanly provided for wood; wherefore I would have you supply yourself at my wood pile till this cold season be over." Then he laughingly asked his friends if he had not effectually cured this man of stealing his wood.

Governor Winthrop was taken to task for such leniency, which seemed an abomination in the eyes of men who were disposed to hold picking up sticks on the sabbath day as an enormity worthy of death. Against his opinion it was decided that a young colony required stricter discipline than a settled state; hence those severe regulations which must have made Massachusetts a very penal settlement for all persons not austerely minded. The Puritans

were not content with imposing their rule of life
upon their own body; they undertook to meddle
with the morals of their neighbours and to keep
their visitors in order. It was a crime even to speak
against their views. The plantation set up near
them by a certain Mr. Morton was an eyesore which
both the Pilgrims and the Bay people felt called on
to cast out from the land. Morton, who seems to
have been an indifferent enough character, was
accused of selling guns and whiskey to the Indians,
a real crime and one which certainly called for interference; but it may be suspected that his main
offence was the setting up of a maypole, which to
the Puritans appeared nothing less than an idol of
worldliness. The fact that he wrote a very curious
book detailing his grievances has given his case
more notoriety than it deserved; but it was only one
of others. The settlers under the charter treated
the country as a club rather than as an open community, and did not hesitate to turn out any one
who was not agreeable to their own habits of life.
At the very outset they expelled two respectable
members of the colonial council for no other crime
than persisting in the use of the Church of England
service. These were not the only persons who had
reason to agree with a saying of one of the settlers,
that he had left England because he did not like
the Lord Bishops, but found the rule of the Lord
Brethren no more to his taste. Uncongenial intruders were indeed unlikely to meet with much
consideration in a community where a minister
denounced his own son for seditious speeches, and

where a magistrate joined in condemning his daughter to be publicly whipped for a trifling offence.

The offenders, thus driven out of the colony for various reasons, did not fail to make complaints at home, which were not unheard. The king, like Pharaoh of old, began to repent that he had let this people go. The eyes of his advisers were opened to the seriousness of what had been done in permitting the establishment of such a refuge for the opinions which they were trying to suppress at home. It was felt that the Puritans were taking too much upon them in imitating the intolerance which seemed one of the prerogatives of royalty. For a time therefore emigration was hindered by the government. It is said that in 1638 Hampden and Cromwell meant to desert their country in despair, and were already on board a fleet which was stayed in the Thames by order of the Council. This story is somewhat doubtful; but it is certain that thousands contrived to come over in some years. The matter began to grow more serious. The king had appointed a commission, with the Archbishop of Canterbury at its head, to regulate the American colonies. This commission got into its hands the general patent for New England granted to the Plymouth company, and ordered the Massachusetts colony to surrender its liberal charter. The demand was repeated, but the colonists had no intention of complying. They made excuses, procrastinated, and showed a stubborn disposition to hold on to this warrant of their rights. The only result was a feeling of uneasiness in the colony and a widening of the distrust which now began to exist between it and the government of the mother country. The Puritan leaders had left England loyal subjects. When Endicott cut the red cross out of the royal standard as a superstitious emblem, he was severely rebuked by his brother magistrates; but before long there was an increasing number ready to applaud such significant actions, and other emblems began to be called in question by men who were in no temper to suffer either the emblems or the realities from which they had fled into this wilderness.

For a time the great bugbear of the colonists was the threatened sending over of a governor-general to control the New England states. This they were determined to resist; and if the necessity for open resistance had arisen, the English civil war and the American war of independence may show us in what a spirit it would have been carried out. Luckily they could adapt to their own case the Campbells' proverb, "It's a far cry to *Boston Bay*"; and the king had enough to do nearer home to keep him from enforcing his authority over the Atlantic. Before long he had so much to do that all danger of this kind disappeared. Then the New Englanders found in Cromwell a ruler with whom they had much more satisfaction in dealing.

The spirit of political independence was thus carefully nursed, but the very idea of religious toleration was scouted. This is the worst of persecution: the persecuted are often found too ready to become persecutors in their turn, and "new presbyter"

when at last he gets his own way proves to be but
"old priest writ large." So the Puritans began to
regard their "platform" with almost as much blind
veneration as had enslaved Laud and Bonner to the
forms of the older churches. They were only less
severe in the punishments by which they thought
to ensure respect for and conformity to their own
notions. Toleration, declared one of their writers,
was the work of the devil, and no practical sin was
so sinful as some error in judgment. Whoever
spoke up for toleration must be an atheist, a heretic,
or a hypocrite. In short, "*polypiety* is the greatest
impiety in the world," concludes this author, who
wrote under the affected name of the Simple Cobbler
of Aggawam, but who was a minister, and held in
such esteem for his wisdom that he was entrusted
with the important task of drawing up a code of
laws for the colony.

Yet where such a spirit prevailed, the duty of
toleration was as specially called for as it was subjected to a severe strain. "It has long been
noticed" by New England writers old and new
"that there is something in the influences, climatic
or other, here prevailing, which predisposes to morbid religious excitement." The English carried over
the Atlantic that constitutional peculiarity which
gave foreigners occasion to rail at them as suffering
from the spleen; and the atmosphere of austerity
by which they were surrounded soon made this
temperament develop itself in extraordinary religious
phantasies. From the first, religious melancholy
found many victims whom it often led to suicide or

confirmed madness. As soon as hardships and exposure had produced a crop of rheumatic limbs and wrinkled old women, we find an outbreak of the witch mania which was to rage so terribly at Salem towards the end of the century. The best and wisest of the Puritan settlers were carried away into an application of the doctrine of special providences, which seemed indeed to be warranted by the remarkable deliverances that they had experienced in their early trials. The lesson of the Red Sea rather than of the tower of Siloam took firm hold on their imaginations. It was noticed with triumph that of nearly two hundred ships employed in bringing emigrants over to the colony, only one was lost; while a vessel said to be destined for their coercion was wrecked in the very act of launching. Other ships were blown up, as they believed, because the sailors were an ungodly crew who mocked the saints or used the Church of England prayers. Gorges and his chief confederate Mason never flourished in their colonial enterprises, because they were not favourable to the Puritan cause. A man who was so unfaithful as to desert the colony might look to be shipwrecked or captured by the Turks and sold for a slave on his passage home. Those who spoke against its institutions were sure to have their barns burned or their crops destroyed. Children were drowned as the result of their fathers making merry or working on the eve of the sabbath. Without drawing on the pages of Cotton Mather, which are stuffed with such instances of judgments and deliverances, often absurd and more often deplorable for the superstition which they reveal; it is plain that these Puritans believed the powers of good and evil to be constantly and visibly interfering in their smallest concerns. Winthrop was not exempt, who gravely records as "worthy of observation" that he, having a Greek Testament, a Psalter, and a Book of Common Prayer bound up together, found that a band of mice, divinely sent for that object as is his inference, had, while not touching the two former, eaten up the prelatical Prayer Book "every leaf of it." Nothing was too great for such credulity. A snake once slipped into the meeting house, and was killed by an elder; this did not fail to be taken out of the ordinary course of things and interpreted as a typical manifestation of the devil's designs and their frustration by the "churches of Christ in New England." Calamities were occasionally observed to happen to persons of the most unblamable character and orthodox opinions, but these cases were explained more charitably; then the Puritan moralists suddenly called to mind that the same event had been said to befall the righteous and the wicked.

On such a soil fanaticism flourished vigorously, as well as genuine religious zeal, and the sober minded conservatives of the community thought themselves justified in using the severest measures to nip in the bud those vagaries of opinion which threatened, as they held, to destroy not only the peace of the church but the very existence of the state. They acted according to the ignorance of the time, not knowing that a man's actions are not always those

which seem the consequence of his opinions. They
did not perceive that the disease was mainly caused
by their own suppression of the instincts of human
nature, and that a little more freedom granted to
cheerful amusement and the kindly affections would
have been a far more wholesome medicine than
penal laws. They did not even take the lesson of
their own experience, that the surgery of persecution is likely to inflame the sore which it is intended
to cure; and when in their own hands such means
had clearly failed, they were blind enough to follow
the same treatment with double violence.

Before the era of persecution was past, old men,
ministers, women had been scourged more severely
than felons for no other crime than that of being
Baptists or Quakers. Some of these sufferers might
indeed have chosen the alternative of a fine, but
they gloried in the disgrace and made light of
the pain. Others were punished for only showing
sympathy towards the victims as they were let
down from the whipping post. The gallows were
at last appealed to in the vain hope of deterring the
irrepressible missionaries of the latter sect. When
all excuses are made, such acts remain a sad blot on
the name of the young commonwealth. Its rulers
were wholly to blame in forgetting that their own
forms of church doctrine and government, which
they defended with such ferocity, had been hastily
agreed to, not without difficulty and scruple, and by
a number of the original settlers far smaller than
that which often came into the country in one year.
After denouncing the separatists for years, they

themselves had borrowed some of the very principles which they had objected to in that body; and now, if the new opinions seemed ever so offensive, they should have considered their own imperfection of judgment and the danger of rooting up the wheat with the tares. They would have done well in laying to heart such teaching as that of John Robinson, which forbade any man or any body of men to think that in their own duckpond they held the whole ocean of God's truth. It is satisfactory to know that the Plymouth people appear to have been laudably behindhand in this work of forcing consciences, though all of their leaders cannot be held free from reproach. It is probable too that the majority of the Massachusetts colonists would not, if consulted, have sanctioned the severities of the ruling class of church members.

The course of our story is now running backwards. Before resorting to these extremities the orthodox Puritans, as they accounted themselves, had tried to secure uniformity by milder measures of coercion, which were yet wholly inconsistent with the spirit of their principles. This outward uniformity had scarcely been established when it was found to be threatened with destruction by various winds of doctrine. Every ship brought teachers to the colony who had not fled from one religious yoke to submit tamely to another. Dissensions sprang up and ran riot through a community where every citizen was a theologian, and where the whole force of intellect, shut out from healthy exercise in almost every other direction, was turned upon theological speculation.

Abstruse and minute questions were argued between parties, "whereof no man could tell (except some few who knew the bottom of the matter) where any difference was." The doctrines of justification and sanctification gave ground for such hairsplitting disputes as vexed the early Christian church on the definition of the Trinity. Like the early Christians, the Puritans thought to arrive at the truth by convoking a solemn assembly or council, which condemned no less than eighty separate doctrines as blasphemous, erroneous, or unsafe. What may be called the opposition party were accused of various *isms*, but the gist of their offending was that they carried the Protestant right of private judgment to a point which has at different times seemed to many its logical consequence; they were on the whole theoretically in sympathy with the tenets of those who have been called antinomians. Anabaptist was another of the ugly names used in this controversy; and an anabaptist was to our ancestors what "a communist" is at the present day, the supposed enemy of all order and respectability. Practical scandals also were the result of this agitation. Women assumed the right of holding meetings, at which one of their own sex did not hesitate to "prophesy" and to pass judgment on certain ministers as being "under the covenant of works." Under show of asking questions after the sermon, hearers were found forward to criticize the preacher in public, so that the church service seemed likely to degenerate into a debating society. The innovators found no little or mean countenance. The majority of the Boston people were with them. Henry Vane, afterwards the celebrated parliamentary leader, who resided for a time in the colony, and in spite of his youth was chosen governor almost immediately upon his arrival, also leant to their side. But the general sense of the voters was against them, as soon appeared when these discordant elements were not to be removed by argument or persuasion. Vane was excluded from office and left the colony in disgust. The General Court, composed of the magistrates and the deputies of the freemen, ordered the leaders of the dissent to be banished, upon such precedents as that of Lot's separation from Abraham and the expulsion of Hagar and Ishmael. Their followers were at the same time required to give up their arms, as a guarantee against rebellion or secession. And that such disturbers might not creep in for the future, the right was assumed of putting a moral quarantine upon all new arrivals in the country, who were not to be entertained till the magistrates were satisfied that they had a clean bill of theological opinion. It was in vain that the victims of such arbitrary measures threatened to appeal to the king. Such an appeal was considered treason in the commonwealth of the saints, who had settled for themselves that the internal regulation of Massachusetts was one of the things nowise belonging to Cæsar.

The leaders of the schism, Mrs. Anne Hutchison and a preacher named Wheelwright, took refuge beyond the bounds of the colony and founded new settlements, after the example of one, their prede-

cessor in banishment, who will ever be held in
honour, both in Europe and America, as the first
consistent champion of religious liberty. Roger
Williams had, almost from the beginning, proved a
thorn in the side of the oppressive majority. Like
them he had fled from England to escape the persecution of the bishops, but he had learned the true
lesson of persecution which they had missed. His
character and his abilities as a preacher were such
that it was confessed on all hands that he had a zeal
for the Lord, yet not according to knowledge, added
these intolerant sectaries, and would fain have
silenced him, even before they knew the length of
heresy to which he would proceed.

Not without opposition, he served as preacher for
a time both at Plymouth and Salem, and scandalized
the other churches by leavening these congregations
with "strange notions," some of which were indeed
strange enough to our thinking, but the strangest
and most offensive of all in the wise eyes of his
contemporaries was the notion of a "general and
unlimited toleration of all religions." It was
persecution, he taught, to punish any man for his
opinions. No one should be forced to worship or
to maintain a form of worship of which he did not
approve. Conscience was the sole realm of religion,
and all dealings there must be between man and
God alone. The civil magistrate had no concern
except with acts which tended to destroy civil
society. Jews, Turks, heretics and infidels had, so
long as they obeyed the law, the same right to its
protection as the most orthodox of believers. Per-

suasion was the only weapon that might be used against error of judgment, and no other weapon could be used with success. These truisms of to-day were the startling novelties which were conceived in the mind of Roger Williams, ten or twelve years before Milton had written the noble words: *" Though all the winds of doctrine were let loose to play upon the earth, so Truth be in the field, we do injuriously by licensing and prohibiting to misdoubt her strength. Let her and Falsehood grapple; who ever knew Truth put to the worse, in a free and open encounter?"*

Alas! our ancestors were only then awakening from the long night through which Truth had been dreamed to be in need of inquisitions and establishments, of stakes and whipping posts, to protect her against Falsehood. Nor is all the world yet come into full daylight.

Roger Williams often saw cause to change his opinions, "it is only fools and the dead who never do," says a wise man; but throughout his life he remained constant to this grand doctrine of toleration. This liberality toward others by no means proceeded from indifference in his own views of religious matters; they indeed were marked by a scrupulosity on minute points which might now be called intolerance by those who have forgotten the former signification of the word. While maintaining the right of all to hold their speculative errors unmolested, he constantly refused to hold religious communion with his neighbours who seemed to him to err. The Church of England, as guilty of persecution, he thought should be openly renounced and held under a spiritual ban. He was so jealous of the freedom of congregations that he objected to fortnightly consultations of his brother ministers, lest these should lead to something like presbyterianism. Davie Deans himself was not more exact to mark right hand deflections and left hand way slidings among his brethren. It is said by his enemies that at one time he would neither pray nor give thanks with his own wife, because she persisted in attending the church of the place, from which he had cut himself off as a protest against its errors. At another time, he found in his wife the only Christian with whom he could consistently join in worship. In politics, as in religion, his conscience was also active in raising awkward questions to trouble his fellow citizens. He objected upon scriptural grounds to the oath of allegiance which the colony thought itself justified in demanding; he took exception to the royal patent, declaring that no one had any right to give away the lands of America, except the Indians who occupied them. He suggested days of solemn humiliation for the wrongful proceedings by which the colonists had taken possession of the country. It must be confessed that he had here hit upon a more important consideration than when he raised dissensions on such trifles as whether women should wear veils in church, and whether the red cross on the king's colours was not a recognition of idolatry.

This was a man in no wise to be silenced, and not always easy to be answered, so it was resolved to have done with him by the summary method of banishment. Not without hesitation was this resolved upon, towards the end of 1635; a respectable minority dissented from the decision, and execution of the sentence was considerately delayed till spring. Williams seems to have been able to excite friendly regard even among those who, in the public interest, felt constrained to enroll themselves among his enemies. Some of the men who had driven him forth from among them, afterwards showed him kindness in the most practical way when he was in poverty. Winthrop, who lived to regret his share in the matter, gave him private counsel as to where he were best to settle after his banishment. Many thought him mad, but found him withal a man of singular piety and lovingness. So great was the charm of his character that it seemed dangerous to allow him to remain under his sentence; he was making converts every day. The magistrates resolved to send him to England at once. In the depth of winter, leaving his wife and children, he fled from their officers and wandered for weeks through the woods, "not knowing what bread or bed did mean." It was well for him that he had cultivated the language and the friendship of the Indians. They now received him with the hospitality which he had deserved, and was yet to deserve at their hands by his generous championship of their rights. These were the ravens, he said, who fed him in the wilderness.

In the country of the Narragansetts, he settled himself at a place which, in grateful recognition of

God's mercies, he named Providence, and gathered round him a little company of persons agreeing with his main principle of free thought and free speech, which, sooner than perhaps he thought, was to leaven the whole country. Thus was formed the nucleus of the state of Rhode Island, still the smallest state of the Union, yet among those which have had the greatest influence on its destinies.

Be it noticed that this was not the first home that toleration found on American soil. A few years before Williams' banishment, the Roman Catholic Lord Baltimore, when founding his colony of Maryland, had, in order to secure his co-religionists in the exercise of their faith, induced the king to dispense with all regulations for conformity. Policy may have had as much to do with this as benevolence; but we must not forget the name of the nobleman through whom the boon of religious toleration was introduced from a quarter whence it migh be least expected.

The plantation at Providence soon found neighbours of the same way of thinking to occupy the island from which the state was to take its name. This territory had been acquired from the Indians through the personal influence of Roger Williams, but it was not in his nature to seek personal advantage. He freely invited all who were willing to share with him, and devoted himself to establishing a commonwealth marked by the widest civil as well as religious liberty. For the first few years there were actually no magistrates in the little state; all public affairs were carried on in meetings of the heads of families. When the colony had grown a little, Roger Williams visited England and procured a charter, under which, though all was owing to his exertions and though he was highly popular, he was not appointed the first governor, probably by his own desire, but accepted the humbler office of assistant. He seems to have been as little ambitious of spiritual power. He conceived some scruple about exercising his ministerial functions, and maintained himself by trade and by hard manual labour "at the hoe and at the oar." He also laboured as an author, writing upon the Indian customs and language, and denouncing the " bloody tenet of persecution " and other errors, in round terms which did not fail to bring forth hot rejoinder from the orthodox church of Massachusetts.

The other New England colonies had no faith in the soundness of their new neighbour's constitution. When in 1643 they formed themselves into a confederation, Rhode Island was excluded. Many were the grim jests passed upon it by orthodox wiseacres, and the fears expressed as to the future of the happy family of heretics who, whatever might be their *ism* or *ology,* found an equal welcome within its narrow bounds. Some bickerings did indeed take place among them, but it was soon shown that good government could exist along with variety of religious opinion, and little Rhode Island flourished as well as the best of them. Time has justified the faith of its founder, and shown him to have been in the right line of the reformers when an instinct of humanity led him to that great truth which is now a commonplace of statesmen and philosophers.

T

III.

In the early history of New England, except in the case of the Plymouth people, the natives seem to play a less prominent part than in the beginning of former colonies. We have already seen how a great part of the country was swept almost clear of its inhabitants and left open to the new comers. After a few years the settlers came over in such numbers and with such resources that they felt themselves comparatively safe, and did not even take the trouble to erect a fortified town in Massachusetts, which according to John Smith's opinion was the first thing necessary. Their most serious apprehensions of danger were from the Dutch to the south of them, and the French to the north. Their Indian neighbours they were able to regard with curiosity rather than dread; the Puritans pitied their ignorance, despised their rude weapons, and with grave humour compared their scalp-locks to the long curls in which the courtly cavaliers took such pride. The narratives of the early explorers had by this time instructed their successors what to fear or expect from the natives, and the unknown was no longer taken for the terrible.

Many controversies have been waged as to the origin of the aborigines of America. The Jews, the Trojans, the Canaanites, the Phœnicians, the Chinese, and many other nations have been supposed to be their forefathers; and the most ingenious theories have been framed to account for their transit from the Old to the New World. Nothing is ascertained on this subject, but it is now known that the Indians of both continents, while showing points of resemblance throughout which go to prove a common ancestry, were divided into many families or races, united by similarity of language, and these again into innumerable tribes, cherishing the same customs but often engaged in implacable and constant hostility. Each tribe was under the government of a chief called by various names, as Werowance in Virginia, Sachem or Sagamore in New England, Cacique in the south. They knew no occupations but war, hunting, and a rude agriculture in which the labourers were always women. They were not very firmly attached to any part of the soil, but, driven by hunger or the fear of powerful neighbours, would migrate to seek new homes in the vast unoccupied regions that lay open to their choice. We have already had many incidental glimpses into their habits and ways of living. Their character is set forth in works familiar to every schoolboy, who must however be warned that such works generally exaggerate its romantic features and do not sufficiently display the brutality, the meanness, and the mental degradation of Indian life.

The Algonquin race, with which almost alone the English had hitherto come in contact, was the most widely extended but not the most warlike of these families. It might have been harder work for the settlers of Virginia and New England if their coasts had been guarded by the fierce Iroquois or Five Nations, one tribe of whom, the

Mohawks, were already a sore thorn in the side of their Dutch neighbours. The Massachusetts tribe of Algonquins, among whom the Puritan settlers first made their abode, had been reduced by the plague to a few scattered villages, and were the more willing to welcome the strangers who brought them not only trade but efficient protection against the other tribes. "Sagamore John," the chief of the Boston district, learned to affect English customs, and his countrymen were soon induced to exchange their coverings of skin for blankets of coarse cloth, and to bring beaver and other furs for English tools and arms. Guns and spirits soon became objects of their ambition, and were bought on the sly, though strict laws forbade any white men to supply Indians with these dangerous commodities. On the whole, the early relations of the two races were here mutually beneficial. It was when the English began to push their way into the more thickly populated districts to the south that they met with serious opposition.

That even among these tribes there was no rooted prejudice against foreigners, is shown by the example of Roger Williams. We have already learned how he was the friend of the Indians, and how they repaid his friendship in time of need. He did not disdain to dwell with them in their "smoky, filthy holes," nor shrink from the labour of studying their extremely complicated language. It was no romantic fancy which led him into contact with savage life; he saw very clearly its debasement, but while he deplored the superstitious ignorance and the coarse animal nature of his redskinned allies, he recognised them as fellow creatures, with flashes of good instinct, latent possibilities of improvement, and certainly with as good right to fair and kind treatment as any white man. This was the true way to gain their hearts, and if the founder of Providence was unable, during a long life of exertion, to do much towards elevating them permanently in the scale of being, he at least secured their constant goodwill for himself, and was often able to mediate successfully between them and his countrymen; his influence was even great enough to make peace for the Dutch with their Indian enemies. No price, it was said, could have bought the lands which were freely given him; and when the strong New England confederacy was threatened by the tribes in the midst of which lay his little state, it was safe, protected not by sword and guns, but by the respect and affection borne by the simple savages towards a man of the wiser and more powerful race, who clearly was aiming at their good and valued their friendship more than their submission. The story of Roger Williams is an honour to human nature, never so dark that some little ray of goodness does not lurk within to be called forth by the warmth of congenial sympathy.

Setting apart the justice of their original intrusion, the behaviour of the Puritan settlers was, on the whole, marked by an intention to deal fairly with the people whom they supplanted. They were scrupulously careful to acquire, by purchase or treaty, whatever title the natives might have to the lands which they occupied. But the Indians' notion of selling was often as indefinite as their rights, and as they easily parted with territory claimed by them, so they were with difficulty held to the bargain when they found their accustomed hunting grounds transformed into farms and villages. A civilized people moreover could not live side by side with restless, cruel, and still unsubdued tribes, without constant danger of disputes and collisions. These did not fail to arise; blood was shed; outlying plantations and small isolated parties were proved no longer safe. Murders were committed, and the murderers were not surrendered upon demand. On the side of the English hostile preparations were deemed necessary; and the fate of the Canaanites furnished the pious soldiers with a precedent which sooner or later seemed likely to be put into practice. The injuries complained of were real; but the provocation which may have been received by the Indians we are not so well able to estimate, since the accounts which have come down to us are all from one side. A superior and victorious race, even with the best intentions, are not always the fairest judges as to right and wrong between themselves and a people whose only strength lies in treachery and bloodshed. We must not expect to find the calmest and most accurate historians among men who had heard the hellish war whoop ringing through the woods, and lived in daily dread of seeing their wives and children scalped and mangled; besides, we must consider the difference of customs, and the imperfect knowledge of each other's language possessed by the two parties, before pronouncing so decisively as did the colonists upon the conduct of their enemies. For the former also it must be said that the position in which they had placed themselves was one where principles of abstract justice could not always be appealed to; the necessity of existence must have often seemed to have no law but the sword. Yet it is deplorable that by a people professing Christianity in a special degree, a few deaths should have been revenged by the slaughter of hundreds of women and children as well as warriors.

In 1636 these troubles came to a head in the southern part of New England, now the states of Connecticut and Rhode Island, then mainly occupied by three powerful tribes, the Narragansetts, the Pequods, and the Mohegans. An Englishman having been murdered by Indians who were harboured by the Pequods, an expedition under Endicott was sent out to punish this tribe. After a skirmish the Indians fled, and their corn and wigwams were destroyed by the English, who then returned, hoping the lesson had been effectual. But the Pequods had only been goaded into designs of vengeance. Incited by the devil (who, according to the orthodox views of certain Puritan divines, was the patron saint of all the tawny race), they proposed to the neighbouring tribes to lay aside their own chronic quarrels and join to drive out the powerful strangers. Their arguments certainly showed the wisdom of the serpent; they pointed out that the tribes united could do what discord hindered, and that delay would aid the English to drive them out one after another. The proposal was listened to, and that it was not agreed upon, the settlements owed to the generous friendship of one at whose hands they had deserved no such service. Roger Williams had just settled down at Providence, after his exile and wanderings, when he learned what was on foot among his Indian allies, and at once forgot his own wrongs in the danger of his countrymen. Not only did he send to warn them of the conspiracy, but he hastened to the Narragansetts to use his influence in destroying it. His life was in danger from the stormy water which he had to cross in a frail canoe, then from the fierce malignity of the Pequod ambassadors, who had arrived before him; but he was rewarded by success in his noble mission. The Narragansetts finally refused to join the league, the Mohegans sided with the English, and the Pequods stood alone in their hostile purposes.

Their insolence and violence now became insupportable. They lay skulking near the Connecticut river, attacked the settlers when at work or when travelling up the rivers; and those who fell into their hands alive were tortured with fiendish ingenuity before being burned to death. The fort called Saybrook, which had been built at the mouth of the river, was kept constantly almost in a state of siege. Men went armed into their hay and corn fields, not knowing but that the dusky foe might start up from his ambush and fall upon them. The newly formed colony of Connecticut, under its young governor, Winthrop's son, found its very existence at stake, and unanimously resolved to "root this nest of serpents out of the world."

The war was entered upon in a stern spirit of religious zeal which boded ill for the enemy. Ministers accompanied the troops, blessed their enterprise, and spent long hours in prayer with them. Massachusetts and Plymouth each contributed a body of men, but the main blow was struck before these arrived. Ninety men were furnished by Connecticut, under the command of Major John Mason, who also had twenty soldiers from the fort at Saybrook and a band of friendly Indians. With these he proposed to surprise a fort where a large number of Pequods were gathered, at a place now called Groton, on the Mystic river in Connecticut. Roger Williams, the good genius of the English colonies, had in the meanwhile not been idle. Neglecting his own affairs he hurried from tribe to tribe, dissuading the other Indians from aiding the Pequods. Poor as he was, he entertained at his house the soldiers sent by his late persecutors. He aided the expedition by his advice, and found them guides through the Indian country. His conduct seems the best warrant for the war, and he was its truest hero; yet his services are ungratefully ignored by the early historians of New England, who show a constant desire to belittle the heretic and the outlaw, and even at the time he would appear to have been scarcely thanked for his pains.

The commander of the expedition has left us an

account of its proceedings. Embarking in pinnaces, his force sailed past the country of the Pequods, who thought their foes were afraid to come on shore and gave themselves up to exultation; while the English, having landed farther east, were approaching their stronghold from the Narragansett country.

On a clear moonlight night the tired soldiers lay down to rest so near the fort that their sentinels could hear the songs and mad merriment of the Indians, who were thus spending what was to be their last night on earth. At daybreak the soldiers rose, and briefly commending themselves and their design to Heaven, took the path shown by their guides, which after a march of two miles brought them to the hill on the top of which was the Pequod fort of wigwams surrounded by stakes and bushes. The Indian allies had slunk to the rear, and were evidently afraid to fight the fierce warriors whom they had represented as well-nigh invincible. Mason desired them to stand still, as far off as they pleased, and only look on to learn whether Englishmen could fight or not.

The Pequods, weary after their wild revels, seem to have been off their guard. The white men, divided into two parties, were allowed to approach within a rod of the gates at either side of the fort. Then a dog barked, and there was a cry "*Owanux! Owanux!* the English!" All within became alarm and confusion. The soldiers rushed on, tore away the bushes by which the gates were blocked up, and made their way into the fort, sword in hand. Little resistance was made; the naked Indians fled into their wigwams, between which the men in armour ran up and down, following the fugitives and slaying all whom they could reach. But this was slow work. "We shall never kill them after this manner!" cried Mason, and snatching a firebrand from one of the wigwams, threw it among the light dry mats of which they were made. They were instantly in a blaze. The fire had been lighted at the windward point and spread fast. The Englishmen ran out and surrounded the fort that none might escape. Fancy the horrible scene: the crackling of the flames, the shrieks of women and children, the volleys of musketry, the whiz of the arrows! Some of the Indians leaped up on the palisades and were mercilessly shot down. A few had the courage to rush forth and meet their death fighting hand to hand. Most of them were burned alive. Seven escaped, and seven were taken prisoners; between six and seven hundred perished. In about an hour all was over, when the sun rose upon a ring of smoking ashes filled with charred corpses. "Thus," says Mason in the true fanatic style, "did the Lord judge among the heathen."

It is said that one of the Indian guides was so overcome by the spectacle of this bloody massacre that he at once became a convert to the religion of the conquerors! Surely to these disciples it might have well been said, "Ye know not what spirit ye are of." With all their zeal and conscientiousness, the Puritans had yet to learn of Him who taught that God will have mercy and not sacrifice, and that even these poor Pequods were the neighbours of the wisest and most righteous men on earth. Necessity may have justified their destruction; but a true Christian spirit could not have exulted over the shambles in which they perished so miserably that bright May morning.

The English in this affair lost only two men and had twenty wounded. They were falling back towards their vessels for water and medical assistance when they found themselves engaged in a running fight with a party of Pequod warriors, who had come out from another fort, unconscious of the catastrophe which had just befallen their friends. But when they came to the place, says Cotton Mather, "where the English had been doing a good morning's work, they howled, they roared, they stamped, they tore their hair; and though they did not *swear* (for they knew not *how!*), yet they *cursed*, and were the pictures of so many *devils* in desperation;" in plain English, they were overwhelmed with natural grief and consternation. A vein of weakness seems to have underlaid the proverbial fortitude of the Indian character. While bearing unspeakable tortures without a groan, they would cry out under the pain of the toothache; and fierce as they were in the heat of battle, one crushing blow could strike them with abject terror.

The issue of the war was already decided. The English, largely reinforced by the arrival of the Massachusetts contingent, had now only to hunt down their enemies. "We have sometimes heard of *a gleaning as good as a vintage*," is the flinty-hearted Mather's hint as to what followed, the raid of Miles Standish against the Massachusetts on a larger scale. The Pequods vainly endeavoured to hide themselves, or to take refuge among the neighbouring tribes whom they had so long held in awe. It was now who should be most forward to avenge old grudges and please the victors by bringing in the head of a Pequod. The chief of the tribe was treacherously killed by the Mohawks, the Pequod country was laid waste, and its inhabitants were almost entirely exterminated. About two hundred surrendered in despair. The last remnant continuing to hold together were surrounded in a swamp and butchered almost to a man. The survivors were sold as slaves or distributed among the other tribes, so that the very name of the Pequods was blotted out of the land. If these poor red men had been Celtic rebels or Polish patriots, history and poetry would have shed their choicest tears over their fate; but there is little romance in the ferocity with which they struggled to defend their woods and swamps against a foreign race.

Whatever may be thought of the humanity shown in this war, it was most effectual as a matter of policy. For forty years no dangerous disturbance was caused by the Indians. The Narragansett and Mohegan tribes indeed soon revived their old enmities, and appealed to the English, unfortunately not always in vain, to take a side in the quarrel. The power of the strangers could not be questioned, but no strong hold was gained on the affections of the native inhabitants. From time to time there were squabbles, and rumours of plots which came to nothing. By this time not only the Dutch but a Swedish colony had firmly established themselves to the south, as the French to the north, and the rival nations were mutually suspected of leaguing with the Indians to destroy each other. In one way the Indians, in their turn, profited by the jealousy and want of union which existed among the Europeans. They began, from one or other quarter, to get firearms into their hands and to grow expert in their use. The danger of this did not fail to be foreseen by the shrewd settlers of New England, yet their sense of justice was such that at one time when men's minds were filled with apprehensions of an alleged conspiracy, and the Indians of the district had been disarmed, the Massachusetts government ordered their arms to be restored to them, seeing that these had been honestly bought from the French or the Dutch; "and we thought it best to trust God with our safety than to save ourselves by unrighteousness." Outrages on either side were conscientiously prosecuted by the settlers. Three Englishmen were hanged at one time for the murder of an Indian; an Indian accused of killing an Englishman was tried by a jury consisting of white and red men in equal numbers. The law, if not the gospel rule, was carefully observed towards the natives. Standing in these relations, the two races kept a watchful eye on each other, and in the time of the troubles known as King Philip's war, it was shown how little genuine goodwill had sprung up between them after half a century of involuntary neighbourhood. It was force rather than friendship that was to make way for the white man in America. A blind instinct may have moved the Pequods, rendering them half conscious of what would be the end of their race. If the Indian pow-wows had indeed possessed the gift of prophecy, they might have raised over the graves disturbed by Miles Standish and his companions such a song of lamentation as has found expression in the words of a modern poet :—

> Ah, little thought the strong and brave
>   Who bore their lifeless chieftain forth—
> Or the young wife who weeping gave
>   Her first born to the earth,
> That the pale race who waste us now,
> Among their bones should guide the plough.
>
> They waste us, ay, like April snow;
>   In the warm noon we shrink away;
> And fast they follow, as we go
>   Towards the setting day;
> Till they shall fill the land, and we
> Are driven into the western sea!

In half a century after the Pilgrims set foot on Plymouth Rock, the white men in New England already largely outnumbered the natives.

We have seen how much the Puritan divines were occupied in controversy. This may be the reason why missionary work was so long neglected by them at a time when the Jesuit missionaries were fearlessly exposing themselves to torture and death in carrying the cross through the tribes bordering the St. Lawrence and its vast chain of lakes. Yet the duty of making an attempt to convert the natives weighed heavily on the consciences of some good men in Massachusetts, and in 1646 John Eliot entered upon the labours with which his name is specially connected. Having acquired a certain command over their language, he began to preach and catechise among the Indians of his neighbourhood, and met at the outset with considerable encouragement. The Indians saw good reason to admit the power of the Englishman's God, and many of them were found curious to know something of the religion which seemed to bear such worldly advantages. Their gravity and attention were most commendable; none of them, records Eliot, slept through a sermon of an hour and a quarter, continued by other exercises to three hours. They had already the groundwork of a belief in a future life, a considerable degree of natural affection, and a vague veneration for the spirits which, as they conceived, animated the phenomena of nature. The shrewd questions which they put to their teacher showed them to be by no means dull witted; some even displayed signs of religious emotion. But beyond this point the devoted "apostle of the Indians" found progress slow. He was not a Jesuit missionary, to be content with outward conformity and such exhibitions of feeling as are easily aroused in a simple people. If forcing them to baptism or hiring them by presents were sufficient, "we could have gathered hundreds, yea thousands it may be, by this time, into the name of churches; but we have not learned as yet that art of coining Christians, or putting Christ's name or image upon copper metal." The heart must be changed, and the

Indian heart was dearly wedded to the immemorial habits and superstitions of the race. Eliot was forced to confess that before there could be much hope of effectual conversion his disciples must be brought to some degree of civilization. To this task he now addressed himself with the most patient diligence, while no way relaxing his spiritual and linguistic labours.

The Puritan scholars were given to that somewhat mechanical form of wit, the making of anagrams. The anagram of Eliot's name was aptly found to be *Toile;* in these days an *e* more or less made no great matter. Toil must indeed have been congenial to the man who succeeded in translating the Bible into the Indian language. It was printed through the aid of a Society which was formed in England, under the patronage of the parliament, for the Propagation of the Gospel in America. No one can conceive the difficulty of this translation who does not know the peculiar character of the Indian languages, their natural poverty in abstract and theological terms, as well as in names capable of being fitted to oriental scenes and objects, and, above all, their structural tendency to form conglomerate or *bunch-words,* that is, long polysyllables, which are practically whole sentences, including article, noun, verb, pronoun, preposition, and other ideas of relation. For example, we may take at random from Roger Williams' glossary, *numamttugehúckamen*, which he translates, "the wind is against me." To master such a language would require a considerable part of most men's lifetime.

When Cotton Mather gravely tried his hand at exorcising the demons by whom the patients, or impostors, of the Salem witch-mania were supposed to be possessed, he found that these evil spirits understood Latin, Greek, and Hebrew very well, but had not been able to attain a knowledge of one of the Indian dialects! Eliot himself was by no means free from the quaint credulity of the age. He firmly believed that the Hebrew language was that spoken in heaven, and also that the Indians were the descendants of the Jews, a belief which powerfully stimulated him in his efforts for their good. There were superstitious fanatics of a gloomier type, who held that the red men, being children of the devil himself, were naturally incapable of improvement and might be dealt with as unscrupulously as mere beasts. Luckily these were much in the minority, though every alarm of an Indian conspiracy brought over some timid minds to their views. The rulers of New England encouraged the missionary in his humane and Christian work, and considerable pecuniary aid came from England, where people knew less about the Indians, and were perhaps more ready to expect their conversion and civilization. About three thousand copies of the Indian Bible were thus published. The translation made with so much toil was into one of the best known dialects of New England. Alas! at the present day there is no living soul who finds in it his mother tongue.

To return to the practical beginnings of Eliot's mission. Such was his influence over the Indians, and their respect for the material prosperity of the white men, that a number of his pupils were ready to submit to an experiment in the restraints of civilized life. They asked and obtained land for a town, and agreed to a short and simple code of laws directed mainly against their besetting sins of dirtiness, idleness, dishonesty, intemperance, and quarrelling. The sabbath was to be observed; the sorcery of the pow-wows was to be prohibited; they were no longer to paint their bodies and dress their hair in fantastic fashions. Grave offences against the moral law were to be punished by death, others by fines, among which we find the penalty of twenty shillings attached to the luxury of beating a wife and of ten shillings to the practice of gambling.

The members of this new community declared themselves most anxious to hear and obey the teachings of Christianity. Naturally they met with bitter opposition from their more prejudiced countrymen, but the movement seemed to take root and to bid fair for ultimate success. Several such towns of "praying Indians" were established. The experiment however had scarcely a fair trial, for in King Philip's war the towns were broken up, and the numbers of the praying Indians dwindled away, the suspicions and indiscriminate anger of the English being almost as hurtful to them as the attacks of their own people; both sides in the heat of war and panic took them for traitors. But the destruction of these communities need not be much regretted, if we are to judge of them by the character of most of the semi-civilized Indians who are at the present day to be found here and there settled on reserve lands among the white men. Missionaries of all sects have done their best, following in the steps of Eliot and Roger Williams. Monks, Quakers, Moravians, Methodists, Churchmen, as well as Puritans, have too often been sorrowfully obliged to recognise that their work was only skin deep; and where any success has been obtained, it seems to have been owing not to the permanent force of principles but to the personal influence of some such patient, affectionate, and simple minded character as that of Eliot.

Education was tried, equally in vain. Much care was taken to train Indian youths in schools and colleges; sometimes they were even sent to Europe, and acquired such a degree of culture that they might be thought thoroughly weaned from the influences of their descent. But the natural instincts almost always proved too strong to be rooted out, and sooner or later the most hopeful pupils broke away to the wild life of the forest and the prairie. It was perhaps more common for Europeans voluntarily to embrace this savage freedom than for the Indian to abandon the ways of his forefathers.

One feature of "civilized" life the Indians were found but too ready to embrace. Whatever reception might be given to the missionary, the whiskey trader was welcome among them from the first, and the introduction of drink became the curse of the one race and the shame of the other. The savage warrior, unaccustomed to moral self control, knew nothing of moderation, and eagerly seized every opportunity of intoxicating himself to the point of frenzy with the firewater which enabled him to forget the monotony of his life. Other European scourges made equal havoc with his hardy frame; and while hundreds fell before the rifle, tens of thousands were swept away by dissipation and disease.

European arms as little availed them as the efforts made to rouse the stubborn natives to a sense of their true interests. Gunpowder but delayed, as whiskey hastened, what was soon seen to be only a matter of time. The restless tribes long continued to be the dread of the pioneer and the despair of the philanthropist. For two centuries they fought fitfully against the fate which pursued them farther and farther into the wilderness, but every war path ended in their defeat, and they shrank from the benefits offered by the conquerors more quickly than they had fled from their arms. If this was the fate of the tribes dwelling near the coast, who possessed among themselves the rudiments of agriculture, what could be expected of the roaming hunters of the great western prairies who knew no mode of subsistence except the chase? There have been happy exceptions both in the case of tribes and of individuals, but in the main the story is a sad one. As the European spread over the continent, bringing industry, commerce, and law, the red man rose from his seats, struggled, retreated, disappeared, leaving scarcely a monument but the names of mountain and stream which he once called his own.

THE AMERICAN COLONIES.

WE have seen how, after struggles and failures, our countrymen gained a firm footing on two parts of the American coast, and began to spread rapidly along the seaboard and to push their way farther and farther into the interior. These two centres of expansion, Virginia and Massachusetts, had from the circumstances of their foundation and the agencies concerned in it, received distinctive characters of their own, which, broadly speaking, were communicated respectively to the two great divisions known as the Northern and the Southern States.

Virginia was more friendly to church and king principles, and its "first families" were held in general estimation. Many of the Cavaliers found a congenial refuge here during the civil wars, as the Roundheads had done in Massachusetts. To tell the truth however, for all its loyalty, the southern colony on more than one occasion showed itself as jealous of its liberties as the northern. The difference was in social rather than in political life. Towns were rare in the south; the inhabitants lived for the most part upon separate plantations, often at considerable distances apart, and some of them of great extent. Many of these planters became rich, and set the example of a free jovial life of profusion and hospitality. Strict morals were not insisted on, education was neglected, nor did the love of industry flourish among the aristocratic sentiments of the dominant class. The labour of negroes and convicts was extensively employed; and the vices inherent in the character of master and slave did not fail to develop themselves and to become a source of weakness. Yet Virginia long continued to take the lead among the American colonies, as her climate and her resources well entitled her to do. But in time it was seen that her prosperity was ill founded upon a social state of which nothing now remains but evils that will be felt for generations to come. Slavery is no more, but it has left its legacy of moral disease and material loss to both the white and the black races. The misfortunes of the late civil war also have fallen heavily upon the Old Dominion; and in our own day Englishmen are again emigrating to help to till those neglected fields which labour and capital may yet turn into one of the gardens of the earth.

The northern settlers, enjoying no such advantages of soil and climate, were driven to seek their welfare in persevering toil and enterprise. They gathered themselves into towns and villages; they cultivated small farms; they introduced manufactures and pushed a keen trade with their Indian neighbours. The qualities of mind thus called into play became habits of life with the New Englander, which, transmitted from generation to generation, have developed that type of the shrewd, practical, helpful, inventive man of business whose favourite motto is "go ahead!" We have seen how democratic principles flourished here from the first, and how the social habits of the community were marked by frugality and homeliness. The prevalent religious notions gave an austere and melancholy tone to the character of the early colonists, the effects of which are still visible. But against the evils which might have thus arisen a safeguard was provided in popular education; it was not long before the people themselves became too well instructed to allow their ministers to hunt out witches and heretics. The founders of the colony had recognised that knowledge is power, and their wisdom was justified by the history of New England. The rich planters of Virginia might sneer at the Yankees, but it was the Yankees who in the end went ahead to most purpose, and set their mark most deeply upon the constitution of the United States. In the march of intellect they have gone so far ahead that it is common for Englishmen to look on them as representing the whole country; the name Yankee is popularly used among us for an American, just as it was first applied by the Indians to all Englishmen, whose name they were not able to pronounce more distinctly.

The plan of our work is now accomplished; and we need not follow, except by a few general observations, the progress of the various colonies which in a century grew into the United States. Some of these colonies, as Pennsylvania and Georgia, have stories of their own well worth telling; but a great part of the record of American colonisation is now filled with a somewhat monotonous chronicle of disputes: disputes about charters, patents, boundaries, disputes between proprietaries and settlers, between royal governors and colonial assemblies, bloody disputes with the Indians, and constant disputes between the rival European nations who thought to find room for themselves on this vast continent.

The latter class of dispute ended in a way not unusual where our countrymen are concerned. The Swedish settlements had already been swallowed up by the Dutch, who in their turn were forced to submit to the English soon after the restoration of Charles II. Thus were acquired the states of New York, New Jersey, and Delaware. Henceforward many communities of foreigners settled in the new colonies, Swiss, Germans, Moravians, French Huguenots and others, but always under British patronage and authority.

One power remained to be dealt with, the greatest of all. Little has been said of the progress of France in the New World; that is a great story which deserves telling by itself. While the English, true to their native bent, were making themselves familiar with every harbour and channel on the coast, the French, once established in Lower Canada, had turned towards the interior for their exploring ground. Their missionaries and traders found their way along the lakes of the St. Lawrence, reached the prairies of the west, and launched boldly out into unknown wildernesses. The Mississippi was discovered, and its turbid waters were traced to the Gulf of

Mexico. In the south the colony of Louisiana was founded, and a chain of posts soon stretched from New Orleans to Canada. France bid fair to acquire a great empire in the west, while as yet the English possessions consisted only of a belt of land extending for a thousand miles along the sea coast.

But two such neighbours could not live at peace in the New any more than in the Old World. In the middle of last century France and England grappled together on three continents. In America the struggle was marked by peculiar horrors and sufferings, as might be expected from the mode of warfare natural to the Indian allies employed on either side. The fortunes of this war were various, but finally victory fell to the English. In 1759 Wolfe defeated Montcalm on the Plains of Abraham before Quebec, both commanders falling mortally wounded in the battle. Soon afterwards Canada was ceded to England, who thus found herself without any rival in America except the now somewhat decrepit Spain, with her little sleepy colony in Florida and certain vast claims which she showed no inclination to put into force and would part with easily for a round sum in ready money. Thus had the wheel of fortune turned since the days of the Armada!

Yet this great conquest soon proved a dear one for British power. The colonists, relieved from the chronic dread of Indian wars instigated by the French, and no longer obliged to look constantly to England for succour against a common enemy, had leisure to stir up the old quarrels that from the beginning had existed between the government of the mother country and its American dependencies. Aristocratic Virginia as well as democratic Massachusetts rankled under a long sense of ill usage; and the truth is that they had fair ground of complaint.

During three reigns the government had done little for the cause of colonisation beyond graciously permitting its subjects to risk their goods and their lives, which perhaps it had first rendered unendurable at home. But when the colonies began to prosper, England awoke to the necessity of keeping them in the leading strings of allegiance. It was too late entirely to destroy the popular institutions which had sprung up beyond the Atlantic, but much was done to temper them by the introduction of those formalities and prerogatives which formed so large a part of the idea of government in Europe. It must also be confessed that our country showed herself a very mercenary mother, and looked on the colonies less as a family to be proud of than as an excellent market for British manufactures. According to the ignorant commercial policy of the time, attempts were made to discourage local manufactures and to force the colonists to import British goods. No foreign merchants might enter into competition; English ships alone were privileged to discharge in American ports; the colonies were not even allowed free trade with each other; many of their products they might sell to no other nation but England.

These restrictions and interferences were very galling to the sturdy offspring who had no desire to forget that England was their mother, yet who could not but remember that they were now grown up and that they owed everything to their own exertions. Ideas of liberty and justice developed fast in this new busy life, where men had to think for themselves and found it easy to shake off many old prejudices. Hence tendencies to political independence showed themselves early. But the British parliament stubbornly persisted in considering that it had full power over all the states, from which it did not admit one representative. At the beginning of the eighteenth century shrewd observers had foreseen what must be the inevitable result.

After the close of the last French and Indian war these troubles came to a head. It was proposed that the colonists should bear some share in the expense of this war, which was fair enough. But it was certainly unjust that the English parliament should undertake to impose taxes on America without its consenting or being consulted. In 1765 the Stamp Act was passed, and was received with a burst of indignation in the colonies, which were determined not to submit to taxation without representation. An American congress met for the first time to protest against this arbitrary measure. Riots took place, the authorities who attempted to act upon the new law were insulted and ill used, and so strong was the popular feeling that it was found impossible to resist it. The Stamp Act remained a dead letter, and by the influence of some of the more enlightened English statesmen it was soon formally repealed.

But the chief advisers of King George III. were not enlightened statesmen, and the monarch himself, though a man of good intentions, was of a singularly obstinate disposition and a narrow and ignorant mind. They were angry and astonished that the colonies should show such a bold spirit, and it was resolved to press the point in dispute, by force if necessary. It was in vain that wiser men and those who knew more about America, urged the danger of driving the colonists to violent measures and denounced the injustice with which they had been so long treated. Fresh taxes were laid upon tea and other articles. Troops and ships of war were sent out to overawe all discontent. The king and the parliament were determined to have their way.

The colonists were equally resolute. The tea, on which the government hoped to exact a duty, could not even be landed; it was thrown into the harbour or burned, or, in some cases, sent back to England. The American patriots refused to use the taxed articles or any kind of British goods. The ill feeling rose apace. As yet a separation between the two countries was scarcely thought of except by a few. But the colonists were mustering men and gathering arms and military stores. It was plain that they would fight for their rights, and the question was, could they stand against regular troops? The English ministers would not believe this, and thought that when it came to the point, the raw militia men would not be so mad as to resist the power of England; the force of the dangerous elements that were disturbing the political atmosphere of America was not rightly estimated till too late.

It was in Massachusetts that the storm first broke. Boston had brought itself into special disfavour by the leading part it took in opposition to the government measures. As a punishment, its port was ordered to be closed, and troops were quartered in the city. A very bitter feeling sprang up between these soldiers and the majority of the inhabitants: the "Tories," or friends of the government, were chiefly found among the rich. Blood had already been shed in a street quarrel, and in the beginning of 1775 the governor and his soldiers found themselves almost in the position of an army beleaguered in an enemy's country. Outside of the walls a provincial congress was sitting, the militia was being regularly drilled, and a close watch was kept upon the movements of the troops. An attempt to sally out and seize part of the stores of the colonial forces, brought on the collision which must have come sooner or later. The alarm was given; the whole district was roused through the night; and on the village green of Lexington, in the grey dawn of the 19th of April, 1775, was fired the first shot of the Revolutionary War.

We all know the end of that war, in which the wisdom, energy, and patience of the great Washington were able to overcome every difficulty and disaster, and to inspire his countrymen with fresh courage when the colonial cause seemed at its lowest ebb. In 1776 Congress issued the Declaration of

Independence, thereby taking up a position from which there could be no retreat. In 1783 Britain gave up the struggle, which had long been unpopular among the majority of the people, and the United States of America became one of the nations of the world.

Thus what had been gained by the courage and persevering labours of private men was lost by the obstinacy of unwise rulers. The States of America were indeed lost to England before she rightly knew what she had gained. It is useless now to speculate on what might have been, or to moralize on what should have been the result to us of this great conquest of the axe and the plough. But while we look back with regret and shame to the manner in which the colonies were treated, we may remember with pride that the heroes who laid the foundation of them were our countrymen, as well as the forefathers of that great nation which unhappily no longer boasts of the English name, though it has not failed to inherit the English nature, with the restless untiring energy that, as in the days of Walter Raleigh and John Winthrop, still sends forth Britons and Americans to seek new homes by sea and land, and to plant for the good of mankind the waste and foul places of the world.

INDEX.

Aberdeen—practice of kidnapping at, 154.
Aggawam — " The Simple Cobbler of "—his opinion of toleration, 261.
Alewives—a fish used as manure, 210.
Algonquin tribes—275.
Amadas, Captain—his voyage to Carolina, 43.
Amadis de Gaul — popularity of, 4.
Amerigo Vespucci — gives his name to America, 22.
Amsterdam — Separatists take refuge at, 172.
Anne, Cape—named Tragabigzanda by Captain Smith, 181; quarrel of fishermen at, 222.
Anabaptists—in Massachusetts, 266.
Antinomians—in Massachusetts, 266.
Argall, Captain — kidnaps Pocahontas, 149.
Armada—the Spanish, 63.
Artillery—of the Plymouth colony, 201.
Azores, the—death of Sir R. Grenville at, 58.

Bacon, Lord—quoted, 32, 143.
Baltimore, Lord—favours toleration in Maryland, 272.
Baptists—persecution of in New England, 264.
Barlow, Captain—his voyage to Carolina, 43; description of a native village, 48; returns to England, 51.
Barrowists—see *Separatists*.
Beards—rare among Indians, 93, 110.
Bermudas, the—old sea saying about, 43; wreck upon, 135.
Bible, the—translated into Indian language, 290.
Billington family—give trouble to the Pilgrims, 198.
Bloodhounds — Indians afraid of, 8.
Bogall, Bashaw — Captain Smith prisoner of, 77.
Boston—foundation of, 240; its name changed, 251; its character, 252; its inhabitants favour the religious innovators, 266; revolutionary spirit in, 302.
Bradford, William—his journal of the Pilgrims' proceedings 103; elected governor, 208.
Brazil—believed to be peopled by Amazons, 6; Portuguese and French colonies in, 24.
Brentford—Pocahontas' residence at, 151.
Brewster, Elder—accompanies Pilgrims as religious teacher, 178; does not

x

administer sacraments, 231.
Bristol—practice of kidnapping at, 154.
Brownists—see *Separatists*.
Burras, Anne—marriage of, 123.
Bryant, William Cullen—quoted, 287.

Cabot, John and Sebastian—their discoveries in the English service, 22.
Cambridge, Mass.—university founded at, 251.
Canada—first explored by French, 23; seized by English and restored, 235; French progress in, 297, ceded to England, 298.
Caribs—accused of cannibalism, 12.
Canaries, the—usual course to America, 43.
Carolina—French colony in, 24; dangerous coast of, 43; English expeditions to, 44, 52.
Cartier, Jacques—sails up St. Lawrence, 23.
Carver, John—elected governor of Plymouth colony, 183; his death, 207.
Cattle—introduced into New England, 230.
Champlain—his explorations in Canada, 233.
Chapbook story of John Smith's adventures, 68.
Charcoal—dangerous fumes of, 131.
Charles, Cape—named after Prince Charles, 83; Indians of, 105.
Charles I.—grants liberal charter to Massachusetts colony, 236; repents, 259.
Chesapeake Bay—English colony arrives in, 82; exploration of, 105.
Chickahominy Indians, —overawed by Captain Smith, 131; become subject to King James, 150.
Chickahominy river—Smith captured on, 87.
Church of England—established in Virginia, 153; Reformation of, 165; Separatists from, 170; denounced by Roger Williams, 269.
Church-membership—conditions of in Massachusetts, 264.
Cod, Cape,—discovered by Bartholomew Gosnold, 171; conformation of, 181.
Coligny, Admiral — endeavours to establish Huguenot colonies in America, 24.
Collier, Samuel—left among Indian tribe to learn their language, 117.
Columbus, Christopher — discovers America, 1; his search for a patron, 3; desires to restore Jerusalem, 7.
Commerce, American — restrictions on, 299.
Commissioners — appointed by the king for Virginia, 159; for the American colonies, 259.
Confederation of New England States, 273.
Congress protests against the Stamp Act, 300; publishes Declaration of Independence, 303.

Connecticut river — colony settled on, 253.
Connecticut colony—resolve to root out Pequods, 281.
Conquistadores, the — their conduct in America, 7.
Constantinople — Captain Smith sent prisoner to, 77.
Controversy—among Massachusetts colonists, 266.
Cotton, Rev. Mr.—denounces sharp trading, 246.
Crim Tartary—Smith's captivity in, 77.
Croatoan, island of—colony disappears at, 65.
Cromwell, Oliver—said to be about to emigrate, 259; friendly to New England, 260.

Dare, Virginia, birth of—62.
Declaration of Independence,—published by Congress, 303.
Delaware — taken from Swedes, 297.
Delaware, Lord—appointed governor of Virginia, 135; his opportune arrival, 141; death, 146.
Delft Haven—Pilgrims embark at, 172.
Delight, the—wreck of, 41.
Democracy—of Puritan Government, 255.
Devon—plays leading part in maritime adventure, 36.
De Gourgues—avenges massacre of French in Florida, 28. [233.
De Monts—explores Canada,
De Soto, Ferdinand—leads expedition to Florida, 21.
Dominicans—befriend the Indians, 16.

Downs, the — fleet detained in, 81.
Drake, Sir Francis—the circumnavigator, 30; relieves English colony at Roanoke, 57.
Drink,—the scourge of the Indians, 292.
Dutch, the—give asylum to exiles for conscience, 173; establish settlement on Hudson river, 175; come into collision with English settlers, 253; submit to England, 297.

Education—provided for in Massachusetts, 251; failure of among Indians, 292.
El Dorado—belief in, 6.
Eliot, Rev. John—begins to preach to Indians, 287; translates the Bible into Indian language, 289; his influence over the Indians, 290.
Elizabeth, Queen—her encouragement of colonization, 35; winks at piracy, 36; prevents Raleigh from going abroad, 38; confirms Gilbert's patent to Raleigh, 42; gives a name to Virginia, 52; heaps favours on Raleigh, 52; worthies of her age, 74; her religious policy, 167.
Endicott, John—governor of colony at Salem, 236; cuts red cross out of standard, 260; leads expedition against Indians, 292.
England—awakes to her destiny, 30; popular hatred of Spain, 31; zeal for plantation, 32; danger of from the

Armada, 63; Reformation in, 165; becomes mistress in North America, 298; treatment of her American colonies, 299.

Fear, Cape, 43.
Finery—savage, 93, 206.
Florida—believed to contain the fountain of youth, 6; Ponce de Leon's expedition to, 21; French colony in, 24; farmed out for conquest to Pedro Melendez, 26; settled by Spaniards, 28; bought by United States, 29.
France—her explorations in North America, 22. 297; overcome by English, 298.
Franchise—conditions of in New England, 266.
Francis I.—thinks of colonizing in America, 23.
French—their conduct and fate in Florida, 24; expelled from New England, 149; attacked by English in Canada, 235.
Frobisher, Martin—thinks he has discovered gold, 35.

Gates, Sir Thomas—wrecked on the Bermudas, 135; arrives at Jamestown, 140.
George III.—his obstinacy, 301.
Georgia—settlement of, 296.
Germans—sent to Virginia, 112; their treachery, 129, 132.
Gilbert, Sir Humphrey—receives letters patent for colonizing America, 35; sails from Devon, 36; second expedition, 38; lands in Newfoundland, 39; sails southward 40; his misfortunes and death, 41.
Golden Age, the—in Carolina, 51.
Golden Hind, the—returns to England, 42.
Gonsalvo de Cordova—renown of, 4.
Gorges, Sir Ferdinand—promotes colonization, 79; aids Smith, 145; his efforts to colonize New England, 234.
Gosnold, Bartholomew—goes to Virginia, 80; death of, 87; discoverer of Cape Cod, 171.
Granganimeo,—visits English, 46; kindness shown to English by him and his wife, 48.
Gravesend—Pocahontas dies at, 151.
Grenville, Sir Richard—his voyage to Carolina, 52; harshness to natives, 53; his death, 58.
Gulf Stream, the—avoided by old navigators, 43.
Gunpowder—puts an end to chivalry, 71; taken by the Indians for seed, 93; Indians cured of meddling with, 132; explosion of disables John Smith, 137; Mayflower almost blown up by, 199.

Hakluyt's voyages—quoted, 37, 50, 62; aid to spread geographical knowledge, 78.
Hampden, John—a visitor to Plymouth, 218; supposed

to be about to emigrate, 259.
Hariot, Thomas—his account of Virginia, 59, 78.
Hatteras, Cape—danger of, 43.
Hawkins, John — relieves French colony in Virginia, 25.
Henry, Cape—named after Prince Henry, 82.
Henry VIII.—his share in the Reformation, 166.
Hispaniola, or St. Domingo —natives of exterminated, 13; visited by English fleet, 52.
Hobbamock—attaches himself to Plymouth colony, 214.
Horses—the Indians afraid of, 8.
Hudson, Henry, sails up Hudson river, 175.
Hudson river—Dutch settlement on, 175.
Huguenots—anticipate Puritan colony, 24.
Hunt, Rev. Robert, his influence with Virginia colonists, 81, 84.
Hunt, Captain—kidnaps natives, 203.
Hutchison, Mrs. Anne—banished from Massachusetts, 267.

Independents, the—rise of, 170.
Indians—their wonder at white men, 8; their helplessness against European arms, 9; enslaved by Spaniards, 10; their "conversion," 14; degraded by influence of priests, 18; welcome the French to Florida, 25; aid them against Spaniards, 28; their intercourse with Raleigh's colonists, 47; become unfriendly, 54; attacked by English, 56, 61; revenge the death of their chief, 60; their habits, weapons, etc., in Virginia, 99; Smith's dealings with, 109, 139; massacre colonists in Virginia, 156; graves of, 189; houses and furniture, 190; no longer feared by Puritan settlers, 274; controversy as to origin of, 274; tribes of, 275; intercourse with the English in Massachusetts, 276; they procure fire-arms, 286; their religious state, 288; their languages, 289; missionaries among, 17, 287, 291; the *praying* Indians, 291; incapacity of for civilization, 292; fate of, 293.
Iroquois, the—warlike character of, 275.
Italian discoverers, 22.

James I.—grants patents for colonization, 79; his respect for royal blood, 151; his dislike of Puritanism, 168; his opinion of armour, 248.
James River—colony arrives in, 82.
Jamestown—settlement at, 83; unhealthy situation of, 85; burned, 103; state of in 1609, 138; about to be abandoned, 141.
Jesuits—courage and devotion of, 287.

Jews—their laws imitated by the Puritans, 255; Indians supposed to be descended from, 274, 290.
John, Sagamore — affects English customs, 276.
Johnson, Lady Arbella—accompanies Puritan emigrants, 239.
Judgments of God—Puritan belief in, 262.

Kecoughtan—Smith "keeps Christmas" at, 122.
Kennebec, the—settlement attempted on, 144.
Kidnapping—154.
King Philip's war, 286, 291.

La Boëtie—proposes to take refuge in America, 24.
Labrador—Frobisher at, 35.
Lane, Ralph—governor of colony at Roanoke, 54; slaughters Indians, 56; returns with Drake, 58.
Las Casas—the champion of the Indians, 16.
Laudonnière, Réné—leader of French colony in Florida, 24; surprised by Spaniards, 26.
Laydon, John—marriage of, 122.
Lexington—skirmish at, 302.
Leyden—Robinson's congregation at, 173.
London—company for colonization formed at, 79; Pocahontas' visit to, 151.
Long Island—Dutch and English settlers on, 253.
Louisiana—foundation of, 298.
Lynn—John Smith apprenticed at, 75; gives name to town in America, 252.

Maine—first settlement of, 234.
Manhattan Island—Dutch colony on, 175.
Manoa—a fabulous golden city, 6.
Manteo—is faithful to the English, 60.
Manufactures—begun in Virginia, 112.
Martin—one of John Smith's enemies, 103; returns to Virginia and is offered the presidency, 136.
Maryland—settled by Lord Baltimore, 272.
Mason, Major John—his campaign against the Pequods, 281.
Massachusetts Bay—conformation of, 181; Puritan settlements in, 235.
Massachusetts Indians—reduced by plague, 202; accused of plotting, 213; reduced to submission by Standish, 228; their intercourse with Boston settlers, 276.
Massachusetts colony—beginning of, 235; charter of, 237; number and character of colonists, 239; early sufferings of, 240; adopts Independent form of worship, 241; their austere manners, 242; dress and manners, 247; houses, 248; description of life in, 249; extension of, 253; politics formed on scriptural models, 254; democratic sympathies, 255; exclusive-

ness, 258; ordered to surrender charter, 259; their credulous belief in special providences, 262; persecution in, 264; theological controversies, 266; leaders of schism banished from, 267; join confederation of New England colonies, 273; intercourse with Indians, 274; quarrels with Indians, 278; take part in Pequod war, 281; justice of, 286; their neglect of missionary work, 287; character of colony, 294.

Massasoit, chief of the Wampanoags—visits Pilgrim colony, 205; his poverty, 209; demands surrender of Squanto, 214; sickness of, 219; reveals plot, 221.

Massawomeks—a tribe encountered by Smith, 108.

Mather, Rev. Cotton — quoted, 183, 254, 284; his absurd credulity, 289.

Mayflower, the — conveys the Pilgrims to America, 180; return of, 200.

May sports—38; abhorred by Puritans, 52, 258.

Melendez, Pedro — massacres French in Florida, 26.

Milton, John—quoted, 269.

Mint—established in Massachusetts, 247.

Missions—the Spanish, 16; French, 287; English, 155, 288; general failure of, 291.

Mississippi, the—De Soto buried in, 22; discovered by French, 297.

Mohawks — troublesome neighbours, 276.

Mohegan Indians—side with English against Pequods, 280; their cowardice, 282.

Monacan Indians — visited by Newport, 115.

Money used in Massachusetts, 247.

Monopolies—47, 52; Parliament's dislike to, 244.

Montaigne—quoted, 8, 28.

Montcalm—death of, 298.

Montreal—named by Cartier, 23.

More, Sir Thomas—quoted, 2.

Morton of Merry Mount— driven out by the Puritans, 258.

Mosco—attaches himself to the English, 110.

Narragansett Indians—declare war against Plymouth colony, 213; Roger Williams settles among, 271; diverted from alliance with Pequods, 280.

Negroes—enslaved without scruple, 12; introduced into Virginia, 154.

New Amsterdam — former name of New York, 175.

New England—named by John Smith, 144; attempts to colonize, 233; attention of Puritans turned to, 235; religious excitement flourishes in, 261; confederation of the colonies in, 276; growth of population, 287.

New Englanders—character of, 295.

New France former name of Canada, 23.

New Hampshire—first settlement of, 234.
New Haven—colony at, 252.
New Jersey—acquired by English, 297.
New York—founded by Dutch, 175; conquered by English, 297.
Newfoundland—fisheries of, 23; annexed by Gilbert, 39.
Newport, Captain—goes to Virginia, 81; returns with supplies, 101; a bad trader, 102; encourages the gold fever, 103; at the crowning of Powhatan, 113; attempts to discover South Sea, 115; threatened by Smith, 121; wrecked on the Bermudas, 135.
Nova Scotia—unsuccessful attempt to settle by Scotchmen, 235.
Nunez, Vasco — discovers South Sea, 21.

Obtakiest—desires to make peace with English, 229.
Okee—Indian name for idol, 100.
Olympagh—siege of, 71.
Opechancanough — captures Smith, 88; his treachery towards English, 126; hatred of the settlers, 152; his death, 158.
Orapaks—Smith prisoner at, 89.

Pamunkey—Smith's adventures at, 91, 126.
Parliament—interferes with lotteries for benefit of Virginia, 149; opposes monopoly granted by king, 234; encourages propagation of the gospel among Indians, 269; claims right to tax America, 300.
Paspahegh, chief of—his encounter with Smith, 130.
Patuxet — native name of Plymouth, 196.
Pecksuot—provokes Miles Standish, 226.
Pennsylvania—settled, 296.
Pequods, The—quarrel with English, 279; surprised in their fort, 283; fate of, 285.
Percy, Hon. George—his description of sufferings of Virginian colony, 85; appointed president, 139.
Persecution—of Protestants, 166; of dissenters, 167; in Massachusetts, denounced by Roger Williams, 273.
Pestilence—on coast of Massachusetts, 202.
Philip II. of Spain—farms out Florida for conquest, 26; proclaimed master of North America, 27.
Pierce, John—patent held in his name, 231.
Pilgrims—John Smith in danger among a crew of, 76.
Pilgrim Fathers, the—take refuge in Holland, 172; their trials, 173; resolve to seek New England, 174; negotiations and arrangements for their emigration, 176; embark at Delft Haven, 178; arrive at Cape Cod, 181; form themselves into a body politic, 183; go on shore,

184; find traces of natives, 186; first encounter with Indians, 193; settle at Plymouth, 195; sufferings of, 199; their defensive preparations, 201; visited by Samoset, 202; make treaty with natives, 206; begin to prosper, 208; joined by new emigrants, 211; give aid to Weston's colony, 215; resolve to make war on Indians, 224; overawe their enemies, 229; become independent of their partners in England, 231; honour due to them, 232; form friendly relations with Massachusetts colony, 241; their backwardness in persecution, 265; join confederation of New England colonies, 273; take part in Pequod war, 281.

Piracy—winked at in Elizabeth's reign, 36.

"Plantation"—popular in England, 32; John Smith's zeal for, 160.

Plymouth,—company formed at for colonization, 79; revived, 233.

Plymouth, Massachusetts—Pilgrims land at, 195; Roger Williams preacher at, 268.

Plymouth colony—see *Pilgrim Fathers*.

Plymouth rock—veneration for, 196.

Pocahontas—her rescue of Captain Smith, 94; credibility of the story, 69, 95; aids the English, 97; sues for peace, 105; warns Smith against her father, 125; saves a boy from death, 139; kidnapped, 149; marriage of, 150; visits England and dies, 151.

Poles—a party of sent to Virginia, 112.

Ponce de Leon's expedition to Florida—21.

Pope, the—assigns the New World to Spain, 4.

Popham, Sir John—efforts for colonization of Maine, 79.

Portuguese — a maritime people, 4; Africa and East Indies assigned to by the Pope, 5; settle in Brazil, 24.

Potatoes—introduced into England, 59.

Potomac, the—John Smith as a prisoner on, 91; exploration of, 106.

Powhatan—visited by English colonists, 83; receives Smith and orders him to death, 93; sets him free, 96; extent of his authority, 99; trades with English, 102; quarrels with English, 104; coronation of, 113; tries to starve out colony, 120; his false professions, 124; flies into woods, 129; seeks peace, 132; slaughters a band of English, 139; finally returns to amity, 150; his death, 152.

Powhatan River; see *James River*.

Powhatan Indians, the, 99.

Pow-wows—antics of, 91; their incantations at a sick bed, 219.

Praying Indians, the, 291.
Providence—founded by Roger Williams, 271.
Providence, special—Puritan belief in, 262.
Punishments—used among Indians, 132; at Jamestown, 147; in Massachusetts, 244.
Purchas, his Pilgrims, —quoted 85.
Puritans, the—characteristics of, 164; their rise, 168; become political party, 169; a division among, 170; their courage and manliness, 194, 211; turn their attention to New England, 235; emigrate in large numbers, 239 (see *Massachusetts colony*).

Quadaquina — visits Plymouth colony, 207.
Quakers—persecution of in New England, 264.
Quebec—seized and restored by English, 235; Wolfe's victory before walls of, 298.

Raleigh, Sir Walter—character of, 33; early military services, 34; his first voyage with Gilbert, 36; detained by Elizabeth, 38; procures confirmation of Gilbert's patent, 42; sends out colonies to Virginia, 43, 52, 60; introduces tobacco, 58; endeavours to find lost colony, 67; his projects in South America, 78.
Rappahannock, the—Smith visits as prisoner, 91; exploration of, 110.
Ratcliffe, *alias* Sicklemore—appointed president of Virginian colony, 86; his uselessness, 104; deposed, 108; returns and plots against Smith, 136; his death, 139.
Rebecca, see *Pocahontas*.
Reformation, the—effect of on the Church of England, 164.
Reformers, the — persecution of, 166.
Rhode Island—foundation and growth of, 273.
Ribault, John—leader of French colony in Florida, 24; massacred by Spaniards, 27.
Roanoke Island—first visited by English, 48; colonies settled on, 54, 60; abandoned settlements at, 60, 64.
Robinson, Rev. John—minister of Separatist congregation, 171; his farewell address to the Pilgrims, 178; regrets the violence of Miles Standish, 229; dies before he reaches America, 231.
Rolfe, John—marries Pocahontas, 151.
Romances of chivalry—popularity of among the Spaniards, 5; their effect on John Smith, 70.
Rottenton—battle of, 77.
Russell, Dr.—cures John Smith, 107.

Sabbath, the—reverence of Puritans for, 204; strict observance of, 242.

INDEX. 315

Sailors—great men among, 2; bad as traders, 103.
St. *Augustine*—oldest town in United States, 27.
St. *Domingo*, or Hispaniola—natives exterminated, 13; visited by English fleet, 52.
St.*John*,Newfoundland—frequented by fishermen, 39.
St. *John's river*—French settlement on, 25.
St.*Lawrence*, the—navigated by J. Cartier, 23.
Salem—founded,236; Roger Williams preacher at, 268.
Salt — importance of to colony, 211.
Samoset—welcomes the Plymouth colony, 202.
Saybrook, *Fort*—beset by Pequods, 280.
Scrivener, Mr.—backs up John Smith, 104; deputed president, 106; drowned, 129.
Separatists—their opinions, 170; congregation of fly into Holland, 172.
Shakespeare—quoted,9,143.
Sigismund, Prince of Transylvania—rewards John Smith, 77.
Slavery—of Indians, 11; effects of in Virginia, 295.
Smith, Captain John—his story little known in England, 68; his romantic disposition and youthful adventures, 70 ; his practical talents, 72 ; his style as an author, 73; a man of his age, 74; birth and education, 75 ; runs away to sea, 75; becomes a soldier, 76; sold as a slave, 77; his escape, 77; his sea-fight against Spaniards, 78; engages with London Virginia Company, 80; quarrels with comrades, 81; accused,but successfully defends himself, 84; his activity, 86, 104, 116, 121 ; fires upon deserters, 87; made prisoner by Indians, 87; taken for a magician, 90; led before Powhatan, 93 ; ordered to death, and rescued, 94; doubts as to his story of Pocahontas, 94; set free, 96; his enemies at the fort, 98; his opinion of Virginia, 101; trading with Powhatan, 102; indignation against gold hunters, 103; overawes Indians, 105; begins exploration of Chesapeake Bay, 105; way of dealing with Indian tribes, 106-110; hurt by sting-ray,and returns to Jamestown, 107; offered the government, but resumes expedition, 108 ; appointed governor, 111; assists to crown Powhatan, 113 ; his rule to cure swearing, 116; his notions of governorship, 117; journeys in search of corn, 121; discovers Powhatan's treachery, 124; visits Opechancanough, 126; his boldness, 127; hastens back to fort, 129; his encounter with the chief of Paspahegh, 130; overawes the Chickahominies, 131 ; punishes his idle soldiers,

134; offers to resign, 136; disabled by an explosion, 137; returns to England, 138; his loss felt, 139; offers his services to the Plymouth Company, 144; his zeal in the cause of colonization, 144, 160; his voyages to, and writings on, New England, 145; his opinion of the Pilgrim Fathers, 146; meets Pocahontas at Brentford, 151; his evidence as to the cause of failure in Virginia, 159; his works and death, 160; his character, 161.

Smith Island — discovered and named, 105.

Somers, Sir George—wrecked on the Bermudas, 135; arrives in Virginia, 140.

South Sea, the—discovered by Vasco Nunez, 21; believed to be near Virginia, 54, 104, 108, 112.

Spain—power of, 3; government of friendly to the Indians, 11; limits of her colonization in America, 21; her claims and possessions in the United States territory, 298.

Spaniards—their love of romance, 5; thirst for gold, 7; cruelties of, 9-16; massacre French in Florida, 27; settle at St. Augustine, 28.

Spanish America — history of, 19.

Speedwell, the — hired to convey pilgrims to America, but returns, 179.

Squanto—attaches himself to the English, 204; his bad conduct, 214; his death, 215.

Squirrel, the—founders in the Atlantic, 42.

Stamp Act, the—indignation caused by, 300.

Standish, Miles — explores Cape Cod, 185; his courage, 194, 207, 227; appointed captain of the Pilgrims' forces, 201; his character, 222; kills Indian braves, and overawes their tribe, 226.

"Starving-time," the — at Jamestown, 140.

Susquehannah Indians — Smith's description of, 109.

Swedes—end of their settlement, 297.

Tattershall—John Smith resides at, 76.

Taxation—resisted by the American colonies, 300.

Tea—unpopular tax upon, 301.

Temperance — encouraged by Puritan colonists, 245.

Timor Bashaw—killed by John Smith, 77.

Tisquantum, see *Squanto*.

Tobacco—first mention of, 25; introduced into England, 59; becomes staple of Virginia, 153; Puritan scruples about, 245.

Toghwoghs—tribe visited by John Smith, 108.

Toleration—disapproved of by the Puritans, 261; advocated by Roger Williams, 268; by Milton, 269; established in Maryland, 272.

Tragabigzanda, Princess—favours John Smith, 77.
Transportation of convicts to Virginia, 154.
Tremont, or *Trimountain*—former name of Boston, 251.
Turks—John Smith's adventures among, 70.

United colonies—of New England, 276.
United States, the—birth of, 303.

Vane, Sir Henry—chosen governor of Massachusetts, but soon leaves the colony, 267.
Verazzani—sails to America in the French service, 23.
Virginia—popular delusions as to, 34; named by Elizabeth, 52; Hariot's account of, 59; general history of, compiled by John Smith, 73; name loosely used, 79; description of, 98; manufactures begun in, 112; strict laws of, 147; progress, 148; great massacre in, 156; transferred to the Crown, 159; character of planters in, 294; prosperity and misfortunes of, 295.
Voting—restricted in Massachusetts, 264.

Wampanoags—the neighbours of the Pilgrims, 205.
Wampum—Indian money, 247.
Ward, Rev. Mr., "the Simple Cobbler of Aggawam"—his opinion of toleration, 261.
Washington, General, 302.
Werowocomoco—Powhatan's residence at, 93; coronation of Powhatan, 113; Smith's adventures at, 123.
Weston, Mr.—sends colony to New England, 215.
Weymouth, *Mass.*—colony established at, 215.
Weymouth colony—bad conduct of colonists, 216; their distress, 217, 224; relieved by Standish, 225; broken up, 228.
Wheelwright, Rev. Mr.—banished from Massachusetts, 267.
White, John—governor of colony at Roanoke, 60; leaves Virginia, 62; returns with aid, 63; his fruitless search, 64.
Williams, Roger—advocates toleration, 268; his scrupulosity, 269; banished from Massachusetts, 271; settles at Providence, 272; procures charter for Rhode Island, 273; his friendship for the Indians, 276; prevents Indian alliance against New England colonies, 280; his services to his countrymen, 281.
Willoughby—John Smith born at, 75.
Wingandacoa—native name of Carolina, 51.
Wingfield, Edward Maria—goes to Virginia, 80; made president of the colony, 83; adjudged to pay Smith damages for slander, 84;

deposed, 86; sent back to England, 103.
Wingina, or Pemisapan—receives the English, 53; changes his name, 54; plots against English, 55; killed by Lane, 56.
Winslow, Edward — keeps journal of the Pilgrims' proceedings, 181; visits Massasoit when sick, 218.
Winthrop, John—appointed governor of Massachusetts, 239; his simplicity, 251; his leniency, 257; his credulity, 263; his friendliness to Roger Williams, 271.
Winthrop, John, the younger —Governor of Connecticut, 281.
Witchcraft delusions, 262.

Wituwamat—insults white men, 224, 226; killed, 227.
Wocoken, island of—English land at, 44.
Wolfe, General—killed before Quebec, 298.
Wolves — taken for lions, 197.
Writing—taken for magic by the Indians, 91.

Yankees—origin of the name, 296.
Yearley, Sir George—Governor of Virginia, 153.

York River—Powhatan's residence on, 93; Smith's journey up, 122.

www.ingramcontent.com/pod-product-compliance
Lightning Source LLC
Chambersburg PA
CBHW021153230426
43667CB00006B/381